THE
WAY OF
THE HERMIT

THE
WAY OF
THE HERMIT

My Incredible 40 Years Living in the Wilderness

KEN SMITH

WITH WILL MILLARD

MACMILLAN

First published 2023 by Macmillan
an imprint of Pan Macmillan
The Smithson, 6 Briset Street, London ECIM 5NR
EU representative: Macmillan Publishers Ireland Ltd, 1st Floor,
The Liffey Trust Centre, 117–126 Sheriff Street Upper,
Dublin 1, DOI YC43
Associated companies throughout the world
www.panmacmillan.com

ISBN 978-1-0350-0981-7

1 3 5 7 9 8 6 4 2

A CIP catalogue record for this book is available from the British Library.

Photographs © Ken Smith

Typeset by Palimpsest Book Production Ltd, Falkirk, Stirlingshire
Printed and bound by CPI Group (UK) Ltd, Croydon, CRO 4YY

Visit **www.panmacmillan.com** to read more about all our books
and to buy them. You will also find features, author interviews and
news of any author events, and you can sign up for e-newsletters
so that you're always first to hear about our new releases.

CONTENTS

THE HERMIT WITHIN

Daylight is a fickle friend.

In the middle of summer, it stretches itself across this land and casts its illusion of an everlasting grace. At its height, you can easily kid yerself into thinking it'll go on like that forever. Bathing your back in its warmth and illuminating the loch as you chop your wood. Daylight is a good friend when it wants to be, but hardly what I would call a reliable one.

It's chopping the wood that underpins the truth of your life in the far reaches of the Highlands. The log pile is your ballast when the daylight is at its longest, and building up your supply of wood serves as a daily reminder that daylight is only a fleeting flight of fancy. Aye, it'll be getting the rounds in at the bar all summer long when it wants to, but as soon as that first autumnal storm arrives, off daylight will scurry, right through the back door without paying its tab or even saying goodbye.

Put your faith in chopping wood. Build up the pile and the calluses on your palms, and always remember: from the moment you first swing your axe in early spring, you're already racing to get your pile in sound order before winter throttles the daylight back out of these moors.

Yep. Put your faith in wood, not daylight. Wood is your true friend, for wood provides light and warmth whenever you ask it to. Even now in May, as the daylight creeps forward and begs for yer forgiveness after another long winter of its absence, I'll continue leaning on the wood for its favours. There is still a bitter chill in the air when the sun sinks behind the mountains and I'll need a fair few logs to weather through the evenings up here.

We've definitely broken the back of the worst of it, though. This winter was rough, underpinned by great storms and torrential rains, but we've endured it all once again. The cabin and its creatures are edging back out of the shadows. The hermit lives to fight on.

I balance a fresh log atop the burning embers of the one that's fading away in the flames below. I like to stack my wood in the log burner in a small grid shape and then watch the livid sparks get sucked right up the chimney. I get through four sacks on an evening like this, but it's all right; the wood pile is full to the brim and within my arm's reach. Fire shadows dance along the length of the log cabin's timbers and my door is closed firm to the world. I shan't need to risk the night for anything other than a pee and a clean of my teeth.

That's good news for you. I've got quite the story to tell and it is going to take me all summer to get it out right.

Nothing good ever comes in a rush, though. Everything starts and ends much later in the high north of Scotland, and is all the better for it. Same for this hermit's tale.

Time for a drink then. Home-brewed beer or birch-sap wine?

A shrew scuttles across my gravel floor. An insectivorous mammal but, in reality, she's far more interested in my Jaffa cakes than the spiders twitching their legs deep in the timber gaps. She tastes the air with her pointy nose. That long conk is of far more use for finding them soft orange dark-chocolate buggers than her tiny coal-black eyes. She can smell one now, over on my desk.

No bigger than half my thumb, off she scurries across all my papers, photo albums and books, piled up high on the worktop. Collective memories of a life very well lived. That tiny shrew won't live beyond a year, but it can cross decades of my life to a Jaffa cake in a matter of seconds.

It can have that cake and eat it. Shrews are a tolerable nuisance. That is, till they cross the line and wade into the box marked 'greedy buggers'. Still, no matter what it does, a shrew is a minor problem next to the bleedin' pine marten. Sharp cheekbones, brown coat with a creamy white breast; they are like a spoilt wee boy-prince decked out for a banquet in his fine velvet coat and bib. They certainly care not for the suffering of their obliging service staff. I can tell you that much for free.

Pine martens might look heavenly but they are a highly destructive, astonishingly intelligent, and very powerful menace of the most supreme order of mustelids. This spring they have already turned one of my barns inside out on their rampage for food. I say they are Beauty and the Beast rolled into one devilish creature. They drive me hopping mad.

I chased one out of the cabin only last week. Do you know what it did as it went? It looked me in the eye, cocked one leg, and urinated all over my door frame. I'm certain it knew *exactly* what it was doing.

Still, we all somehow muddle through together in this wood. A little under forty years I've been living off-grid out here now. My neighbours and I, together in this thumbprint of trees on the bankside of Loch Treig.

You have to surrender to the fact that you're not going to be the master of the land if you choose to live in a place like this. A bit of your food is a peppercorn rent to pay to be a part of the natural order. Instead of constantly railing against it, it's easier to just embrace the most basic facts of the wild and share a bit of what you have. Mind you, there is a limit to the amount of my food I can donate to my furry and feathered friends – and once that limit is met, away it'll go into my locked cupboards and secure tins.

I'll have a glass of my home-made beer tonight, I think.

Something from the barrel and not the demijohn. Just enough to lubricate the mind for a few stories without becoming a boorish, drunken old fart.

I turn the tap and it trickles out into my glass. It's a beautiful tawny-coloured liquid. All grown and brewed within a stone's throw of this barrel. Can't remember what fruit I've brewed this from though. It tastes like an apricot. It looks like apricot. But is it apricot?

Anyway. Here's to the story of the so-called hermit of Treig. May he live long and all that. Cheers!

(I'm not sure it is apricot actually.)

———

People say I am a hermit, but it isn't really true in the strictest definition. My dictionary says a hermit is someone who lives alone (true in terms of people, untrue in terms of all the other living things I'm up here with), apart from the rest of society (mostly true, but not strictly so), and especially for religious reasons (depends on your definition of religion, I suppose, but it's a bit of a stretch for me, I'd say).

I know what they really mean when they say I'm a hermit though, what with my scruffy 'Wildman of the Woods' looks and apparent social isolation. I exist in the popular image of what you might think a hermit would look like and how a hermit would live. Probably, even how you imagine they'd talk, too.

I don't mind being called a hermit, it makes me laugh, but am I really a hermit in the truest sense?

For a long time, I was more of a homeless nomad – 'The Tramp of Treig' rather than 'The Hermit of Treig'. A vagrant man who haunted the local mountain bothies and existing as legend in the visitors' books that were kept in those isolated huts. Whisperings of this odd fellow written in pages sitting up on the shelf; the unofficial bothy history lying among the cobwebs, puddles of candle wax, empty gas cylinders, and all the other useless and unwanted crap that's been left behind by generations of hikers.

It wasn't till 1986, the year before my fortieth birthday, that I was finally granted permission to build this cabin in the woods. That was when I found my home, and my hermit identity evolved and grew arms and legs all on its own.

I don't shun the outside world at all. I quite like most people and very much welcome the company of the few close friends and family who come here to stay and get away. Every few weeks I'll hike out to the local shops for supplies, and get my post, too. I am no stranger to a pint or two at the pub either. It's just that I prefer to meet people on my terms, or rather, I like to be in control of my own day; deferring only to what the weather wants to do or what the seasons have in store; *how I feel*, rather than bending to the wills and whims of other humanoids. If you can grant me that, then you can call me a hermit as much as you like and you'll always be appreciated here, and that's about it.

Well, it isn't really. There are some obviously *hermit-like* behaviours in the way I choose to live. My log cabin in the woods has no clear pathway to its doorstep. It just emerges from the trees when you are only a few paces away from the gate. In fact, if you didn't enter these woods already knowing I was hidden in here, you'd likely miss my place entirely; but again, none of that is because I don't necessarily like people.

It is quite funny how incapable we are as a species of seeing anything from any other perspective than how it might directly relate to us. My decision to immerse myself in this place is not one based on pulling away from all of you, rather it is to give myself wholly to this wild space instead. To be a part of the nature here, not forever set apart from it in some sanitized domestic setting, with all its noise and problems.

I came here to find solace. A sanctuary of sorts. A deeper understanding of what this part of Scotland really is. Warts and all.

None of that means I'm necessarily armed with a higher wisdom or that I have developed some spiritual enlightenment or religious purpose – like that hermit fella from the dictionary definition. I don't think I have a unique insight anyway, but I'll let you decide that for yerself.

I may live alone, but I'm far from alone in the rich history of loners. The outsider, isolating themselves from the collective in some outlying place, is a consistent theme that stretches right back to the dawn of collective human civilization. For, as long as we have chosen to live together, there are always those who have chosen to live apart.

In ancient times, most populations would have had themselves a semi-professional hermit. Back then, they were celebrated as someone who sat outside of politics, corrupting influences and wider social ills. The hermit was the keeper of the stories, an important standard-bearer and comprehensive archivist of the history of a community. Most significant of all, they were taken as the ultimate barometer as to what was right and what was wrong. Their ability to live without reliance on anything, or anyone, meant they were the ultimate source of apolitical and acultural opinion. The only people truly on the moral high ground. In reality, their chosen lifestyle probably meant they struggled to give constructive advice on any social direction, anyway; as really, what's the point of sparing any thought for all that rubbish if you've already seen how senseless it all is? I know that's how I feel.

You don't have to stick up a cabin in the woods and isolate yourself forever to feel the benefits of a little time alone. There are hundreds of thousands of religious scholars, thinkers, creatives and leaders who have headed to the wilderness part-time to form, reflect and refine their world views and ideas. In Christian belief, Jesus of Nazareth was said to have taken to the remote Jordanian desert for forty days and nights, as did Moses on Mount Sinai. Islamic tradition tells the story of the Prophet Muhammad receiving his first angelic revelation while living alone in a cave near Mecca, and Hinduism has seen millions of Sadhus, Hindu holy people, living a monastic existence, in a near-permanent state of prayer, whilst receiving trickles of well-wishers and worshippers.

Much art, science and literature has been produced by those people who chose to temporarily execute their ideas without inter-ruption. Famous recluses, such as the scientist Charles Darwin, writer Emily Brontë, philanthropist Howard Hughes, director Stanley Kubrick, even the Beatles guitarist George Harrison, all found some form and presence through their occasional voluntary seclusion from society.

'Not till we have lost the world, do we begin to find ourselves, and realize where we are and the infinite extent of our relations,' American naturalist Henry Thoreau wrote back in the nineteenth century. Prophetic words, which might as well be inscribed into hermit law (if there were such a thing) because, honestly, there really is a little hermit waiting to be released out of us all (before they can promptly disappear for a while to figure it all out).

Protest at the direction of society is probably the biggest influence on the decision to go hermit full-time. A feeling that stretches from a general malaise, right through to a downright disgust, at wider mankind's environmental destruction, our predilection for warfare, our generally regressive political directions and increasing disregard for others. All fair enough, I'd say, but in modern times I'm afraid its various manifestations have given the formerly good word of the hermit a very bad name indeed. More often than not, introversion and reclusion, the fundamental character traits of a hermit, have become closely associated with those who have a real visceral anger and forceful hostility towards humankind. I hear about them on my radio from time to time. People the news describe as 'lone wolfs'. These hate-filled fellas who get guns and knives and occasionally go out on these awful killing sprees.

This is absolutely *not* the way of the hermit, and is a dreadful smear on all those who prefer the quiet life – all introverts, as well as hermits and recluses. This violent phenomenon has taken the former idea that we are gentle, and gently enlightened people, quietly and peacefully engaged in seclusive thought, and then bastardized it as simply time for us to manifest our menace. According to that typecast, some of us are at best weirdos, and at worst potentially dangerous criminals. Today public opinion and press speculation too often paints the hermit, in all their guises, as someone who should be feared and avoided; no longer a person to venerate, and certainly not someone to emulate.

I hope this book helps undo some of the damage because, in truth, both the positions – either that we have some special mystical power or prowess, or that we pose a threat – fall well wide of the mark. It might be tempting to put us all in one convenient box, but ultimately I am afraid we are all individuals, with our own individual thoughts, feelings, and reasons for living as we do. Speaking for myself, I certainly don't believe I'm particularly special. I'm not armed with some higher knowledge or a greater sense of purpose, nor do I possess a highly evolved set of survival skills, or harbour superhuman abilities to hang tough in terrible conditions. I am just Ken Smith, a man who prefers to do things his own way.

I hope in your reading, you might see some parts of this life that you may wish to adapt or adopt into your own. The freedom of a grand horizon, the taste of something gratefully and sensitively taken from the wild, the liberation to be had from discovering that not everything that is good has to cost you money.

I don't want you to ever think that my way of life is unattainable and unique to me. It certainly isn't, and there is absolutely nothing wrong with you seeking the metaphorical or physical wilderness every once in a while for yourself, too. If I can do it, you can do it. After all, as I've already said, people like me have existed within every culture on earth. We are just as much a part of human history as we are fundamental expressions of the human condition. We are not an oddity or curiosity that somehow sits enigmatically and inexplicably outside normal human society. We are as much a part of you, as you are of us.

Argh, maybe this beer is going to my head after all (and I can't even sober up now that the bloody shrew has stolen my last Jaffa cake!), so let me finish on this, and then I'm letting the fire die out and climbing into my bed.

I've spent the majority of my life living outside the conventions of mainstream society, and I'll tell you what I think is weird, and it ain't the hermit. It's how entire generations of people have been conned into believing that there is only one way to live, and that's on-grid, in deepening debt, working on products you'll probably never use, to line the pockets of people you'll never meet, just so you might be able to get enough money together to buy a load of crap you don't need, or, if you're lucky, have a holiday that takes you to a place, like where I live, for a week of the happiness I feel every day. And then they have the bloody cheek to guilt you into somehow being grateful for it?

No. I'm pretty certain I'm not the weird one, and yet here we are, my friends. Let's be honest, you didn't buy this book just because you were curious about me, did you? You're here because that small part of you, the hermit that sits within us all, wants to know if there is something more, and if it can be done.

Well, it can.

PART ONE

Where It All Began (and then Began Again)

DERBYSHIRE BOY

I was born on 28 October 1947 in a small house in the village of Whatstandwell, Derbyshire. It sits close to the River Derwent, about five miles south of Matlock, with the Cromford Canal running right past it. I believe that canal was the main navigation to and from the sewing mills that had their heyday during the industrial era, but these days, most comings and goings are either along the B-road that joins Whatstandwell to the A6, or the small train station stop, just on the village's fringe.

I say village, but back in 1947 it was little more than a row of stone-built, slate-roofed terraced cottages. Hardly even a hamlet. In those days it was only really your dad who worked, while your mam stopped at home to look after the kids and do all the housework. My dad worked at Lea Mills spinning mill, which made fine knitwear, and later he went on to work at the wire works, walking the canal towpath to and from work on a six-mile round-trip each and every day. Before the mills he'd worked in the Royal Navy, and Mam had also been a Wren, a member of the Women's Royal Naval Service.

I was one of four. Brother Dave came first, born during the war, then came Mike, me, and finally my sister Patricia, who we called Trisha. Trisha and Mike are still here, but my brother Dave sadly passed away. We were close and played together very happily, but the house I was born into was not a nice place. I can't remember huge amounts of detail about the inside, we moved away when I was still young, but I knew I didn't like it there at all. It was rented off a wealthy man who lived in a luxurious mansion somewhere nearby, but sadly the living standards of his tenants were in marked contrast.

Still, we were the lucky ones. We were the house at the top of the row and sat detached from the rest of the terrace. The poshest house of the lot, or, more accurately, the least worst. Not only were we detached, we were the only ones with our own private washing block. The washing block was this square lump of concrete with a large, cup-shaped copper tub inside. Us kids would go down to the well, where all the residents would draw their water, and then carry it back to fill that tub up. The water was then heated by a fire built with logs chopped by Dad in the local woods, which, like the water, had to be carried back up to the block by us children.

When the water in the copper tub was hot enough, we would have our bath. It would be Mike and David first, then Trisha and me. Work was shared, so was food, water, muck, and head lice. My upbringing taught me the value of graft from a very young age, but there's not a whole lot of romance about that way of life. It could be a very hard existence, especially for my mam and dad, but it was also pretty typical of how a lot of working-class people were expected to live after the Second World War, and we were very happy for the most part.

We mucked along together. There was a lot of camaraderie in that community. A sense that we were all in it together. You knew everyone on your street would help each other out back then. If you were short of anything, food, soap, even a bit of cash, it was always there to be borrowed. You just found ways to split and share the little you had, and make it go as far as possible. Mind you, I can't personally remember helping anyone out as a wee toddler. I do remember once blocking up all their keyholes with bread when they were all off down the pub, though!

———

Our house wasn't just inhabited by people. There were ghosts, too.

Most children have a happy early memory. A hug from their mam, a favourite bit of food, maybe a holiday, but mine was waking up in the middle of the night to the sensation of someone stroking my head. I opened my eyes to see this man in braces, with a little boy stood right next to him, both standing over me.

It was far from a one-off occurrence. I recall it happening several times during my childhood, but, strangely, I was never once scared. I didn't shout out. I didn't bury my head in the sheets. I just lay there watching them as they watched me.

One day though, we experienced something as a family that really did unnerve us. Mam, Mike, Dave, and I, were all down in the wash block. Mam was up the steps trying to get some clothes washed and us kids were left to our own devices at the bottom. In the corner of the room sat this small three-wheeled trike that all the children used to peddle around while their parents did the washing. Unbeknown to us at the time, that trike had actually belonged to a young girl who'd fallen into the well and tragically drowned.

That day, while we were all happily playing, the bell of the trike started ringing out all on its own. We looked over, absolutely struck dumb, and suddenly, it began to pedal itself right across the washroom floor.

That was quite enough for my poor old mam. She was horrified. 'Blow the washing,' she cried out, before bounding down the steps and rushing us all into the house. It would be many hours before she eventually built up the courage to go back to the washroom to get our clothes, and none of us felt particularly comfortable playing with that little trike after that.

I know for a fact that similar things happened to the other tenants that followed us into that place. Thirty years later, I was sat in a pub, and overheard a conversation between a husband and wife. They were actually recalling the time they'd lived in that exact same row of houses in Whatstandwell. I couldn't quite believe my ears, and had to interrupt them just to double-check I'd definitely heard them right.

It was the most remarkable coincidence, but we soon started comparing notes about our respective time in that place, and, when

I finally felt comfortable enough that they wouldn't think I was a *total* nutter, I chanced my arm and asked,

'So, did you happen to have any spooky experiences while you were there?'

The atmosphere changed in an instant.

The wife went pale and a dark cloud descended over the husband. 'Oh no,' he opined, wagging a finger, 'don't bloody start on that thing again.'

He then went quiet and stared angrily at his pint, but his wife began to open up. 'My hair was stroked at night,' she ventured nervously, 'by a little boy and a man.' She went on to detail experiences identical to mine, and her husband eventually admitted defeat and started chipping in too. 'We even swapped bloody beds,' he said, 'and she was *still* getting woken up by these bloomin' people stroking her.'

At the end of our chat, the wife elbowed her husband in the ribs so hard he spilled his beer. 'See?' she said in a triumphant tone, pointing at me, her chief supporting witness and new best friend, 'I told you Albert! It *were* haunted!'

Children, I think, have a far greater connection to whatever it is that sits outside our known universe. They are naturally much more open and accepting. Able to take things at face value without feeling like they have to explain away the true mysteries of the universe. Adults don't come forward with their paranormal experiences readily, not because they don't believe in what they saw, but because they dread the judgement and ridicule of those people who weren't even there. Naysayers, that seek to disprove and dismiss anything you've ever experienced that is a little, well, less than ordinary.

'Judgement' is not really a concern for me, given my chosen way of life. I have the privilege of being able to be completely honest about everything I've ever experienced, as I will suffer absolutely no ill-consequences from the conclusions of others about what I have to say. Quite honestly, though, if you cared less about what people thought then you would be a lot happier – regardless of whether you live as a hermit or not. Tell your truth, and blow the lot of them, I say.

My childhood experience was not to be my only encounter with spooks in my life. Another happenstance came much later, shortly after I'd returned to Scotland from all my travelling. That was a deeply unpleasant event, and one that truly did shake me to the core, but you'll have to wait a little while before I can tell you about that.

—

I was about five years old when we finally moved out of Whatstandwell. We only headed three miles down the road to a council house, but the relief in us all was palpable. Finally, we were free of that primitive place and off to the relative civilization of the village of Crich.

Crich was where my education really began. I had attended Whatstandwell school for a year before we'd moved, but I can't remember learning anything of note. It was a brutal place, where corporal punishment was the norm. On my very first day of school, I was caned just for running out into the road to get a ball. A mistake certainly, but one worthy of beating a small child finding his feet in a new school? Most certainly not. That was the way it was done back then, though. Victorian ideas of education persevered right into the middle half of the last century, until the practice of caning was finally outlawed in the 1980s.

There were two primary schools placed on the hill at Crich: top school, for the infants, and bottom school, for the juniors. They were both built in the late 1880s, a time of great economic and population growth in Britain's industrial heartlands. As workers grafted in the pits, mills and docks, the need to make provisions for the education of their children grew. Soon these thick stone, brick and slate-roofed buildings began to pop up in the working communities spread out across the land.

They were typically small, cold and functional. In my first school you could get all the children in just one room, and we only had four teachers in total; but that didn't mean education wasn't taken very seriously. Traditional ideas of education persisted, and learning was by rote, but I was exceptionally lucky that once we'd moved I found the best teacher I ever had. Mr Florey communicated his lessons brilliantly and I flourished under his stewardship. Better still were his ethics. He was a man who cared about his students' feelings and did not believe in teaching through fear. The cane may well have been the norm in the 1950s, but Mr Florey was one of those few liberal-minded teachers who broke the mould (and not the skin on our hands and arses).

It was a sleight-of-hand trick he'd play. 'Smith!' he would shout when I'd been acting up (which I did a lot of, I can be honest with you about that). I'd look up and it was as if he had a look of pure evil in his face – a truly thunderous rage.

'Come over here and put out your hand!'

There he'd be, stood over you ominously with a thick wooden ruler. I'd hold out my hand and, theatrically and deliberately, he would miss wildly.

'I've missed!' he would cry. 'Hold it out again!' he'd demand, before missing again. 'Right, that's taught you a lesson. Now go and sit down!' he'd bark dismissively.

Every time, to everyone, he would always do the same. It was dramatic, a deliberate show put on for the benefit of the other teachers in the building, but we were all well in on his ruse. He never once beat a child and we loved him for it. I think we all respected him that much more too. I know I did; he was an excellent educator and we hung on his every word. If you misbehaved, you felt ashamed of yourself for letting him down. A far greater punishment than the cane ever could be.

I did have one very big problem though. One that no conjuring on earth could get me out of. I was left-handed.

It seems utter madness, but in those days being left-handed was considered to be a deficiency that required curing. This fear of 'leftness' is documented in many ancient cultures, but in British society it most likely had its roots in the Bible, and Jesus's proclamation that the blessed would sit by the right hand of God, with the cursed stuck on his left. It didn't take long for an almighty leap in judgement to be made, and pretty soon it was the accepted wisdom that the Devil himself was left-handed, and that he, and all other evil spirits and curses, could be roused with gestures from the left hand. Even the English word 'sinister' originated from the Latin word for left.

The way my teachers went about solving this 'problem' was as cruel as it was simple. If you were left-handed your left arm was tied behind your back and you were forced to write with your right hand. Can you imagine? Five years old, having your first experience in education, having already been caned just for running after a ball, and then having one arm roped behind your back?

It continued throughout my education and eventually worked. I can still easily write with my left hand as well as my right. In fact, the whole exercise has made me ambidextrous, to the extent that I can actually write with both hands at the same time, forwards as well as backwards. I haven't quite found a specific use for that very odd talent, but it's a decent party trick all the same, and has secured me a few free ales in its time.

I might have been left-handed but I was far from daft. I was top of the class quite a few times through school, in pretty much every subject barring Maths. My spelling was very poor, though. I'd never want to break the creative flow and rhythm of a story I was working up in my mind by stopping to ask how a word was spelt and, as such, I'd constantly be reprimanded for being unable to spell correctly.

This is going to feel like such a poor excuse, but I believe it is an allegory for what I see as an issue with our formal education system generally, in which functionality and form, exactness and precision, are rewarded over any semblance of imagination.

—

10 February 1962

*The pond is very large and deep, with a sludgy sandy bottom . . .
[it] contained many weeds and water insects, as well as amphibians.*

*The amphibians were frogs, but which now lay dead on the
surface with bites in them. Some had no heads on, others with no
legs, and even some with bleeding tummies.*

*It was evident that there was some kind of fish in this pond,
probably a pike.*

*We could not see it, but we cast a line into the pond with a worm
on the end hoping to catch it, but we knew pikes do not like worms,
so we hoped it was hard up on food, then it would like worms.*

*We left the pond with the line securely fastened to the bank and
went on to the newt pond, hoping to return tomorrow to see what
was in store for us.*

———

11 February 1962

*It took me about thirty minutes to reach the pond, and by now it
was drizzling.*

*My hands were wet and cold and the rain made constant ripples
in the pond, but I wound in the reel we had put there the day before,
only to find the worm on the hook still intact.*

*My feet sank in the wet clay as I cast out again, and the fine
spray of rain came on.*

*I made another line with some string, only this time I tied on a
dead frog on the end, but as I had no luck, I went home.*

It was plainly obvious from a very early age that I was never
going to be someone who was stuck indoors in a suit and tie,
trapped behind a desk, working for some fool that didn't even
know my name. A fascination with nature and the outdoors was
deep in me from birth – as I'm sure it is for many children before
the world of school, work and adulthood squeezes it right out of
them.

It was very important to me that I brought wild things home to study, and I would spend all my free time outside, collecting all sorts and stowing them away in the cardboard-box-cum-treasure-chest beside my bed.

A small gang of us would head off in search of adventures and animals, usually in any of the old abandoned quarry sites spread out around our home, or the woodland that we called 'The Strictly Private'.

Not one of us seemed to make the connection between those 'Strictly Private' words marked on the sign at the entrance to those woods and what 'Strictly Private' actually meant in English. Even if we had, though, I highly doubt it would've made a difference in our trespassing. They were some of the most beautiful woods I'd seen. Far too nice to be shut away from the unwashed public, at any rate.

We all piled in and created absolute havoc in those great trees, chasing each other and playing hide and seek around the rhodo-dendron bushes. We used to find these huge old stone wheels hidden in the undergrowth, too; giant things they were, some six feet across and impossible to move. Quite what they were used for we never really figured out, but they made for brilliant centre-pieces for all our games and adventures in The Strictly Private.

Crystals, fossils and rocks; all came to my collection from the quarry (Crich and its surroundings were a fascinating place geo-logically, where sandstone and limestone bedrock met), whereas snail shells, feathers, acorns, roots, pine cones, leaves and seeds all came from The Strictly Private. I would pore over all of them for hours on end, studying their lines and intricate details under a small microscope till my eyes were sore.

In the pages of several well-worn Royal Mail notebooks, I recorded my first handwritten notes of my discoveries and obser-vations, alongside diaries of my dreams, and I had a whole book dedicated to things I saw from my bedroom window. *Many things have happened lately around Crich, although nothing has around the windows*, I penned in the late 1950s. I decided not to commission a second series of that particular book, but it all marked the start of a lifelong sense of duty to record all my comings and goings in detail.

I'd always use my finest handwriting, and also included elaborate maps of the very best of my stomping grounds. Clearly, I took natural history, and its meticulous recording, very seriously indeed. *I got my acorns by climbing an oak tree and picking them off one by one*, I noted, aged seven, before lamenting how the bulbs found beneath a railway bank died because I didn't plant them in time.

I also became quite passionate about growing mould; using the old English word 'fust' to describe a clutch of recipes for what, it is fair to say, was quite a singular and unusual hobby. It seemed lemon juice had the finest result: *a shiny, and very delicate fust*, I recorded with my curly handwriting – with more than a touch of boyish glee, I imagine.

It was a carefree time, but not entirely without incident. I soon collected all the garden-variety bumps, bruises and scrapes; and once tore a ligament jumping out of a tree while scrumping apples (an injury that left me pigeon-toed for life); but the worst accident by far came very early on in my life as an explorer. I was only five when I fell down the flight of sandstone steps outside the Whatstandwell washroom and fractured my skull.

I remember very shakily regaining my feet and staggering back up the stairs to find Mam washing our clothes. 'Mam, I've fallen down the steps,' I announced. I have no idea what I looked like, but her face almost instantly resembled the one I'd seen with the washroom ghost encounter. It was a picture of abject horror, but we couldn't flee this scene and pretend it hadn't happened – it was almost the worst nightmare for any parent and required her immediate attention.

'Right!' she cried, hurriedly packing up all the washing stuff, 'we've got to get you to hospital!'

Now, in those days it wasn't a case of just getting in a car or ringing for an ambulance. We didn't own a car, or a phone to make a call, for starters, but I don't believe there was an ambulance service back then anyway. We needed to tell my dad what had happened as all the other children were at school and it was clear that we were probably going to be gone for some time. We walked a track for three-quarters of a mile down to the canal, with my mam gripping my hand to steady me as I stumbled along with my concussion. We crossed a bridge over the canal and followed the towpath for another mile, and finally started the descent to the wire works where Dad was working.

'Stop here, Ken,' she commanded, leaving me with my fractured skull on the pavement by the A6. Mam then went into the wire works, found Dad, told him what had happened, and returned about twenty minutes later. Now we could make a start for hospital, so off we went, south on the A6 towards Ambergate, with the thumb out and in quite desperate need of a hitched lift.

Soon, a lorry stopped, and this next part of the story was kept from me for many years. It is a horrible tale, and not something any child would ever want to think about their own mother having to go through. From my side, all I can really recall was that the lorry took us to Derbyshire Royal Infirmary, the X-ray revealed a fractured skull, and I was told I was going to have to stay in hospital to recover. Mam headed home to look after the rest of the children, but her side of the story was very different.

What she would tell me some years down the line was that the lorry driver had said the lift to hospital was only on the condition that she would have sex with him. With her little boy bleeding in her arms, she was in a truly desperate situation. 'Look,' she said pleadingly, 'please. I've got to get him to hospital. My son, I think he has broken his skull.' By that point, now some time after the accident, my head had started to swell up with all the blood. Thinking quickly, she added as a closer: 'I'm also pregnant.'

This wasn't a lie. Trisha was on her way, and it was a fair assumption that this might put this man off, or at least generate some sympathy. This lorry driver, though, was undeterred and insistent. Those were his final terms for carriage: a leg-over or no lift.

It was disgusting and disgraceful, and makes me absolutely sick to the stomach to even think about it. My poor mam was terrified. Terrified of him, but also terrified of what might happen to her son if she didn't take the lift she so urgently needed. This sexual predator knew all this, and was using our extreme vulnerability solely for his own gratification.

Mam tried to trick him. She agreed to have sex with him, but only after he'd taken me to hospital. 'If you feel the same way once you've dropped us off, meet me at the Belper Triangle,' she'd offered.

The Belper Triangle was an intersection on the A6 and a very popular bus stop just outside the small town of Belper, a little north of Derby. The lorry driver knew that Mam would have to pass through it to get back home to Whatstandwell, and that the bus was certain to stop at this terminus to pick up and drop off passengers. 'Wait there with your lorry and I'll join you on the way back,' she added, in a final act of desperation.

With me under the doctor's care, Mam got on a Trent bus for the journey home and, as she sat down, she began to pray. 'I hope, please, that this bus does not pick anyone up from the Belper Triangle,' she asked of God and, as the bus made its journey northwards, her anxiety and prayer peaked.

To her horror, as the bus approached the Triangle, she spotted the man waiting there in his lorry. She slunk down in her seat, trying to shield herself from his view, sure that she was about to be busted, but to her absolute astonishment and amazement, the bus did not stop. No one got on or off at the Triangle, the man didn't see her, and she was carried away home. It was a miracle. Mam was saved. I would like to think that truly horrible man waited there for many an hour and ended up in prison at some point, but justice can be hard won in this world and I'm just glad Mam was safe.

There were occasional hard times growing up, and parenting then, when compared with parenting now, might even seem a little crude, but our mam and dad always gave us everything we really needed: unconditional love, and – as much as they could afford – their time and attention.

Mam had absolutely no choice but to get that lift. Over everything else, it stands as a testament to what she was willing to go through for any of her children. I am proud of the incredible dignity and composure she showed in such a terrifying situation but, above all, I'll always know how much we were loved. I am in no doubt though that, once I was old enough to discover the truth of what had really happened, it sowed the seeds of a generally healthy mistrust for some human beings into the earth of my being.

COMING UP FOR SCOTTISH AIR

11 *March* 1963

*It was the rays of early dawn that awoke me, we were approaching
Dumfries, and no more did my journey worry me. I sat looking into
the hills and moorland, such a contrast to the cities in England,
and little did I know at the time, that I would grow to love these
desolate places.*

I left home and school and started working at just fifteen years
old. Young, by today's standards, but not such a big deal back then.
I loved my family and we all got on well together, but we were
growing older and in need of our own space, as young adults so
frequently are. It was claustrophobic in our little house with
everyone still living there, but then my dad, encouraged by my
other brothers and sister, went out and bought a sheepdog called
'Ricky'.

I'd told them I didn't want to share the house with a dog, and,
as it became increasingly clear that I was going to have to take on
some of the responsibility for the upkeep and walking of young
Ricky, it soon became me or the dog.

And the dog won.

It took a few months of sending letters out to the four corners
of the United Kingdom via a truly feckless Youth Employment
officer, but eventually I landed a job. I wasn't hugely precious about
where the work was going to be, as long as it took me away, was
outside, and had some prospects. It was 1963 and I was fifteen years
old when I boarded the midnight train and headed to the true
north for the first time. I was to start work in the Forestry

Commission at Bridge of Gaur, planting woods right up in the Scottish Highlands.

I was taken to a Forestry hostel where my weekly wages of thirty shillings, about thirty pounds in today's money, didn't even cover the cost of my board. I did eventually get a grant from the education authority to help with my living expenses but there was virtually nothing left for spending after I'd deducted my board, my food and my laundry. That didn't matter, though, I was there to graft and learn – earning could wait.

I worked for them for four years in all, planting, fencing and ditching the Rannoch woods, trees that are still spreading out all over these moors today; but the early weeks of that first job were brutal. The lads I lived and worked with were merciless bullies, especially to newcomers or people they marked out as a bit different from the rest, which I most certainly was. I was quiet and a bit introverted as a teenager, more focused on the natural world than carrying on like a lout or following the football scores, and I was frequently doused in buckets of water and flour, stolen from, woken in the middle of the night, or just plain beaten.

Many times I was brought to the verge of tears and, as much as I wasn't missing home, or Ricky the dog, I still came very close to quitting. If it wasn't for what we had in our backyard, there is no way I could've seen it through. I sought solace in the hills, and wound up finding my self-confidence instead.

I loved those windswept hills, for I myself was a legend among them, and being the legend, [I] could tell these stories I possess, and as time drew on more stories of deer, wild cats, and fishing expeditions came known to me in those wild and desolate Grampian mountains.

I wrote romantically in my diary. I didn't have the foggiest where I was going to end up at the time, but there is certainly a nice serendipity to the fact that my first job took me to work just fifteen miles, as the crow flies, from where I'd eventually settle for life.

Instinctively, I felt immediately at ease while wandering alone in those mountains. Even at aged fifteen, they spoke to me in a way that nowhere else had before, or really, in Britain, has since. I loved the Scottish wilds from the very first time I stuck on my boots and took to their embrace and, my god, did I need them for those first few months.

As the weeks passed, I came to feel like I was truly home, and the hard start faded in my mind. Looking back, it was hardly surprising that a big group of teenage boys and young men would cause trouble amongst each other. There was no social life to be had up there, and the nearest town with anything like conventional entertainment was sixty-three miles away in Perth. The living situation soon settled down and I was gradually accepted as just another one of the lads.

I came to learn how lucky I was to have the opportunity I did. These days, if you did a fraction of the things I was doing in that job at fifteen, you'd be instantly dismissed for not having the correct certificate or having passed the appropriate course. In those days it was very much a case of 'see one, do one', with little time for anything else. You'd wake up in the morning and it was: 'Right, out into the hills, lads. Today I'll show you how to dig a drain', and off we'd march. You learnt from getting out there and doing it, not from acquiring the correct paperwork or being told about it in a classroom. So many times in my later working life, I'd have people turn up on the building site without the first clue what they were doing, despite apparently having passed a course. It would take weeks to get them up to speed and unpick all their bad habits; far better, I say, to learn on the job, actually doing the work, than waste time and money learning in a classroom.

That all said, whenever you hear people bemoan how workplaces today have gone 'health and safety mad', with all their red tape and paperwork, it is best not to look back on the past purely with rose-tinted spectacles. We did have safety practices and were absolutely expected to follow instructions to the letter, but some of the work we did was very dangerous, and, at times, unacceptably so. I had several industrial accidents in my lifetime and worked with people who lost limbs and lives to machinery. The consequences of not doing as you were instructed could be fatal, and often there were very good reasons not to put yourself in harm's way in the first place – but sometimes colleagues did so regardless, and did so with awful consequences. Unfortunately, it was a hard lesson I would learn right at the start of my career.

It was in my first year working with the Forestry Commission and we had been tasked with driving all the deer off the land known as The Cruach. The saplings had been planted, the trees were growing, and the whole place had been surrounded by a perimeter boundary fence for its protection from grazing animals. However, there was a large herd of deer roaming around the interior that needed to be shifted. As long as they were trapped in the enclosure, the freshly planted and fragile trees stood no chance; the deer would simply chew right through them the moment they sprouted from the ground.

A plan was hatched. It seemed straightforward enough: the forestry workers were to be spaced around forty feet apart, forming a long line that spanned the width of the enclosure. All we needed to do was march forward as one, from the back to the front, making enough racket to scare the herd right out of a gap in the fence that we had created at the far side.

Things went okay at first. The deer started to flee ahead of us towards the gap in the fence, but it soon became apparent that not all of them were about to play our game. As we pushed forward, some of the herd about-turned, charged back down towards us, broke through the gaps in the line, and went right back into the depths of the enclosure.

Time for Plan B. Alongside the forestry workers, a group of top deerstalkers, men charged with leading hunting guests on a nearby estate, had also been recruited to help with the deer removal. Turning on our heel, we flushed the animals back towards the stalkers who were lying in wait with their rifles.

It sounds like a crazy plan when written down plainly on the page. Dangerous, too, to be walking right behind a group of animals that were about to be blasted by guns. But these men were among the best shots in the business, and all we really needed to do was follow the instructions: hold our line, stay visible to stay safe, and get the job done quickly.

Shots rang out as the stray deer were picked off one-by-one and it didn't seem like we would be on that job for too much longer, when one young forester in our line decided he wanted to shoot one of the deer in the testicles with a catapult he'd hidden in his pocket.

Aside from being a very stupid idea in any circumstances (all he would've achieved is angering or scaring the animal, for zero benefit to anyone), it was needlessly reckless given what we were already doing at the time. With no one close enough to set him straight, though, the young man broke free from our line, dived into the heather and started creeping forward on a stag.

With his stealth and cover, the deerstalkers didn't see the lad as he crawled right up into a firing position next to an animal, and, in the fraction of a second he took to leap up in front of the stag with his catapult drawn, one of the deerstalkers had also just squeezed his trigger.

The rifle's bullet whistled directly through the chest of the young man and dropped him right where he stood. We all rushed over, but it was already too late. One of the lads looked at him and grimly pronounced, 'We might as well say his peace now. There's nothing we can do for him.'

It was horrendous. One young man – with his whole life ahead of him – was now dead, and then there was the poor man who had made the shot and killed him, left behind with the memory of this needless disaster for the rest of his time, too.

That deerstalker was a very good and kind man. There really was nothing he could've done, given the circumstances, but he would never hold a rifle in his hands again.

—

I left the Forestry Commission in 1967 and went to work for Scotland Nurseries, but the nursery itself was actually just east of Matlock in Derbyshire, so it was back to living with my parents. Soon, I'd left that job and gone to work on a cattle and dairy farm near Crich.

I adored all those jobs. They were fascinating learning experiences, which, when taken in sum, offered lessons in both self-reliance and the effective management of a landscape and its animals. All of which would be crucial knowledge for when I did go completely off-grid. I learnt the Latin names for all the plants and started working my own allotment, regularly taking cuttings of plants, shrubs and vegetables, and growing them on myself. You couldn't go on the internet in those days, but I was surrounded by people with real expertise and a knowledge of what I needed to do, and pretty soon I had a surplus of plants that I could sell on for a bit of extra income.

The wages though, remained very poor. Even working six days solid you could scarcely make ends meet. The most I ever earned in a week was nine pounds, but you could still get a pint of bitter for twenty pence from The Dutchman pub back then, so it wasn't all bad. In reality, though, I wasn't going to get very far on that money, and saving was impossible. That's when good old brother Dave got a hold of me. 'Look Ken,' he'd said after a particularly galling week of very hard work, 'you need to pack in the farming and come join me in the building trade. You'll earn a lot more money.'

Dave soon got me a job in his company tiling and laying floors. Dave loved a pound note, so it was more hard work with very long hours and travel right across the country. I didn't have anything like the same passion for that work as I did for all the jobs outdoors in the countryside, but Dave wasn't wrong about the money. My wages tripled overnight.

BORN AGAIN

On the 14 October 1974, everything in my life changed.

Until that point, barring a few crazy experiences, I'd had a pretty regular time for your average working-class lad in the post-war, post-industrial years. There had been a fair few ups and downs, but nothing that was going to push me off the straight and narrow course that's laid out for so many young people from humble beginnings like mine.

There are always those people that break the mould – politicians, heads of business, top sports people – but for most of us you feel like your entire future is mapped out by the time you get into your twenties. Graft, drink, find a partner, graft, have some kids, graft, pay the bills, graft and die.

You don't ever stop to question it because you can't stop. Just getting by day-to-day is a big enough challenge, without hand-wringing about your future, your direction, or who you really are as a person. There's no time for any of that navel-gazing, lad, just get your head down and get the work done.

I was twenty-six, a couple of weeks off my twenty-seventh birthday, and was finishing up a good night out in Ripley. They'd just kicked out at the local discotheque, and admittedly I'd had a few. Nothing out of the ordinary there for a single working man in his mid-twenties.

No one back then would be wasting their drinking money on the frivolous expense of a taxi, so I was just starting the five-mile walk home and heading up Church Street when it happened.

I can't have been more than 600 yards from the disco itself when a gang of eight lads with shaven heads set on me. The first one head-butted me square in the face and shoved me right through the window of the local bakery and down onto the floor. Shards of glass rained down on me, cutting into my skin as my broken nose bled.

That would've been plenty enough abuse to take my money, but they wanted more than that. I felt one of their big working boots connect with my face, sending a claret fountain spewing out onto the floor. Another boot came stamping down on my crown with force, and then more blows started to fly in. Boots drummed into my head and body. Boots crunching into bone and spraying more blood. They were wild and completely out of control. Like a pack of wolves fighting over the rights to tear apart a carcass.

My memory of the events in the immediate aftermath is hazy. They stopped eventually and I was left crumpled in a puddle of blood and glass. Somehow, I made it home. I was in a quite dreadful state, but come Monday, it was time to get back to work.

My injuries, I thought, looked bad but were mostly superficial. Cuts and lumps and blackened eyes, nothing that wouldn't heal with time. At least I hadn't broken any bones, I thought. I had a headache though, but I wrote that off as just a touch of the flu.

Three days later and I was laid up in bed with a pain in my head that was so bad I thought it might explode. Unbeknown to me at the time, the damage to my brain was extremely severe. As those boots had hailed in, my brain had been tossed around the inside of my skull as if it were a tennis ball trapped in a cement mixer. Eventually my brain had begun to bleed out, and as the days had passed, the pressure from the build-up of all that blood trapped within my skull completely overwhelmed me.

I crawled from bed and managed to raise enough determination to slide up my bedroom wall and flick on my light switch before I collapsed. It was night-time, and I knew Mam would come into my room to switch off any lights before she went to sleep. I couldn't speak or move. I just lay there, slumped behind my door, as I heard her slowly coming up the stairs in her slippers and nightgown.

Soon, she was shouting down to Dad. 'There's something wrong with Ken! I think he's on the floor behind his door!' Dad rushed up and gave my door an almighty shove. I looked up at them both, sure that I was dying but no longer capable of forming the words.

It was the one and only time Dad left the house via the front door. Sprinting out and fumbling for loose change in his pocket, so he could make the emergency call from the public payphone down the street.

I was rushed into Derbyshire Royal Infirmary. The conscious world I knew, one of light, sound and colour, had already started to shrink away as the ambulance tore up our road. Eventually, everything I knew, my entire conscious being and all my memories, sat as small and vulnerable as a candle's flame flickering away in the night sky. I would try and cup that light, hold onto it, shield it, keep it alive, but eventually the smallest breath of wind left nowt but smoke and shadow.

That was it then. I collapsed back into an abyss of the deepest shade of black.

—

Sometimes, sitting here in my cabin alone at night, I'll think back to that day and shed a little tear. Not out of sadness or self-pity, although either would be reasonable emotions to feel given the circumstances, but at the immense relief that I did not lose my life.

I had so much more living to do, and it marked the biggest change in my life's direction. I honestly believe that had that event not happened, I doubt I would've ever found the courage to truly put myself first and prioritize adventure. But all that was yet to come.

First, I became aware of light. My eyes were open and I was lying in a hospital bed on my right side. My lips tried to form a word, but I was still unable to speak and actually quite unsure of what words really were. I made an effort to move and discovered I was entirely paralysed down one side.

My sight was limited, and my vision was doubled, but I was aware enough to note that I was staring directly out of the window beside me. The rain was bucketing down, hammering the window-pane and sending steady rivulets of fresh Derbyshire rainwater snaking down the glass.

At least my eyeballs could move. At the top of some stairs, I could see a nurse dressed in a white cotton uniform. I knew I was definitely in hospital then. She had a smart white hat on top of her head and was just about to disappear down the stairs, when something instinctual must have made her glance over in my direction.

'Oh!' she said with a start. 'You're awake, Mr Smith!'

It did not matter that I had no way to respond back to her. She continued with the warmth and generosity of spirit that is so typical of so many who work within the nursing profession. That underrated, underpaid and overworked army of staff that really run the hospital wards – tending wounds, and healing spirits too.

She crouched down by my side and fixed me with eyes filled with compassion.

'These,' she began, reaching for something piled on top of my bedside cabinet, 'are all your "get well soon" cards.'

She read them all out loud. One by one. Then found another fistful. 'And these are all your birthday cards.'

She gently held my hand and fixed me with her eyes once more. I'd had four operations on my brain. Nine hours under the knife, and almost two weeks in a coma.

'Tomorrow, Mr Smith, is your birthday. But today. Today is the day you were reborn.'

———

17 January 1975

I went to hospital on 14 Oct 1974 . . .
I was seriously ill and was dying fast. The doctors gave me four serious operations on the brain with a small chance of living . . .

I hope now I continue to recover and soon I hope entries in my diary are entered in joy, for besides the doctors, it is God who saved my life, and I thank them all for the help they have given me.

The road back towards full health was set to be a long one. Not only could I not walk or speak, but I'd also lost two-thirds of my memory and could not write. The consensus among the doctors was that I might never recover. That my injuries were so profound that a degree of disability was going to be with me forever going forward. That, though, was not how I decided I wanted to see out the rest of my days. I had been gifted a second chance at living and I set to my rehabilitation like a man possessed.

I was determined to prove the doctors wrong, and so, thank goodness, were the nurses who cared for me. Every day one of them would come to give me encouragement to try and get a little bit of my movement back. At first it was just for five minutes, then ten, then twenty; but slowly, working together, we got there.

At first, I only focused on controlling the little things that I could. Incremental daily improvements in my physical state and well-being: wiggle my toes today and don't worry if you are going to get up and start walking around tomorrow. Repetition and discipline slowly paved over the significant cracks in my broken mind too.

The first challenge was getting well enough to get out of hospital. That took a fair few weeks in itself; then I had to salvage my memory and learn how to write and talk again.

I started with the very basics of how to grip a pen, and then taught myself the simplest turns of phrase and everyday words. It took immense patience and discipline, but it was like being back to day one at Upper School, just without the cane or the bleedin' left arm tie. Once I had grasped the basic letter sounds and elementary words, I graduated towards some seriously laborious rote-learning sessions with what became a very well-worn dictionary.

If I couldn't spell a word, I would drill it to the point that I could. Rewriting it hundreds of times on sheets of paper, and even on the dictionary pages themselves, in the smallest handwriting I could possibly muster. Eventually I had worked my way backwards from Z to A, so I started again. Again, and again. Until I felt my level of literacy was no longer embarrassing.

It would've been far too easy to hide my problems and do nothing to help myself. I had the perfect excuse, after all. But learning how to walk, read and write, for the second time in my life, instilled in me a single-mindedness and determination to win that would drive me forward in the wilderness. After all, if I could get through all this, then I could get through anything.

—

I ultimately spent forty-nine days in hospital and had almost ten months off work. The skinhead gang were eventually caught. They were made to pay £300 for the baker's window, and £10 each in a fine. It doesn't sound that much today, but that was more than a week's wages alone back then. Mind you, you could argue they took more from me out of my life, but there's no point wasting your thoughts on retribution, I can tell you that much for free. Focus on what you have that's good, never on hate.

My parents cared for me as I rehabilitated myself from their council house in Crich, and my employees, Bowmer and Kirkland, could not have been better to me. They made sure I was paid all my entitlements and kept my job open for me to return, but I knew that my days in the building trade were numbered.

As if I needed any more evidence that it really was time to go, I hadn't been back at work too long before I fell thirteen feet from a steel post onto a bed of industrial steel spikes. The spikes punctured my body every six inches from my ankle to my shoulder, and I still have the scars to this day, but miraculously they somehow missed all my vital organs. Five days inside was the charge sheet this time, but how that fall didn't kill me I do not know. There was not a single witness to that accident at my work who could believe I was not a *very* dead man indeed.

That marked my last hospital stay of any description for the next twenty-nine years. There's something in that, you know. The decades that follow were my most extreme, my most adventurous, my wildest, and yet nothing ever injured me enough to put me back in hospital for a stay. The truth is, you are always more likely to die from something mundane in a very trivial-seeming domestic environment. It isn't when you're hyper-alert and vigilant about risk that you end up coming a cropper, it's when you least expect it. Beyond accident, the biggest killers in the Western world are the symptoms of our own perpetual boredom and dissatisfaction with life's mundane direction. A slow death through the grinding monotony of a routine that does us absolutely no favours. Booze, gambling, junk food, drugs or smoking, all just to mask the tedium, while accelerating us closer to the grave, deepening our depression, and stealing away the simple joys of being alive. Renting us back two weeks of annual holiday, and then having the cheek to tell us we should be glad of it, before locking us all away again.

Back then, smoking was something everyone did. It was just another part of life; like having a pint after work or eating your breakfast; but today we really do know what a dangerous and deadly habit it can be, and it cost my family dear.

I was thirty-one years old when Mam had the heart attack. I just came home from work early one day, and there she was, pacing around the house holding her chest. I rushed over and she managed to mutter: 'I'd rather not speak'. Those were the last words I ever heard her say. The doctors arrived but she died soon after.

The whole family was devastated and a dark cloud descended on our household for some time. They said her arteries had hardened from all her smoking.

Bloody smoking. I've never smoked. We had a bet among us kids that whoever smoked would have to give the non-smoking sibling thruppence. I stuck to it, and was the only one among us who didn't take up the habit; but I never did get that thruppence, and that addiction stole away poor Mam before her time.

I knew I needed to escape that system, and all its trappings, as quickly as I possibly could. I spent a couple more years working and saving, cutting back on absolutely everything, barring the very barest essentials, before the early summer of 1979 finally ticked around. I went around all my friends and family and told them we would all be having a pint together in The Black Swan pub in Crich.

I didn't tell them it was going to be a leaving party, or that I'd decided to put a load of money behind the bar, and so it went that all the people closest to me in the world filled that place and drank long into the night on my tab.

I recall many came back to my place afterwards too, filling up on my home-made apricot wine many hours after the bell for last orders had been and gone. The next morning it was a scene of total devastation in my front room. Bodies everywhere, and plenty of pools of amber liquid puddled on the floor. Luckily, it was all apricot wine, and the sign of a proper send-off. I said my final goodbyes then, thinking, quite reasonably, I'd see them all again when I was back. But I got that quite wildly wrong. It was the last time I ever saw most of them and that party marked the end of my life in Crich. Really, I suppose, it also marked the end of my time as a reasonably 'civilized' and normal member of society.

I knew, from the day I awoke from the assault, that my life had fundamentally changed. No matter what, I would never put myself in a position where one person's actions could have such a terrible impact on my life.

If I was going to be born again, you'd better believe I wasn't going to live on anyone else's terms but my own.

PART TWO

The Wilderness Days

CANADA, THE GREAT WHITE NORTH

My first trip to the high country of America and Canada came in May 1979 when I was thirty-one years old. Back then, I had a very loose plan to travel 2,000 miles through Canada via British Columbia, the Yukon, and their portion of the Rocky Mountains. My great Scottish friend, Roy Stephen, had jacked in his job at the Fordoun sawmill to join me, and the grand, six-month adventure we shared would leave an indelible impression on us both.

Roy and I had spent many of our holidays from work hiking together in the Scottish Highlands; but there was always that pull to try and learn more, to truly test ourselves, to find a place that was bigger and wilder than anything we could ever experience on our own small island. We imagined the iconic mountains and forests of Canada would provide all that we sought – a wide-open place to be released, to feel truly free. What we couldn't have known was that it really would be all that, and so much more too.

We walked till the soles dropped off our boots, hitchhiked as much as we could, and only dipped into our pockets for a bus fare when we were truly out of all other options. There were only two nights where we didn't sleep outside under a flysheet or staring up at the stars. We carried everything we needed on our backs, and learnt to cook all our food over an open fire.

The experience was profoundly inspiring but, looking back, I can see that when I arrived, I was brimming with the most brilliant brand of misplaced self-confidence, probably suffered by most young men on their first grand expedition away from home. So, the learning curve was steep for both of us and, in the cool of the high north, we were in for a baptism of fire.

It was the evening of our first full day in Canada and we'd already travelled about seventy miles from Vancouver, up the Fraser River, and on into an area somewhat ominously called 'Suicide Creek'.

Roy made camp, and I took a wander upstream to go fishing. I hadn't made too many casts when I spotted a man leaping out of his truck and headed my way at some pace. Assuming I'd broken some local fishing law, I did the honourable thing and immediately did a runner. Back through the bush, through an area of marsh and fallen logs, for about half a mile down the creek, and back out onto the road; where I was immediately apprehended by a simply enormous human and his very lively looking Alsatian.

'What's going on here then, and where's your identity?' he bellowed. This man-mountain was, in fact, a Mountie, a member of the Royal Canadian Mounted Police. He didn't have a horse, just his equally massive dog (which someone of my size probably could've ridden, if they were in an utterly suicidal mood). It was loosely roped to his wrist, and appeared particularly keen for some fresh Derbyshire meat.

I came clean with my fishing crime, and he looked at me as if I was some sort of blithering idiot. 'Son, you don't have to pay to go fishing in these areas,' he declared, sweeping a hand across the almighty expanse of backcountry, 'and, even if you did, can you imagine a bailiff trying to police this place? It would be impossible.' I discovered then that any explanation of any wrongdoing in any British accent whatsoever, even one as thick and northern as mine, was an instant passport to an extraordinary degree of leniency, especially when backed up with an actual British passport, which I only too hastily produced as the Mountie continued to flex his muscles.

I was marched back to the camp with Roy, and it was explained to us both that the reason for him turning up was because a local farmer had spotted me fishing in the river, and had tried to warn me about a cougar that had just been spotted prowling in the area. They had only recently sent out a hunter and the wildcat had killed both his dogs, so the conscientious Canadian just wanted to let me know, lest I be on the menu next. But I'd simply run off.

That had caused the farmer to panic, as it turned out there were also two escaped convicts in the area. That brought the phone call to the mounted police and ushered forth my muscular new friend and his dog. We soon settled it all with the Mountie and were left to kip beneath a derelict hen shed (which I presume was somehow cougar- and convict-proof), but honestly, we had scarcely been in Canada twenty-four hours and there we were: camping in the wilds, prone to animal and criminal attack and, thanks to me, already in trouble with the law. It suddenly seemed a very long way from home . . . and it felt absolutely *bloomin' marvellous!*

Our adventure through Canada continued. Days became weeks, became months, and I had never been so happy. We moved north to Cache Creek, a vast desert wilderness filled with cacti, sagebrush and tumbleweed (and many rattlesnakes beneath the rocks), before hitching and hiking our way higher and deeper into central British Columbia.

We found huge lakes filled with large rainbow trout, and forests carpeting the mountains in every direction we turned. We built rafts and fished; spotted the nests of bald eagles, beavers, and the spectacular crimson-eyed diving bird, the loon. Alongside the fish, we caught grouse, and once trapped a squirrel, but the meat was so tough that it was not going to be an animal we ever bothered with again. We became friends with the local indigenous people too, the First Nations, who netted the lakes and caught enormous charr – a member of the salmon family, with dark backs and bright orange bellies – which they then gifted to us, alongside loans of their boats, chainsaw, and invitations to their homes and churches. They never once asked for a cent in return.

It wasn't pure paradise, of course; we had some awful weather to contend with: monumental downpours that pinned us beneath the flysheet, sometimes for days at a time, and clouds of mosquitoes. At one point, we were even plagued by flying ants, which filled our camp and sleeping bags. And one morning, Roy was almost crushed by a charging bull moose that was fleeing a gang of First Nation hunters and their dogs.

But the most dramatic moment came not too far from the town of Smithers. We had just stocked up on food for the long trek ahead and entered what felt like a never-ending region of swampy marshland. Eventually, we reached a creek with waist-deep water. Roy had fallen into a river earlier that day, so was already soaked through, and didn't think twice about plunging right in; but I quite fancied keeping my boots dry, so, after spotting a convenient fallen pine that seemingly bridged the two banks, I attempted to mimic a tightrope walker.

Two things became instantly apparent. The first was that the log was absolutely soaked, and the second was that the creek had transformed into a raging torrent in the section immediately beneath my makeshift bridge. I attempted to edge across and discovered, to my horror, that not only was the tree wet, the bark was rotten. Away it slipped, like the skin off a split banana, to reveal a marble smooth interior. It was like balancing on a horizontal pillar of polished marble and down I went, plunging sideways into the angry water.

Believe it or not, I can't actually swim. We did have a few lessons at school, but I never swam again once I'd left. No doubt I would've been cursing that decision, had I been able to think about anything other than my chances of survival rapidly vanishing before my eyes. I got lucky and was swept into the bank on the other side, but our freshly purchased jam, bread, cheese and fruit were not so fortunate. I looked to Roy, and could see him suppressing a laugh. I should've been relieved I wasn't dead, but I was absolutely furious I'd lost our things in the river *and* that Roy thought it was funny; doubly so, when I realized I had also lost my brand-new fishing rod.

We made plans to head up the isolated Stewart–Cassiar Highway that cuts a route through the north-west corner of the province, and then on up to the Yukon province. By this point, I was suffering with a leg injury, and we were both concerned about the distance between settlements on a road that was untarmacked due to the presence of permafrost. Again, the kindness of Canadian strangers came to our aid. Roy settled on the idea of us building a trolley to help us walk with our packs, and a gentleman, who had seen the state of us and our camp, drove him around the local dumps to salvage any useful bits of scrap. Two bicycle wheels, a school-desk frame, an old bed, a lawnmower handle, a bar stool later – and the trolley was complete. Truly, it was an education in what you could build simply from the waste of others; and we were well on our way.

Higher and deeper into the Canadian north we went. We were becoming increasingly resourceful backwoodsmen and competent long-distance walkers. Our fish diet had expanded from rainbow trouts to include Arctic grayling, suckerfish, lake trout and Dolly Varden trout. We became skilled at setting snares for rabbits, and learnt which were all the edible species of mushroom and berries. We made jams of wild fruits, and for greens, we consumed vast amounts of dandelion leaves alongside the fresh shooting leaves of young fireweed plants, the purple-flowering beauties that sprung forth in all this undisturbed boreal forest.

With each month that passed, I could feel myself changing, not only in terms of the skills I was acquiring, but physically and mentally too. We entered the Yukon and I became far surer of my feet. Our hair grew long and our beards thickened. I forged fresh muscles, honed from carrying loads, hiking and hunting, and felt myself shedding the burden of all the former abuses to my body of the years past. My mental horizons expanded exponentially too. I felt free and experienced a rarefied sense of belonging that I hadn't ever felt anywhere outside of the Scottish Highlands. Of course, it helped that I was in an awesome area of iconic wilderness vistas: snow-capped peaks, turquoise lakes and enormous trees; and that Roy and I were travelling at a time of year when it was possible to live very well just from that land's natural bounties alone; but there was an authentic rawness to this way of life that was undeniably seductive too – addictive, even.

Even the dramas: the enormous electrifying and terrifying storms, the day Roy was hospitalized by bee stings, a car crash at the hands of a drunk driver, all our close encounters with wild animals (more on that later . . .) added to the pure excitement of it all. It was intoxicating, invigorating, and utterly liberating.

Our last six weeks were spent in the Rocky Mountains, but the weather was turning. The snow was no longer confined to the caps of the mountains and, as the mercury plummeted, so crept in the snow, and then the rain. It was undeniably spectacular: a land of glaciers and towering peaks, the height of which we hadn't witnessed before. We hiked as much as we could, but the nights were closing in and it soon became punishingly cold. With our flysheet encased in ice most mornings, wild food was harder to find and, at times, so was ice-free water.

Returning towards Vancouver, the rain was relentless. My pockets were empty and my wristwatch was worn halfway up my forearm, such was the amount of weight I had lost. It had been one hell of a journey, but it was clear we were being ushered off the land by nature.

It was time to head home.

GRIM AND GRIZZLY

I had a feeling within me . . . a strange feeling that my home in Britain was not as I had left it.

I had felt that feeling before, back when Roy and I had been wandering in the Rockies in 1979, but I had tried to force it to the back of my mind. After the plane touched down, and Roy and I had made it through customs, there were my brothers, Dave and Mike, waiting.

I could see from their ashen faces that something was very badly wrong. They explained they'd tried to get a message out to me, but by the time they'd received a postcard with my whereabouts, and hastily written back to that location to try and share the awful news, Roy and I had already long since departed.

I still wish I could've somehow seen it coming. I wish I could've known what was going to happen while I was away. My dad had died from cancer and that was it. Both my parents had passed in the space of little more than a year. Mam to the heart attack and then Dad to a cancer I didn't even know he'd had.

I'd missed his funeral and was overwhelmed with grief. Losing Mam had been absolutely awful, but I had buried down my emotions as my brothers and I lowered her into the grave. Just a few months later I was away in Canada with Roy, and I was able to distract myself to a degree, but now back in England, without them, there was nowhere left to hide.

It hit me really hard, that did. I became deeply depressed and, for a good while, I believe I was quite lost. I didn't write in my diary for a very long time. In fact, I didn't do very much at all.

—

There's only so long anyone can run from grief before they are eventually forced to confront it. My whole life was put on hold for a year. I was consumed by a depression until the day eventually arrived where I had to let all my sorrow in. I bought a bottle of whisky and cried it all out.

No matter the circumstances, losing your parents is hard. You never really get over it, least of all losing both almost back-to-back.

I had to try and get on with my life. I had no money, the council were wanting to repossess my parents' council house, my home, and putting huge pressure on me, and I was soon left with mounting bills from rent, gas, electricity and food. Escape had been at the forefront of my mind before I'd made it back to England, and was doubly so now. I wanted to return to the wilderness and stay there for as long as I possibly could. Maybe I was running away from the reality of the situation I'd come back to but, whatever it was, there was no way I planned on hanging around for any longer than I needed to. There was even less tying me to a life here now than there had been before.

I wanted to get back to the place where I had been happiest, to go even further into the North American country than I had with Roy; but first, I needed to return to the building industry to work and save harder than ever.

The three and a half years that elapsed from coming home with Roy, to finally having enough money to return to Canada, were quite possibly the hardest period of my entire life. To add to the grief and other difficulties, I was living in a squalid, damp-filled home, with a toilet that would not flush and pipes that burst from the frost over one terrible winter. It was the sort of place where your breath crackled like ice: a three-bedroomed stone tomb.

Trying to save, I invited in a lodger to help with the bills, but he turned out to be an alcoholic womanizer, who fled the home when one of his many 'conquests' eventually discovered where he lived and served him up some well-deserved just desserts. The only plus turned out to be that – because it was often *so* cold – I had no need to waste money refrigerating the stock of hare, rabbit or wood pigeon that I'd harvest with my rifle for a bit of extra meat. But that was about the only positive. The amount I was paying out in bills, even living as meagrely as possible, could've kept me in the Canadian wilds for months; but, working back in construction, I grafted as hard as I ever had and saved everything I possibly could.

Finally, mercifully, the day of my departure came around again. I was thirty-five years old and itching for another adventure.

—

My solo trip took me through British Columbia and the Yukon once more, and then north, far north, to the Arctic Circle, Canada's North-West Territories, then back to the Yukon; north again to Alaska, then back once more to the Yukon. I had an open return plane ticket, so no fixed date to come back to the UK – the plan was to go where I pleased and stay away for as long as my funds would last. In the event, I was gone for a year.

I bounced up and down the hinterland of the continental north-west, tracing the mighty Fraser and Teslin rivers, and traversing the major mountain ranges. I tramped over snow-capped peaks and through the immense boreal forests, and met many of the legendary creatures of North American folklore.

Often, it felt like I was in an elemental wilderness that was still somehow capable of repelling man's most malign influence; but, for many generations, outsiders have arrived in these lands desperately seeking something. Some sought out the promises of great riches in the gold rush; others wished to discover something deeper about their true selves: a *wild man* survivor image, reflected back against the jagged mountains and vast lakes. But that land is undeniably indifferent to us. It cares not for our will; and for every man who found their fortune, there were many more who left empty-handed, or who were never seen or heard from ever again.

For me, my adventures in Canada and America were the most transformative of my life. They hauled my existence out of the

Derbyshire grey and into the technicolour. I was alive and profoundly inspired.

I flew to Seattle on 3 May 1983 and immediately boarded the Greyhound bus to Vancouver. After that it was back to Suicide Creek, up the Fraser River to Hope, before fishing and hitching a path east to Banff. Next I looped north, returning to the Yukon via Whitehorse and making Dawson around the time of the longest day, 21 June, to climb a hill and photograph the bright sunshine at exactly midnight.

I fished the Klondike and found fool's gold, and eventually passed through the gateway to the Arctic Circle, and beyond to Inuvik, in Canada's extreme North-West Territories.

I was always humbled by the generosity of the people who lived in some of those extreme outposts, especially the indigenous Inuit. Even when times were tough, and the communities were very poor, a lift, a meal, or a can of beer was readily offered to the outsider. Back then, I wondered whether it was pure surprise at seeing someone new in such lonesome places, or if it was just my Derbyshire accent, but I have since come to realize it was most likely a willingness to impress on others that community's values of kindness and hospitality. I carried those sentiments with me, and strove to use them in my own life going forward.

As when I travelled with Roy, I made my way mostly either by foot or by hitching. I aimed to sleep out in the open and under the flysheet, but this adventure was to be double the duration and distance of our trip back in 1979 and I could never have imagined how much this experience would ultimately change me as a man.

There were changes I welcomed, like learning lessons in self-reliance, self-belief and independence – but I had not anticipated that those holiday skills would one day form the foundations of how I would wind up living the rest of my life.

I should say though, there were some very obvious differences between the specific skills I needed to develop for Canada, and the ones I carried forward with me to my later life here in Treig. In Canada, walking and sleeping alone in the forest and bush, 'death by bear' was never too far from my thoughts. However small those odds actually were, I still thought I should come up with at least something to lessen my chances of becoming a meal, and, as it happened, there were several opportunities to test my strategies.

—

One of my more extraordinary bear encounters came during that 1983 trip. I had returned south to Whitehorse, where my old travelling partner Roy had actually settled. Since our trip, he'd found God and the love of a good woman, and he and his wife were the proud parents of two children too. He was eager for a break and together we took off for the most lonesome waters of the Yukon; together again: camping, fishing and gold-panning.

The following day began early, around four a.m., with Roy jabbing me in the back with a finger.

'Ken. There's a bear in the camp.'

'Can you see it, Roy?'

'Aye, I can.'

'What's it doing?'

'It's stuck its head in my rucksack.'

'Well. What ya gunna do about it?'

'GRRRRRRR! Ger outta there!'

We scurried from the tent, as the bear, presumably a grizzly, made a hasty retreat through the bush, carrying within its mouth two loaves of bread, a half-roll of sausage, cheese and, believe it or not, a packet of tea bags.

It usually doesn't take anyone long to nudge the conversation towards an imagined scenario where – roaming the wilderness of North America – I might have been ripped apart by a grizzly bear, wolf, mountain lion or, at the very least, trampled by a giant moose.

Regular people have a strange preoccupation with the idea that death in the wilderness is likely to come from the tooth or claw of some bloodthirsty, rampaging predator. The truth, though, is always much more benign. Truly wild encounters with the creatures most capable of ending our lives are usually fleeting snapshots: a flash of fur here, a heavy, crumbling rush through the brush there, as whatever-it-was crashes from the scene the very instant it becomes aware of your presence.

Predators are pragmatists. They are lethally armed to quickly dispatch far weaker prey in an instant, but they will predominantly target the lamest, sickest, smallest, slowest and stupidest. In that way they maintain and sustain the health and balance of an environment or herd; and you can be sure that when an ecosystem is beset with myriad problems, the apex predators – those at the top of the food chain, without predators of their own – will almost certainly be missing from the scene.

Luckily for us, their highly selective hunting strategy writes a hefty chunk of life insurance into your policy whilst out wandering in their territory. To them, we offer up a pause for thought. Superficially we look lame, sick, small, slow and stupid, but we are not their regular prey and could well be hiding a weapon. If a predator can't be absolutely sure you offer no conceivable threat to them, then they'll nearly always steer well clear, and target something else instead.

Statistically speaking, in modern times, the chances of dying while out on some backcountry adventure are extraordinarily low. In the United States, if you exclude the tragedy of suicide, the likelihood of you dying in a National Park hovers somewhere around one in two million; ten thousand times less likely than you losing your life in a car accident in the same country. Bears are by far and away the most dangerous of all the mammalian predators, but even then, they account for less than 1 per cent of total deaths in the wilderness. We are talking about, on average, just eleven deaths in North America every year, and, although bear attacks never cease to shock with their brutality, the chances of you being attacked are still incredibly remote.

In terms of animals, you are far more likely to be killed by bees than bears, and over half of the deaths in the wilderness are caused through either falling, being trapped in an avalanche, drowning, or simply getting lost and then subsequently dying from heatstroke, hypothermia, starvation or dehydration. All are truly appalling ways to meet your maker, but none quite have the same star-power Hollywood draw as a good old-fashioned bear attack. They feel somehow pedestrian by comparison, and yet that is precisely what makes them so dangerous. While you're out buying your bear spray and bells, you neglect to do the really simple things like check the weather forecast, get a good coat, or bring adequate food or shelter.

In fairness, though, falling from a slope or getting a bit cold and thirsty are all things you're highly likely to experience at some point or other while you're out on a big trek. They are usually very trivial, very survivable events that happen with a certain degree of frequency when you're walking for weeks on end; whereas being attacked by an 800-pound grizzly bear . . . well, that only needs to happen once.

I had maybe twenty encounters with bears during my travels. Most were passing affairs: a bear peering from behind a rock before scuttling off, another vaguely plodding around the camp, or a mother and her cubs spotted roadside as I hitched a ride; but a few really did get the pulse racing.

In the Rockies a black bear sniffed my rucksack for food, and in Alaska it took a lot of shouting and gun-toting to get one shifted from our camp. Once, while fishing, I turned a bend in the river and met a black bear head-on. Fortunately, it shot up a big cotton-wood tree and we both made our escapes.

The worst moments were when the bears were unafraid. Four occasions really stick in my mind. Once I walked within twenty feet of a black bear, which simply roared back at me, and sent me hurrying off. One night-time camp invader was so persistent, I had to set fires all around the flysheet to try and ward the bear off. And the one with Roy was pretty extraordinary. Despite all our attempts to scare that bear away, it still opened Roy's pack and took half our provisions in a single mouthful. That was a big grizzly, and was almost within touching distance of where we lay. As soon as it disappeared off with its hoard, we were up. Lighting fires and sitting up till dawn, absolutely quaking in our boots.

The best single piece of advice I can give if you are ever in a threatening position with *any* potentially violent wild animal is, whatever you might be feeling inside, you *must* fight the urge to run away. Running shows weakness and fear, two emotions that are near certain to escalate the predator's idea that you are a very easy meal indeed. They could, in fact, lethally execute you long before you could ever make it to a climbable tree. You could never outrun a bear, a wolf, or a mountain lion; and, even if you did manage to get to a tree, a bear or a mountain lion would come straight up after you and peel you open like a can of beans.

What you need to do is play to that pragmatic part of the predator's mind, which I mentioned earlier. You are looking to convince it that, however soft and fleshy-looking you may appear, you are still not worth the risk; that you could fight back; that you might somehow have the ability to maim and wound.

Stand your ground, slowly back away, if you can, and the mountain lion or wolf will very likely back down too. The only exceptions could be the bears. You are definitely giving yourself the best possible chance of survival if you don't show fear, but bears – especially the grizzlies – are much more aggressive.

If you stand still but the bear still attacks and is black, then give it absolutely everything you have: shout, scream, target the eyes and ears, punch, kick, and use any available weapons like sticks and stones. If it is the much larger brown or grizzly bear, though, for god's sake: *just play dead*. Don't get me wrong: a black bear is no teddy, and anyone trying to fight one off is still in *almost* the deepest trouble imaginable, it's just that, in this truly dire game of mammalian Top Trumps, the person with slightly worse luck is definitely the one stuck beneath the grizzly.

To give you a very brief natural history lesson: generally speaking, your brown bears are in the coastal areas of Alaska, whereas your grizzlies (which are also a type of brown) are found inland and have no access to marine foods. Either way, they are up to double the weight of a black bear and twenty times more likely to cause injury. They are armed with huge teeth and curved claws that can extend up to four inches in length; twice the size of the black bears'.

A grizzly 'attack' is most likely to be a pure defensive reaction to that bear having bear cubs somewhere in the area. In which case, a fightback is not only pointless, but it is far more likely to confirm to the bear that you are indeed a threat to their children's safety and need to be neutralized for the sake of their progeny. Quite often, the grizzly will come bowling over, knocking you, 'the threat', to the ground to firmly establish your weakness (and their dominance) before it then simply moves on with their cubs.

According to the established wisdom, only when it becomes obvious that the grizzly attack really *isn't* a test should you fight back; but I think it is fair to say that finding someone with that level of composure, in the heat of any bear assault, is about as slim as their odds of survival.

If you have been unlucky enough to be attacked by a grizzly and have somehow survived, then I hope you can count yourself fortunate to have at least escaped with your life; but I'm sure things are never quite the same after an ordeal like that.

As humans have greedily extended our own territories out into the homes of these animals, degrading the environment and removing the naturally available food sources of many predators, we have caused an upswing in the amount of contact we wind up having with these potentially dangerous animals. The scarcity of their natural food is forcing many predators to look elsewhere, and when a phenomenal sense of smell, a degree of intelligence and increasing desperation all meet in the middle, it doesn't take too long before you start seeing an apex hunter in some very unexpected places indeed.

Which all leads me neatly on to my very best near-death bear story.

It happened while I was stopping at Whitehorse, the capital of the Yukon, and I was indulging in one of my favourite money-spinning escapades. I was down at the local rubbish dump looking for useful things that people have thrown out. Anything that could help me in any way. You would not believe what gets thrown away down there. Humans are incredibly wasteful, but, as the old northern saying goes, 'Where there's muck, there's brass.'

Over many years of dump-diving, I've found clothing (including brand-new boots), in-date tins of food, pots and pans, full batteries and loads of electronics; I've even found money. Industrious people with flat-bed trucks would be backing in and out of those places all the time, lifting kitchen appliances, old motors, wiring, whole carpets, and then making simple repairs, or giving them a clean before selling them on, almost good as new.

This particular dump was enormous. A large twelve-foot-high fence spanned the perimeter, while JCBs moved around inside, managing mountains of rubbish that were so high they towered over you and frequently blocked out the sunlight.

The trick for a good haul was to head for areas that had been freshly dug or piled by the diggers: either the mountains of newly turned treasures, or the craters left behind in the waste. That fateful day I was deep in the dump, walking up a hill of rubbish to get to an area where a new pile had just been created. I was strolling along a plateau, and couldn't have been too far from my destination, when a movement to the left of my makeshift path stopped me dead in my tracks.

My heart rate danced as my focus was pulled towards the source of the movement. I could see immense bulk, and brown fur moving backwards. This was not a trick of the light, a cuddly toy, or a hallucination brought on from the stench of the dump. What I was looking at was the giant arse of a simply enormous grizzly bear as it reversed its way backwards out of the hole it had just created in the tip.

Clearly, it had been looking for food and, judging by the look on its face, it had been unsuccessful. I stood motionless, not due

Right: A true monster of a king salmon in its fine breeding colours. My long trips to the Canadian and Alaskan wilderness in the late 1970s and 1980s were defining periods of my life. They gave me the skills and self-belief to go on and live the life that I have had.

Below: Out for a stroll in a whole world of white. That's Luibeilt bothy in the distance. They reckon it's Scotland's most haunted, but I'd beg to differ.

Above left: My work as a ghillie mostly revolved around the deer-stalking season, but I did help on the grouse shooting too. Here two shooters wait patiently for a bird, with Stob Coire Easain mountain watching over their backs.

Above right: A late summer light illuminates the vast fells at the head of Loch Treig.

Below right: A stunningly still day on Treig. When the water provides a perfect mirror image of the mountains, it can be tricky to work out where the land ends and the loch begins.

Below left: Corrour Station back in the day. Notice the old hand-operated levers for changing the tracks and the signalman's house where I used to get my post delivered? Corrour remains marvellously isolated and is the highest mainland stop in the United Kingdom.

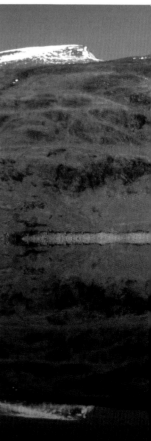

The walls of the guest cabin start to take shape in the long grass. If you look in the corners of the structure you can see the 'saddle notch' technique I use in all my building. It is just a case of repeating the process log-by-log till the whole wall is complete.

With the walls finished, freshly cut log-ends pile up as I smarten up the building's edges with my saw – leaving the structure looking neat with its uniform corners.

Once the building reaches its full height, I have to be really careful – no one wants to fall off the top of their log cabin while they are busy building the roof frame. With the window and door cut in, I just need to get hold of some corrugated metal to finish the roofing.

The cabin that marked the start of a new life of isolation on the banks of Treig. Forty years later, I can't say I've regretted a single thing – but losing this cabin to a fire in 1991 was one of the hardest moments of my life up here.

Left: The toilet is half constructed on the new cabin build and I look very stressed here. I had to construct the cabin under huge time pressure – winter was coming to the Highlands and I needed a roof over my head before the snow descended.

Below: An aerial view of the cabin. Easy to find if you're a bird, I suppose, but only a few steps into the curtain of trees could leave you scratching your head and wondering where on earth you were when on the ground.

The back of the 'new' cabin, complete with a window, deer antlers and a small wind turbine that didn't really stand up to the Scottish elements for very long. Working flat out, it would take me about six weeks to get the basic cabin structure standing – but the outbuildings, loch-stone pathways and gardens took many more months of hard graft.

A bountiful garden heaving with root vegetables, herbs and the shoots of future fruit and berry trees. There are few things more nourishing for your belly, or pocket pennies, than growing food for yourself.

My cabin has had to withstand some serious weather over the years.
Huge storms, sub-zero temperatures, snow drifts, even the occasional heatwave.

The bath arrives on the shores of Treig. I hauled it up to the side of my cabin and
built a small log burner around its base to heat the water. If it was placed next to some
fancy luxury cabin you could probably charge a fair bit for such a well-placed tub,
but luckily it doesn't cost me a thing.

to my superior knowledge of staving off death by bear, but because I was quite simply stupefied by terror.

We were face-to-face on the same pathway, and now the grizzly was slowly, but very purposefully, advancing towards me. Clearly, I was in very deep trouble indeed. I was hemmed in by the dump's fence on all sides and, at twelve-foot-high, as much as it might seem theoretically possible for me to scale the barrier without being eaten, I could only make it there if I could first negotiate my way around the labyrinth formed by all the dump's rubbish.

If the bear didn't catch me before I got to the fence, which seemed highly likely, it would almost certainly catch me as I tried to scramble over. This fully grown grizzly stretched some eight foot in height from its feet to its claw-tips. It would pluck me off and crunch me as easily as I'd pinch an apple from a tree.

It left me with just one credible option for escape. I needed to go right back the way I'd come. Back along the plateau atop the rubbish mountain, then down the pathway till I made it to the sole entrance and exit: the main gate in the fence. It seemed an almightily long way away right then, but, through the fog of cata-tonic fear I knew, no matter what I did, I could not make a run for it.

The bear might have been moving on me with serious intent, but it wasn't charging me. Not *yet*, anyway. Given a grizzly can sprint at up to thirty-five miles per hour when it wants to, the best chance I had was if the bear maintained its measured plod. This was obviously no grizzly defending her cubs. This was the far rarer example of a grizzly actively engaged in stalking a human. If it made it to me, which it absolutely was going to if I remained still, 'playing dead' would quickly result in performance art becoming dreadful reality.

In terms of human bear interactions, this was the most dangerous position you could possibly be in, with the absolute worse brand of bear: a giant adult grizzly that held no fear of humans and was *very* hungry.

With the gap closing between me and the bear, I slowly started to pace backwards. Remaining calm in my body language, making no rapid movements, and giving no reason for the bear to bolt forward, while very deliberately moving away and keeping my eyes fixed upon the animal. Luckily, as I began to move, the bear's pace did not quicken, and we entered a curious dance where we maintained a distance between us by matching pace: me backwards, the bear forwards. I just had to hope I didn't trip over on some lump of trash, otherwise I was definitely history.

It is a curious experience, being confronted with your total physical vulnerability. Our lifestyle, our technology, our houses and cars all shield us from our actual, feeble reality. They create a reassuring gap between now and the time in the past when we all lived in caves and trees. Back in prehistory, the spectre of a very violent death at the hands of a sabretooth, cave hyena, or short-faced bear was omnipresent; but today, most humans, and especially those who live in the Western world, can easily go their entire lives without ever realizing quite how fragile and feeble we really are, especially when held up against the apex predators of the wider natural world.

It was highly ironic that, trapped within this colossal mountain of human engineering, the visual metaphor for all our 'progress', there was not one single thing at hand that could've staved off the murderous advances of this bear. Most of the waste I walked within had been created purely for our living convenience, improving *our* lives on the one hand, whilst degrading the planet's habitats and condemning this bear to hunt the tip for food on the other. I was in a truly pitiful position. A highly intelligent tortoise who had forgotten to put on his shell.

Walking backwards, I made it across the plateau and became aware that I was heading back down the slope. That was my eureka moment. If I maintained the gap now, there would soon be a very brief moment where the bear would disappear from view over the brow of the hill; the only time in my retreat where I wouldn't be able to see the bear and, crucially, it wouldn't be able to see me either.

I stared back at the bear as I paced down. 'Can't see its ankles now,' I muttered to myself. 'Can't see its legs now,' I continued. 'Can't see its belly . . . can't see its head.'

And in that moment, I broke the golden rule of grizzly attack and ran as fast as I ever have in my entire life. In Derbyshire parlance, I ran like *absolute buggery* – straight back through the gate and down onto the road outside the tip. There, I met a V-shaped junction cutting around a small wood but, filled with adrenaline and panic, and certain the bear's breath was hot on my heels, I didn't even deviate from my course. Instead, I ran straight through the wood, straight out the other side, and almost got flattened by a truck.

The man slammed his anchors on and exploded at me in a rage of brake-pad fumes and dust. 'There's a grizzly inside!' I screamed back at him. 'GRIZZLY BEAR!' he shouted back, his countenance doing an instant about-turn as he quickly grasped down the back of his vehicle for his gun.

This man was armed and ready in a way that suggested he might've been waiting for this moment his entire life. With one hand on the steering wheel, and another on the trigger of a rifle that looked capable of dispatching a T-Rex, he blasted his truck all the way to the front gate and ran inside.

I was safely back in the human world of faux superiority through working technology, but I didn't hear a rifle shot and the bear had already escaped. I'd been very lucky and so had the bear. The municipal rubbish dump was no place to die for either of us.

ALONE IN THE WILD

The memories are dimmer now, but during that trip in 1983 I had two good chunks of time all alone in the wild – one in the summer and one nearing winter. The first saw me follow a section of the Peace River between British Columbia and northern Alberta; the other was along the River Teslin in the Yukon. Both were for a few weeks at a time in an achingly beautiful area of real wilderness that I felt very privileged to get to know. I'd decided to turn away from the sanctuary of civilization, to cut the umbilical cord provided by the main roads and access to people, their shops, bars and banks and those few weeks were my first taste of true self-sufficiency and what a life lived off-grid might really be like.

I must confess, I have mislaid the diaries for a lot of what happened during the period of roaming solo among those trees and mountains. Luckily for me (and you) I do still have the boxes of slide film from the photos I took at the time, and simply by placing them in a battery-operated viewer, I can close one eye and pour myself right back into the memory of that whole marvellous adventure.

I love photography. Before my travels began, I took evening courses in photography and carried a single-lens reflex camera and film with me wherever I went. Photos can capture everything from the widest vistas to the very tiniest details; can store it all and keep it forever. A photo is a moment in time, frozen at the point you clicked the camera; but the release of memory that the image can draw out of your brain is like pulling a great, beautiful fish up from an immense depth on the very thinnest of lines. I can see an image and remember weeks on a mountain range, or the sharp taste of some freshly picked wild berries. I can feel the magnificent pain in my feet, and recall the toughness of my muscles as I pressed forever forwards. I can remember it all through a single photo; then just close my eyes and feel as if it is happening to me all over again.

Practically speaking, heading away from the towns and highways, and off into the woods was one very obvious way to save money. Roy and I had done this from the off on our first trip, but this was going to be about far more than just eking out my cash in the forest fringes. I wanted to know what proper adventure felt like, in one of the most exciting places on earth. I wanted to go much deeper than ever before. I wanted to find out how I would fare, truly out on my own, and to be utterly independent of everything and everyone. Immersed in nature; neither spending a cent nor seeing a soul.

There was no established route, I just wove my way through the bush, loosely following the course of those two enormous rivers. This was the adventure of my dreams: solo in a grand theatrical hinterland, where you could be cutting through dense forest one day, or out in wide open mountain country the next. No compass, no map, no track; no real idea of a firm destination, nor formal plans about how long it would take. The risks were very real though. In the summer on the Peace River wild food could be abundant. Seasonal berries filled the trees and bushes and fungi might flood the floor, but that meant the larger animals were out too – sometimes to eat the smaller animals that foraged those same fruits of the forest, other times with freshly born young, or behaving aggressively as they approached their autumnal breeding seasons.

Early winter on the Teslin brought occasionally deep snowdrifts and the potential for killer cold and very bad weather. The big dangerous beasts may have been scarcer, but that meant wild food was much harder to find too. Being able to set snares for the few small mammals there were, and catch fish from high rivers, was as imperative as learning how to adequately ration the small supplies I carried with me.

It may sound suicidal, but for those who feel it, there is a magnetism to the truly wild. It isn't machismo, there's just something about being right *out there*. A deep sense of calm purpose and a connection that is almost religious in its feel. I found a confidence in myself and my own abilities. The stakes were high – this was the sort of place where a silly mistake could cost you everything. A misplaced step and a slip into the river, a heavy fall on a mountainous slope, a severed finger from the clumsy use of your knife; all could wind up guaranteeing you would never be seen by human eyes ever again. Perhaps it sounds a bit daft given the risk I'd accepted by walking off into the bush in the first place, but once I was there I learned to take absolute care at all times. In a potentially dangerous and unpredictable environment, you should at least try and control the controllable hazards. Take no chances. If a river looked too deep to cross, the route forward too dense or steep, I would simply take the extra time to find another way round. Looking after myself and sticking to my limits became my norm. I hold those life-preserving lessons dear today; but being alone also allowed me to explore the line between an over-confidence, that could get you in deep trouble, and an excessive degree of caution, that could suppress your most fantastic dreams. I highly recommend it.

Once you have found your rhythm and established your routines, you feel like you could conquer anything, and possibly even go on forever, were it not for winter. Sometimes I'd meet areas of dense, impenetrable bush, these thorny, twisting, almost fairy-tale-like monstrosities, with spikes an inch and a half long; or I'd encounter natural obstacles: deep-sided creeks to navigate, or cliffs to traverse. With experience, though, came the growing sense that I really could do it. In many respects, once I'd slipped off the main road and allowed myself to be swallowed by that landscape, I had no other choice but to find a way, and that, in itself, liberated me from all my fears about any shortcomings I might have.

It was totally committing, and therefore required my total commitment.

—

I had very few possessions going in, which was fortunate, as travelling light was absolutely the key to moving with efficiency. All I took was a good knife and billhook, a few bits for fire-lighting, flour and sugar, a cooking pot and bottle, the snares, fishing gear, flysheet, sleeping bag, and the clothes on my back.

With so few things at my disposal, I had to be industrious to survive, and that meant looking to the traditions upheld by the true custodians of this land. One of the slides shows a strange-looking fire laid out on a flat and dry forest floor. This was a First Nations technique that I was shown right back on my first trip with Roy in 1979, when we were fishing alongside the indigenous locals in central British Columbia. The 'Indian Star Fire', they had called it then, was beautifully simple.

You gather logs of a similar thickness and length and arrange them in a star formation, with the inward-facing points almost touching in the middle. You then light your fire in the centre, and push the logs further inward as the wood burns away. The real benefit of the Star Fire was just how much control it gave you over the burn rate and intensity of the flame.

For a less intense fire, I was taught to pull the logs ever so slightly apart at the centre; for a stronger burn, you just pushed them together. The arrangement of the logs makes it easy to keep the fire ticking over without burning right through your fuel, whilst still giving you the option of a period of intense heat whenever you were ready to cook. The real trick was to choose wood that still had some greenness to it, that was relatively freshly cut or fallen, and not completely dry. It ran counter to everything I'd learnt about wild fires so far. Green wood is so full of moisture that you'd ordinarily stack it in a pile to dry for at least a year before using as fuel, but in the Canadian wilderness, using the Star Fire technique, it worked brilliantly. If the wood was totally dry, you lost all your control; it just kept burning through, even when the logs were parted, but the right amount of moisture just gave you the right sort of burn and, once you had that down, it was pretty much the perfect backcountry fire.

I also learnt the traditional technique for building a simple tripod for hanging a pot over a fire, or making a wooden spit-roast for any wild-caught meat. All of that meant my cooking really could be executed with just one pot and a sharp knife for a construction that, once you'd done a few times, could be assembled in a matter of minutes. I have a slide here of a large lake trout cooking on one of my hand-made spits. All I've done is to make a cut right around the circumference of its head, just below the gills. A good firm pull removed the head, and pulled out all the guts with it. Then, I've skewered it lengthways on a thick, sharpened stick. Next, I've cut two sticks with Y-shaped heads and placed them in the ground on opposing sides of the fire, and laid the stick holding the fish right across these. I would turn the fish as it cooks, and right below is my small pot, collecting the fat as it bubbles from the body, ready for reuse as a cooking oil.

Gathering was hugely important, especially during the summer excursion on the Peace River. In that area, edible berries and fruits, like wild strawberries and gooseberries, were prolific. I would fill my pot and then boil them down with the sugar and make absolutely delicious jams to carry along with me. Mushrooms too: great horse mushrooms, which can grow to the size of my palm and be found in large rings; and the common field mushroom.

There were many times I'd find more wild food than I could ever eat in my lifetime. Great bushes of berries, and trees flush with fruit; or a grove of mushrooms that was so dense it would turn the forest floor a snow-white and seemingly went on for days. Imagine. A belly full of delicious mushrooms, as you lay down to sleep in a white ocean filled with so many more. There were times the Peace River really felt like a living paradise, a Garden of Eden of sorts.

At other times, especially on the Teslin River at the start of winter, life in the wild could be a struggle, and I'd be much more reliant on the bannock. The bannock became a key part of my diet. It is, in essence, a flatbread, made from a very basic dough mix, which you can cook directly in a pan. I believe the bannock is a northern thing. It is certainly well known among the Scots, which was where I first learnt to make it, but it was also a staple among the earlier settlers and fur traders in Canada; most of the First Nations and Inuit peoples seem to have their own twist on a bannock, too.

The beauty of bannock is in its simplicity. You make your dough by mixing flour and sugar (and a bit of that fatty cooking oil, if you still have it) with incremental glugs of water, till it is all bound together – but not too sticky you can't pick it up. You might want to rest it for half an hour or so, but then all you do is roll the dough out into balls, which you flatten to about 1-cm thick, place on the pan with a bit more oil, or cook using a stick, for usually just a couple of minutes per side. Then you can spread your jam thickly on top, or eat them just as they are.

I'm looking at the next slide, which shows a horrible hairy caterpillar with black ends and long white whiskery lashes sticking out along its body. It is split in half by a garish yellow band. I saw these often, and were warned that they were poisonous. They aren't, though. It is the spotted tussock moth caterpillar: not actually poisonous, but those hairs are well known to be highly irritating, and will cause a very itchy burning rash and welts if they brush against your skin. Other slides show the animals I caught in my snares: rabbits and a perfectly white snowshoe hare; but I also took duck and grouse with my catapult.

Another slide shows a moose with her young calf. I remember that so well. They were close enough for me to hear them breathe. Extraordinary beasts to behold. The largest deer on Earth; standing over six-foot just to the shoulder and weighing up to 1,500 pounds; moose were not a creature you'd ever wish to startle. They are incredible swimmers, but their eyesight is utter crap. As long as you are downwind, which I was, you'd be so surprised at how close you can get. Moose will come at you if they've got a young one, though; so I wasn't going to push my luck here. Their antlers are massive, up to a metre and a half wide, and I once found a huge pile of them on the forest floor. I assumed someone had been out shooting them, but I later learnt that male moose actually drop their antlers in the exact same location every time. They'll do that, then regrow them, before shedding them all over again.

I pretty much saw every iconic animal species you'd care to think of. The bears and moose, of course, but also bald eagles, wolverines, elk, wolves and coyotes. I saw beavers building immense dams and encountered western garter snakes that slithered one metre long from forked tongue to tail-tip. I watched herds of caribou that stretched up to a mile in length, and salmon runs so dense that they completely blackened the crystalline rivers. Soon, I came to notice how extraordinarily confident some creatures were when they were well away from the threat of humans. Often, squirrels would climb up onto my arms and I would frequently pass within feet of birds and deer; but, when it came to the predators (or just potential accidental killers, like a startled moose), I always maintained a respectful distance, and was very careful to store away what little food I had, high up in the trees.

I might not have encountered people, but that wasn't to say I was in virgin territory. Occasionally, I would find these curious dwellings, abandoned right out in the middle of nowhere, surrounded by bush and appearing like they'd simply dropped from the sky. Some were fifty years old or more: deserted log cabins constructed from local timbers, usually with a bear-proof storeroom built on stilts, and derelict hunting and fishing outposts, leaning over and slowly rotting on the banks of the rivers; all built with ambitions that had long since departed. A romantic dream, perhaps, that turned into a nightmare? Or something more prosaic? Once, I found a wooden cross driven into the earthen floor inside one such shelter. Possibly the grave of some poor unfortunate; who knew what the story was there?

One of the slides shows what must once have been a beautiful log cabin. It was large, inviting and well-built, with at least a couple of rooms, thick timbers and a solid roof of tiled wood shingles. At a first glance, it would have been an obvious place to rest and looked like it could stand for another half a century or more; but staring down from the trees was just about the roughest form of natural security because, right there, in the trees, hung several great horned owls (also known as tiger owls) – one heavy-set and barrel-bodied beast of a bird. With a wingspan that can exceed 150 cm, and one of the largest sets of talons of any owl, this is not a species that you want to get on the wrong side of. Local hunters told me they are very dangerous – animals that would attack without the warning growls, or tell-tale body-language cautions, you might expect from other species.

They will tear apart porcupines without a problem, and will violently defend their territory too, especially if they have young present. Many hikers have been known to feel the sudden force of those talons when they have unwittingly stumbled onto their home turf, and I wasn't about to make that mistake. I pitched my flysheet well away from, what was now, very much *their* cabin, and took some lovely photos of them staring sternly down my lens.

Another slide shows my best effort at a photo of the Aurora Borealis, the Northern Lights. It was something I'd always hoped to see and then capture on film; but that wasn't going to be easy. These extraordinary solar flares light up the night sky with flowing pink, green, purple and red waves of swirling, dancing colour. Their movement is almost continuous, but after a few performances I noted a split second where the action might stop but the colours remain: the eye of the storm, I thought; my opportunity. After dozens of efforts, one night I lay in the snow, locked my arms as a tripod, and opened my aperture as wide as it would go. The movement stopped, I pressed, counted 'one, two', released; the shutter closed and it all started again. 'Yes!' I howled into the festival of colour as a wolf at the moon. I had the shot.

There was such a sublime richness to that land that it often felt like a throwback to times past. I had finally found the wilderness of my imagination and was frequently awe-struck by the vistas that folded out before me. Angular sharp white peaks stretched for many miles in every direction, like a wolf's jawline, all unclimbed by man. Thick boreal forests and swathes of balsam poplars with their pale barks, towering up to a hundred feet high. Huge lakes that could be mirror-calm one minute or whipped up by a storm the next, their surfaces lashing skywards, as if they were being whisked by a giant hand. Sometimes I'd pad through the snow, leaving my prints. Just mine and the animals', side-by-side, without a single other human set to be seen.

It was almost as if I'd discovered an entirely new planet; and it changed the way I felt about the wilderness profoundly. It no longer felt like a place to be conquered or feared; rather, it was a place where I could understand my own small significance in the grand scheme of the great life on earth. In all that humbling, I learnt to really look, understand and appreciate what was right there in front of me for what it truly was – and for as long as it lasted.

Even then, as Canada approached the mid-1980s with an economic recession biting hard, there were still vast tracts of untamed wild places that teemed with wildlife. One of the most emblematic animals of the nation, particularly in the Yukon region, was its king, or Chinook, salmon. I can't tell you what it was like in the breeding season. The sheer amount of salmon in those rivers was often breathtaking. You felt like you could walk right across their backs from one side of the river to the other; and the bald eagles and bears would feast till they were so fat they were unable to move. I heard how entire forests would grow off the back of nutrients from the many millions of post-spawning dead fish, and the smokehouses of the natives were filled wall-to-wall with salmon, as were their nets; yet no matter how many were taken, it never looked as if any animal would be capable of putting a dent in the sheer volume of salmon entering those rivers.

I hear now on the radio that salmon numbers have gone into a precipitous state of terminal decline. Everything – from man-made barriers in the form of dams, to global warming affecting their hunting grounds, to overfishing, to disease – has combined to absolutely decimate their numbers. Today, there are parts of the Alaskan Yukon river catchment where there are no salmon running through whatsoever. It seems impossible to believe. To go from what I saw, to this, in just forty years, is completely crazy and extremely scary to contemplate.

One of my favourite photos shows me standing with my telescopic fishing rod and a king salmon gripped through its gill. It is a spectacular fish, decked out in its bright red spawning coat, and is truly enormous. I grimace at the camera, straining to hold it up as it stretches fully from the tip of my left earlobe down below my left knee. It was the biggest fish I have ever caught in my life; but it wasn't even that unique back then. When the season was right, giant kings were simply everywhere. That fish wasn't even the biggest I hooked.

I don't want to think of that picture as a relic of times past, to be viewed in the same way as all those Victorian images of tiger-hunting expeditions, or the black-and-white photos of the car-sized halibuts they used to catch every day off Alaska in the fishing industry's heyday. But I have to face facts: many of the places I roamed back then have long since changed beyond all recognition.

———

I shouldn't imagine they'll come for me now, so I might as well just admit it. Nearing the end of my trip, I jumped the border illegally to get back into Canada. The States was no problem. I could always pick up a new tourist visa with no questions asked at the border, but I actually wanted to spend more of my time travelling in Canada, where I couldn't seem to get one for any more than three months at a time. By the end of my journey through the wilds of Canada, I'd overstayed my three-month visa by half a year. I didn't think it would be such a big deal. I crossed back over into Alaska, where the American Customs stamped my passport without any issue; but when I came to return back into Canada, the reception was altogether different.

Apparently, I had broken the law, and if I now wished to return to Canada I would have to go back to England and reapply for a whole new visa from scratch. Well, I wasn't about to do that and, despite them claiming I had insufficient funds, I now knew just how far I could go on virtually no money whatsoever. I looked at the map for the Alaska Highway leading back over to Canada. All I needed to do was head into the area next to the road and then cross over in the gap where there were no highways or border posts.

It only looked about ten miles, so I didn't think it was going to be a problem; but I hadn't really considered the height of the bloomin' mountains. I was going up over 10,000 feet just to jump back into Canada from Alaska. Huge, rocky, windswept peaks, capped with snow, formed a formidable natural border where guards were obviously not necessary. You couldn't see the summits most of the time as they were all so high in the bleedin' clouds. It might've been tough going, but at least it eradicated any sense of nerves about the possibility of getting caught for my rule-breaking. Up and over I went, more than likely among only a handful of people to have gone that way; not that it was something I was ever going to publicize, till now.

This final slide in the box is a picture of my toes. My first and second toes are twisted horrifically from all the many months of walking. When you use your feet over distance, daily, it will alter their shape. They change from the feet we've moulded within our modern-day footwear, and largely sedentary occupations, to those of our nomadic past, when the very greatest human migrations were made. They grow harder, wider, flatter, more gnarled, and shaped back to their original purposes: tools to help us balance and walk tremendous distances with weight and without complaint. Mind you, I gag a little at that photo. Good grief, they really look horrendous.

On one trip alone in the wild, I bumped into a remote hunting party. They were out on the River Teslin and looking for a grizzly bear to shoot for its meat. They gave me a handful of plums and jolted me back into a civilization of sorts. In the party were a lovely couple called Bob and Ida, who I met again on my eventual return to Johnson's Crossing. They explained they were soon leaving to go to Mexico as it was getting too cold to work, and asked whether I could look after their remote log cabin and their dog, Duke, right through the Canadian winter.

I didn't need asking twice, and that was how I saw out the next six months, living in a snow-locked log cabin, with a fat and flatulent Labrador. We ate huge, eel-like burbot fish, caught on dead-lines from deep under the ice, or the occasional duck or snare-caught jack rabbit. I romped with Duke along frozen rivers and through waist-deep drifts. I was alone in a white paradise, but I knew that, as soon as the spring thaw arrived, the clock really was ticking down on all my time upcountry.

The expiration date on my open return plane ticket to England was starting to burn an unignorable hole in my tattered pockets. I wrote one final entry in a diary which I copied and left behind for Bob and Ida. After that, I made one last trip to say goodbye to Roy and his family, and a heel-dragging journey back to the American border. I boarded a very long flight home with a bag containing little more than a journal, some clothes, and a clutch of photos to develop. I knew then that I was going to have to face a future filled with much uncertainty.

29 March 1984

Well Bob and Ida, this will be my last entry I'm sorry to say. I'm like one of the many clusters of perched young swallows upon pylon lines, undecided, but know that magnetic pull urges them.

One day they're there and the next day they are gone. That's how it is with I, so, ending this so-called epilogue, I write as I felt sitting upon the banks of Teslin during mid-February, a flicker of brain on the spur of the moment to endeavour my attempt of the following words donated to you both Bob and Ida called, 'A Repose of Freedom'.

It's got beauty and movement that glisten,
On a cold winter's night of the moon.
To stand by the Teslin and Listen,
To the call of a lonesome young loon.
When burgs grind their wrath in their anger,
And crunch with the breaking of ice.
To flow past the Creek they call Squanga,
With the grip and the power of a vice.
Yes – there's nothing on earth that is like it,
There isn't and not ever will be.
With banks that are shaded and moonlit,
For the whole of our world left to see

K. Smith.

PART THREE

Tramping About

THE POLTERGEIST OF BEN ALDER

I returned to England in 1984, aged thirty-six, homeless and jobless, with a very straightforward choice to make. I could go right back to the working-class graft – accept my predestined place in the lifelong tradition of earning little whilst giving over my body, mind and most of my time to paying rent and bills – or I could take that man, born in Derbyshire but made in the wilds of British Columbia, Yukon and Alaska, and get him to replicate that new-found way of life on his own island.

Remarkably, I still had some savings left, so I knew I could keep my nomadism going a while longer, but what would come after that? Could I really go on living indefinitely with next to nothing? At some point I would need to find a home of sorts, but how could I afford that without any income?

Superficially, you might think it easier to 'go wild' over here. The extremes in temperature aren't as great in Britain when compared to Canada or Alaska, and the wilderness isn't anything like as vast, or potentially violent, but that would be a very simplistic read on the reality of my situation.

Any sub-zero temperature makes wild food very hard to come by, and even low single digits can kill you from exposure if you're not suitably equipped and homed. The fact that it might be minus not-a-lot in an average British winter, as opposed to minus thirty in the pits of one in the Yukon or Alaska, isn't hugely significant in terms of what you need to do to stay alive if you choose to live outside. Yes, the British environment itself is inarguably more benign in terms of its size, climate, and the ferocity of its wildlife. We also have a National Health Service, some forms of benefits for citizens in need, and there is a far higher chance of rescue if something did go drastically wrong, but the flipside is that it is *far* harder to work and live off the land.

I knew I had the requisite abilities to survive, and the right mindset, too. The time in the wilderness, and alone in Bob and Ida's cabin, was proof of how comfortable I could be in my own company. However, practically every aspect of backwoods wilderness living would require breaking British law to execute it properly. I was under absolutely no illusions that I couldn't just disappear into the countryside here, build a house on some random patch of land and start hunting, trapping and growing wherever I liked. However, there could be no going back to how things had once been. I had seen enough of both sides of the coin to know which side I wanted it to land. Whatever it took to make it work, I'd rather be freezing cold, hungry, poor and free; than freezing cold, hungry, poor and trapped.

That was it then. A really easy decision to make. I landed in Heathrow and took to roaming the land as soon as I could, reasoning that the sooner I hit the road, the sooner I could figure out a solution to my longer-term problems. It sounds paradoxical, but sometimes your biggest barrier to making a major life change happen is planning it to within an inch of its life. Too many people have dramatic and truly brilliant ideas that never take the leap from the blueprint of their minds because they've already persuaded themselves it's going to be impossible, long before they ever start to try. Sometimes you just need to get going, with little more than a 'hope for the best', and then simply see what happens. Don't get overwhelmed by where you want to be in a decade from now, just start living as you see fit tomorrow, and then try and do it all again the next day too. You'll get where you need to go eventually.

At first, I headed south, down to the extreme tip of Britain's coastline at Land's End, before steadily working all the way back north. I explored many of the outlying places of the British

Isles, and I learnt to avoid cities like the plague. Dreadfully expensive and suffocating places, filled with busy, mistrustful people. Not good places to pitch a flysheet or hitch a lift.

Eventually, by foot and thumb, I'd wound my way to the Scottish Highlands. Of course I had. The Highlands, for a resourceful homeless man who loves the great outdoors and is happy in his own company, was an exceptionally hospitable place to be. I'd not forgotten my magnetic attraction to this place when I'd first worked on Rannoch Moor aged fifteen. I'd been back plenty of times since then, whenever I could afford a holiday from work, in fact, and my affection for the region had grown exponentially. The biggest plusses, from a purely practical perspective, were the open-minded people, the natural spaces, the fact wild camping was still legal, and, best of all, the sheer number of bothies.

Bothies are simple buildings in remote and very beautiful parts of the country. They are usually ex-homes of farmers, crofters or estate workers, which have since been repurposed to offer free shelter to anyone out walking and in need of a night's rest. You won't find much inside a bothy: a sleeping platform, an area to cook, perhaps a fireplace or wood-burner; but when held against a flysheet (or sleeping in the street or on a park bench), they are absolutely palatial.

Strictly speaking, bothies aren't meant for long-term use – a night or two before moving on is generally the norm – but I felt I was unlikely to run into any trouble as long as I made every effort to maintain their upkeep. For now, I only needed to find a bothy that was within a day's return walk from a place with shops and a bank. The year 1984 was fast coming to a close and winter was well set in; just getting a roof over my head was becoming vitally important to my survival, and to my savings – at least till the warmer weather arrived in spring.

November trickled into December, and I made what I thought was quite a sensible choice. However, for reasons that were impossible to foresee at the time, it would become a decision that would mark me forever.

Thursday 29 November 1984

In Pitlochry. I wandered around all day thinking to myself where shall I go? Where shall I spend this winter? Time is getting on, and soon harsh, northbound wind of snow shall designate the Grampians to a wilderness of bleakness and desolation.

Just as dusk began to fall, a decision, which has been under consideration for some time, became my determination, but a hard one. Thirty miles north of Pitlochry is a small village called Dalwhinnie. Which upon a journey west brings nothing but moorland and an eighteen-mile walk alongside Loch Ericht to the base of Ben Alder mountain. There, hidden by a towering structure of rugged crags, a sudden turn into Ben Alder Bay reveals a calmness upon the water and a welcome of Ben Alder Cottage.

If all goes well, food will be bought tomorrow, and if no rain falls, I will depart.

———

Friday 30 November 1984

After a morning of preparation, hiking began, and out with my thumb to take in thirty mile before arriving at Dalwhinnie come midday.

Upon calling within the one and only café called The Ericht. A good meal of fish and chips filled my stomach before beginning an eighteen-mile walk towards Ben Alder Cottage.

By early afternoon my hike was underway via the banks of Loch Ericht, now churning its white-topped waves in heavy wind.

Blowing winds forced one to travel in a horizontal position.

After two hours of walking in such a rainy, windswept area of desolation, I had to pitch my flysheet as dusk had almost fallen. Everything within my rucksack was damp, along with a wet bag of flour for bannock making . . . only to alter the inside colouring of my rucksack to a mixture of white and ripple the waters of Loch Ericht with curses.

———

Saturday 1 December 1984
It was such a cold, rainy, windswept night, it's a wonder my flysheet
withstood such powerful gusts.

As the grey light of morning penetrated the grey horizon and
the Grampians, a calmness hit the air. All my belongings were
saturated, especially my sleeping bag, so, packing my rucksack with
wet belongings, a tiring three-hour walk began to arrive I at Ben
Alder Cottage by 11.30 a.m.

Little wood was within the bothy, but enough to light a small
fire to reward I with a warming cup of coffee, a most desired drink
to calm my motions and ache within my shoulders.

There I was then, after three days of pitiless travel, finally sequestered in the Ben Alder Cottage-cum-bothy for the coming winter.
That building has stood firm since 1871. It was originally built as
a home for workers and navvy labourers employed on the Ben
Alder Estate, before its location on two popular hiking trails gave
way to its modern-day use as a bothy.

In terms of settings, it doesn't get much more spectacular. The
pretty, natural stone walls and slate roof are backdropped by the
dramatic granite bulk of Ben Alder Mountain, and the waves of
Loch Ericht practically lap up to the bothy doorstep – if this was
a commercial rental, it would cost you an utter fortune, yet there
it stands, free for all who make the walk.

If your tramp has evolved into a slog, that bothy appears as a
tiny beacon of hope hidden hard against a sea of bog, loch and
rock. A welcome respite for weary limbs at any time of the year,
but with that winter's snow and rain blasting the landscape into
a mushy pulp, it felt like a safe harbour would to a ship's crew
caught out in a storm.

It was in a bit of a state, so I spent a couple of days making it
more homely: sweeping, collecting wood, and cleaning the log-
burner, as the occasional hiker blew in through the door with the
tempest snarling at their back.

I dried out my clothes and sleeping bag, and took to fishing the loch for a few trout, but I was quite dishevelled. Not quite 'drowned rat' yet, but certainly somewhere close. I was hungry too, and matters were certainly not helped by the fact that all my flour supplies for making bannocks had spoilt in the walk over. My combat jacket was most symbolic of the story so far. It was comprehensively battered. More hole than coat, with a broken zip, no buttons, no straps, and a ripped armpit. These were predictable outcomes for a poor man hanging tough in a Scottish winter, and I felt I could endure the worst of it all (and more on top if needs be), but on the night of 5 December 1984, my troubles truly began.

The rain was relentless. There was something about it that really set it apart from your bog-standard Scottish downpour. It felt like it was coming from a supernatural place; direct from the depths of hell and not from the heavens above. For days, unyielding, wind-driven sheets of wrath thumped the bothy and blew out all vision through the windows. It brought its own brand of blackness, and a feeling of isolation that was near other-worldly. I put that all in here now for context, as it was in the days building up to 5 December that I became aware of another presence in the bothy, which was now otherwise empty, except for me.

I felt I could hear someone, or something, creaking on the bothy floorboards and mumbling away in an indistinct voice. There was an atmosphere too, and it most certainly was not friendly. I felt on edge and tried to busy myself as much as I could. I am a practical, rational man, and this whole thing, I told myself, was purely down to my overactive imagination and the unique circumstances conjured up by the truly vicious weather. I even joked how those factors alone could very well drive a sane person mad, especially way out on that lonesome moor. It was nothing a good bottle of rum couldn't soon put right, I thought, without any conviction whatsoever.

I knew I was lying to myself, but I didn't yet know how wide of the mark I truly was.

The daytime of 5 December passed without event. The wind actually eased off, and the loch was soon mirror-calm, barring a few ring-shaped ripples from feeding trout. A very positive sign that brought a very good day's fishing too: five fish fed greedily and were very gratefully consumed by my starving self; but, as darkness fell, I returned to a bothy that was crackling with dark intentions.

My diary entries from that night are incomplete. The words 'Have you ever felt fear?' were among my last, scrawled out inside my diary alongside a hurried explanation of what had just broken out before me; but, by that point, the fear that was coursing through me was so intense that 'writing' was landing very low on the list of things that I should immediately do. I genuinely thought I might die in the bothy that night.

This is what happened.

Night had fallen and I was sitting comfortably by the fire. Two large boulder stones had been rolled into the bothy for walkers to rest their feet on, and I was leaning on one of them so I could write. The fire was flickering away in front of me, and the rain had been replaced by heavy snow. Inside everything was warm, but deathly quiet. It was unnerving. The sort of quiet you might experience sitting in a town on the verge of being ravaged by war. Superficially peaceful, but in reality anything but. A heavy anticipation was in the air. A knowing silence.

The first indication came shortly after I'd written about catching the trout.

'By gum, it's bloomin' cold!' I exclaimed out loud. I looked for an open window or door, and double-checked the fire, but there was no obvious logical explanation. It was like there had been a very sudden change in weather conditions from right within the bothy itself. Someone had flicked a switch and all the warmth in the room had been sucked right out and now, despite the fact I was beside the fire, it actually felt colder inside Ben Alder Cottage than it did outside in the sub-zero snow.

I felt a very real, very primal sense of foreboding deep within me. A primitive dread that acts as a warning of potential confrontation from beast or being. The signal to be ready. To be on high alert. But no sabre-toothed equivalent was forthcoming.

The extreme cold clung to the air, so I shuffled as close to the fire as I dared. 'Why has it gone this bleedin' cold?' I said, trying to break the heavy silence with my own words, but then I heard this terrible noise. It was coming directly down the chimney stack, a deep rumbling, a tumbling, and then BOOM! The fire exploded into a bright orange ball of flame.

I leapt to one side as a whole series of stone blocks flew into the fire, sending out a great molten cloud of ash, smoke and flaming sparks; but there was no time to regain control of my senses. A terrible metallic crunching noise from behind saw me swivelling around, only to observe two metal deckchairs walk their way right across the room.

They clanked across the floor in an impossible jolting animation; like an unseen hand was gripping at their backs; right till they smacked into the wall on the other side.

It was absolutely and utterly inexplicable, and still is. I can't remember how I reacted next, if I screamed out loud or what, but I can remember how the adrenaline in my body was raging to such an extent that my hair was quite literally standing on end. I was bristling with a brand of absolute horror, the like of which I would quite frankly not wish on anybody.

It might have been the middle of winter, and pitch-black outside, but I scrawled in my diary and packed my bags as fast as I could. Out into the snow I fled, without ever looking back. I marched through the dark for eighteen miles straight, fuelled by five trout and fear; up the river behind Ben Alder Cottage, along Loch Ossian, down through the bogs to skirt the head of Loch Treig, before finally moving upstream to an all-new bothy called Staoineag.

There was no wood to light a fire as I crashed through the door, but, frankly, I didn't care about that. I was just hugely relieved to have escaped Ben Alder Cottage with my life. Regardless of anything, I could've dropped dead from sheer fright alone.

I pulled my sleeping bag tight around me and slept fitfully through what remained of the night.

—

Almost forty years have now passed since that terrible experience but it still feels so raw.

I had stayed in Ben Alder Cottage before during my many holidays in Scotland, and for a few nights prior to the disturbances, all without incident. I'd heard of the bothy's reputation for being haunted, but it honestly wasn't something that bothered me. There is scarcely an old building in the wilds of Scotland that doesn't have a ghost story attached to it. So, knowing that I had to bed down somewhere that winter, and Ben Alder Cottage was a well-placed bothy that offered warmth, wood and decent fishing right on the doorstep, it seemed an obvious choice.

The well-worn anecdote ran that the place was haunted by the ghost of a Joseph McCook. McCook was a former deerstalker and ghillie who worked on the Ben Alder Estate in the early 1900s. He had lived in the cottage, and it was alleged that he'd hung himself from the rafters. Virtually everyone in the area seemed to know about it; it was mentioned in the guest book in the bothy itself, and people had written and spoken publicly about the hanging and subsequent haunting too. I fully admit, it was poor Mr McCook who I initially blamed for all the carry-on in Ben Alder Cottage that night as well.

Several years later, I came to learn that Mr McCook had not, in fact, died in Ben Alder Cottage at all. According to a direct descendant, McCook's death came in 1933, while he was peacefully at rest in a retirement home in Newtonmore – a village some thirty miles from the building. Somehow, though, the suicide myth prevails to this day. The true reason the legend of the McCook haunting became so pervasive was actually down to the story-telling nous of the estate's head keeper and a local novelist. Working in cahoots in the late 1930s, they spread the myth to discourage would-be deer poachers from entering Ben Alder Cottage. A good ghost story, they hoped, would be enough to put them off a night in that building, which was the only obvious place from which to launch an illegal night-time assault on their animals. However, as the decades past, the rumour stuck, and then it grew into something else entirely.

Regardless of the origins of the hauntings, for decades now, hikers have gone on record with their strange experiences from a night spent at Ben Alder Cottage. Some say they clearly heard footsteps in adjacent rooms that were subsequently found to be empty. Others spoke and wrote of how they heard footsteps coming right up to the front door outside; or even an opening of the door, without anyone ever entering the bothy itself.

The same sudden and intense feeling of cold that I'd felt was very common in many of the accounts, as was the feeling of a hostile and unseen presence. Things being thrown and moved around was less common, but, the year after my ordeal, a Canadian man also fled the bothy after lumps of stone had flown down the chimney at night. One mountaineer reported a packet of biscuits flying from the mantelpiece to the other side of the room; others experienced the slamming of doors, tappings, scratchings and groans. Someone else reported seeing a ghoulish face at the window during a storm, and one of the more disturbing accounts wrote of waking at two a.m. to the sound of loud, old-fashioned music being played in the room next door, alongside sounds of dancing, shuffling feet and jumping. However, when they got up to investigate, the room was found to be vacant. That witness swore they would never return to Ben Alder Cottage again. Some of these phenomena were later attributed to the behaviour of a lone stag, which apparently liked to rub and bang its antlers along the outside walls of the bothy; but that stag, or its behaviour, has never been credibly documented.

You could see how the scenery and setting of Ben Alder Cottage could be ripe for a yarn, though. Bleak hill-tops and a tendency for thick mists to form without warning. A whistling wind with loud driving rain, strange animal noises, unexpected hikers tramping past. A simple stone building set on a desolate loch edge, plus the McCook hearsay? You've got conditions that are more than capable of whipping up a phantom of the mind's eye; especially after a long hike and one too many drams. I'd all but said so myself, in the build-up to my own fateful night.

Those events tattooed something terrible deep into my soul and it took me some time to settle back down to normal. Just thinking about it now can still make my hair stand on end, and it's been almost forty bloody years! Back then though, I had to try and bury the memory of that night and move on, and given it was December in the heart of the Scottish Highlands, I had plenty of distraction with just finding wood and enough food to survive in an entirely different bothy.

THIS IS THE PLACE

The sun never shines on Staoineag bothy.

It is sunk in the bottom of a valley, with hills hanging all around and the Rath River snaking past one side of the threadbare building. The exterior didn't look anything like as homely as Ben Alder Cottage. Gravestone grey, concrete pebbledash walls propping up a corrugated roof. Inside, a boarded floor sat on top of granite bedrock, with wood-panelled walls and a basic fireplace in each of two rooms. No tap water, no electricity, and one window in each room – but at least the windows were large. Twelve square panes of glass in each, enough to catch some of the very limited light from outside. I remember in the past you used to have to pay rates based on how many windows you had in your house. Maybe that explains why there's so few windows in Staoineag? But nonetheless, I would have happily lived in a dustbin as long as it was warm, waterproof – and devoid of ghosts. Staoineag might not have been pretty, but it was at peace; we were going to be a good match.

It was Christmas and I was somewhere entirely unexpected. There were trout in the river and the walk to the nearest shop was much shorter than it had been from Ben Alder. The village of Kinlochleven was nine miles away to the south-west, as opposed to the eighteen miles from Dalwhinnie to Ben Alder Cottage. Yes, I soon felt that, in spite of all the drama, I might actually be better off wintering in Staoineag than Ben Alder, and soon took to making myself feel more at home.

Despite my initial misgivings, there was a cosiness to the place that had obviously been absent at Ben Alder, even before the haunting. As the weeks of winter rolled forward, I slipped into an easy routine of walking, gathering, fishing, and occasional shopping; but there was one very obvious pitfall of living in a bothy, especially if you are someone who is slightly more introverted than your average person: I had to share my space with a lot of other humans.

I was extremely grateful to have a free roof over my head under any terms, and was in absolutely no doubt that the bothy was never mine to lord over alone. I had as much or as little right to the place as anyone else who came through the door: that was bothy law, whether I liked it or not. The problem was you never really knew who was going to come through the door next.

For the most part, the people I met were friendly, well-meaning, and often very kind too. We shared drinks and food. There was usually a real sense of communal spirit, and I had many very enjoyable times. However, there were also plenty of occasions when the bothy guests fell well short of what you might consider polite company. There were those who treated the place, and anyone else trying to sleep, with absolute disrespect. All-night parties, fuelled by alcohol, marijuana and magic mushrooms took place frequently. I didn't mind a drink myself, and sometimes a bit of revelry was appreciated, but not at the expense of others who wanted a bit of peace and quiet. That, I thought, was just downright rude.

There were other drugs too, and occasionally you'd be sharing a night with people who had profound issues with addiction. There was a real heroin problem in Scotland during that time, and it wasn't too hard to get out to Staoineag from the cities by fare-dodging on one of the local trains. I always tried to give addicts my time and a sympathetic ear, but when people were on really hard drugs, it's not easy, and you never really know what someone might do when they are really high. Once I used an old gold-panning technique I'd picked up in Alaska to pan the ground around the bothy for valuables, and I must've found fifty needles buried in the mud. It made me feel quite sad and very sorry for them all, really. I'd say it is always worth remembering that people can have different reasons for escaping into the wild, and not all of them are conventional.

Hardcore drug users were in the extreme minority; it was your basic bothy idiot who provided the biggest regular nuisance by far. On a weekly basis, I'd be cleaning up the litter of people who seemed to think the place worked like a free hotel, with a full-time staff member ready to do all their dirty work for them. I didn't want to sleep in their filth, so I always got on and did it, but the most offensive and blatantly selfish acts always revolved around the fire.

Before I go off on one, it is worth remembering that I'm not just being a grumpy old bugger. Warmth in the Highlands is one of the most important necessities. The bothy is a shared space, as are the very few resources that are held within it. I felt it was my duty as a longer-term resident to do a bit of extra work in the bothy, but there was a line, and it seemed to be continually crossed when it came to the firewood.

Firstly, and most frequently, were the hikers who would burn through all the firewood without ever thinking to go out and collect a single splinter for others. I understand that gathering firewood is a nuisance when you're tired from a long day in the hills, and it is fine to light a fire to dry off and warm up with what's available fireside, especially if you have just come through the door with a storm raging outside; but it is not acceptable to then do absolutely nothing to replace what you've used up during your stay. Especially when someone else will likely be hot on your heels and hopeful of wood to burn for the exact same purpose as you.

I can't tell you how many times I got back to Staoineag to shelter from foul weather, only to discover the previous guests had burned through all the wood before leaving without gathering any more for others. After that first winter, I had to take matters into my own hands, and I began to stash a personal supply of timber in the hills around the bothy; just so we wouldn't all freeze to death if someone had torched every scrap of wood in the place.

The second, more extreme, group of offenders were those who would burn through all the wood, and then think absolutely nothing of burning the wooden furniture, floorboards, and the walling too. That was the height of selfishness, and there were a few times it led to huge arguments (and almost blows) between me and the other guests. Can you imagine? You've got a free night's stay with only the most basic of codes of conduct to follow, and not only do you ignore that, you start to destroy the place too? It was near unbelievable behaviour, yet it happened more times than I care to remember. I knew though that, whenever it did happen, I would have to make the repairs as quickly as possible. It seemed like there was nothing that encouraged wanton destruction more than idiots following in the footsteps of other idiots.

Sometimes it would be less selfish behaviour and more just downright foolishness that led to issues with the fire. People building needlessly large fires without realizing that a big fire needs a lot of wood and, before they knew it, all the available wood would be gone and a very cold night would lie ahead for everyone was one problem. But the bigger issue that arose with a very big fire was the very real risk of causing a chimney fire. Chimneys that are well-used and not regularly swept out have a tendency to collect dust and debris on their inside walls. If someone then builds an enormous fire beneath, it doesn't take much for a lick of flame, or a spark, to cause all that flammable material to burst into flames.

I have a photo somewhere of the sight that greeted me on the return to Staoineag one evening. An inky dark sky, and the shadowy outline of the bothy, punctuated by one almighty exclamation: bright red volcanic flames erupting out of the top of the chimney. A fire so large, it had ascended from the very bottom of the grate all the way to the rooftop and beyond.

It was so incredibly dangerous. A chimney fire's flames can easily cause a roof to catch light – I accidentally did it myself once with a load of coal I'd salvaged – and from that point forward you're in a real fight to save the building. Luckily, though, that chimney fire subsided after a few stern words and a bit of water; but the potential for fire to devastate when in the hands of daft people should never be underestimated.

Another cause of accidental death and destruction are inexperienced hikers and their gas stoves. Everyone knows (or at least they should do) about the potential for asphyxiation from carbon monoxide poisoning if a gas stove is lit in a tight and unventilated area, like a tent or a snow cave, but sometimes people will follow all the basic safety precautions without actually knowing how their stove operates at all. The most dangerous of outcomes comes when a gas leak, from an insecure seal between the canister and gas ring, ignites on lighting. I can recall one evening in particular, when a lady saw her whole gas stove catch ablaze, and, in a panic, she just hoofed it across the wooden floor of the bothy. As the stove rolled, it left a trail of flames in its wake, but there she was: doing nothing other than screaming her head off, as I flung the door open and kicked her flame-ball of a stove outside before dealing with the fire on the floor. How we didn't lose the bothy to the chimney fire, or that incident with the stove, was down more to luck than anything else, but I was at least glad I'd been there to act as quickly as I could.

Stupid hikers. They really make me mad. But living in Staoineag meant I was always at their mercy; and, by god, I knew I was ready for all the madness to come to an end by the time that first winter in the bothy was over.

Not all the hikers were completely selfish, far from it. As I said before, many were really good people who went out of their way to express their gratitude when I'd help them with their things or build them a fire, or just give them a laugh and a mug of tea. Slowly, the Staoineag bothy book filled with memories recorded by other guests.

23 February 1985–25 February 1985
Arrived having been blown off the top of some hill above Corrour Station – tent in rags. Soaked to the skin, I would've been content merely with a roof over my head . . . but what was this? None

*other than the previously mentioned Ken O'Staoineag, presiding
over a roaring fire. Both the tea and my dry clothes were much
appreciated. Ken must surely go down as an important part of the
history of this place,*
    Mark Hallam

Nice, isn't it? But it wasn't enough for me to hang on in there.
The very moment I could make my escape, off I went.

———

As soon as the first shoots of spring arrived, I took out my battered
old flysheet and headed off to wild camp. I didn't want to stray
too far from my useful supply route to Kinlochleven, but I needed
a break from humans, especially now we were fast approaching
the busiest season for hiking.

The loch at the end of the Rath River seemed to provide the
answer to my practical problems. It was just a snip over a mile
from Staoineag; close enough to get back for the occasional food
run. I knew it was a pretty and quiet place, and the fishing was
good too; but I could never have anticipated that it would become
my eventual home, a place where I'd grow to know every boulder,
bay and burn on those banks.

It wasn't exactly an easy start for me at Loch Treig. In my haste
to get away from Staoineag, I left the bothy a few weeks earlier than
I should have, and the spring showers of 1985 gave me a pummelling.
On one occasion my flysheet lost its tether and all my belongings,
clothes and sleeping bag were as soaked as they would've been if
I'd just chucked them directly into Treig's dark waters.

I wasn't exactly cursing the place, but it wasn't till I'd built a
small lean-to shelter with a salvaged scrap of corrugated zinc
roofing and a plank of wood that the kernel of an idea started to
take shape in my soul.

Subconsciously, I pressed myself into the loch's banks as that
summer inched forward. We'd got off to a rocky beginning, but

I started to see Treig in a different way. It was like having a brand-new pair of boots that gave you blisters at first, but, after time, you broke them in to the point that they felt like a vital extension of your body.

A real change for the good was happening. I no longer felt the need to get moving elsewhere as soon as warmer weather arrived. There was something about this land that told me just to hold on a while longer. It might've been just a whisper at the time, but I knew it was definitely worth heeding, and I am so glad I did.

One late summer's day, I stood on the banks of Treig and I just knew that this was it.

This was the place.

———

Loch Treig was hollowed out by the enormous glaciers that hugged this land during the last Ice Age. About 15,000 years ago, Scotland warmed, and those great glaciers retreated; grinding, scraping and ploughing away at the bedrock as they went. This loch, a five-mile elongated glacial comma, was what was left behind.

Treig is enclosed by mountains. On one bank the Easains loom large: Stob Coire Easain and Stob a'Choire Mheadhoin; and over on the other, Stob Coire Sgriodain and Chno Dearg keep a careful watch over the water. In winter, their lumpen, snow-capped summits and lesser summits are creased upwards like the white knuckles of a troll. They offer a natural fortress that hides the loch, while their waterfalls and burns endlessly feed it.

The 'lonely loch', I've heard Loch Treig called. It looks unfathomably deep. A seemingly abyssal sheet of black that sucks water into a bottomless shadowland. I wondered if all the water in Scotland would ever be enough for this thirsty place, before I discovered it bottomed out at 436 feet at its deepest extent. Still, that's undoubtedly deep, and the loch retains a harsh cold all year round. Even at the height of summer, it takes nerves of steel to dive in for a wash.

There were once a couple of communities located on the bank-side, before the loch was dammed in 1929. It was all part of the Lochaber hydroelectric scheme, which effectively turned the loch into a reservoir and flooded all the land that those houses once stood upon. Those poor people were all rehomed, but the thought of all their houses submerged under the water makes this place feel somehow lonelier. Ossified homes. Pathways that are impossible to walk down, doors that will never be opened, fireplaces that can't ever be lit. I saw it all in the heatwave of 1985, when the lake level dropped low enough for me to walk right up to the old school building. Amongst the sodden ruins, I found old clay pipes, porcelain, and a penny date-stamped 1881. Remnants of a community tragically ousted by man's needs.

In Gaelic, Loch Treig translates to 'the lake of death', but as much as the crown of mountains surrounding it might seem to superficially cut Treig off from civilization, the isolation here is far from complete. The image of a wilderness landscape utterly devoid of people, especially of local people, is an old trope cast the way of the Highlands by outsiders. This place may be remote by the standards of our congested island, but that cliché of it being somehow 'untouched' or 'forgotten by man' would be a lie.

The dam aside, there is an historic network of man-made pathways puncturing this land. In the past they were trade routes; drovers' roads to and from distant farms and hamlets, linking farmers and labourers with local market places where they could sell their wares. A big change was heralded with the Victorians, who encouraged the idea that Britain's mountainous places were adventure playgrounds (for those not living in the purest poverty) in all their writings, paintings and poetry. Highland pathways changed dramatically after that. A clutch of the summits around Treig became added to a list of mountains known as the 'Munros', denoting a Scottish mountain with a height in excess of 3,000 feet, and by the time Sir Hugh Munro's 1891 *Munro Tables* was popularized, the enthusiasm among hikers to 'bag them' had grown with some gusto. The Scottish Highlands became a place of pleasure walking and mountaineering from that point forward. The most famous Munro of all, Ben Nevis, the highest mountain in the British Isles, sits just ten miles to the west of Treig, and sees some 130,000 ascents every year. 'Forgotten by man', this place is not.

This is very much hill-walking country then and, mountains aside, there are several lower-lying long-distance footpaths joining the dots between fell, loch, village and road; all the way to the bustling town of Fort William and beyond. Good news for the local economy, which was boosted further by an upswing in transport infrastructure.

The Victorians established the train track that runs along Treig's eastern slope. A life-giving artery to the towns and villages that came to rely on the West Highland Line for work, travel and trade; but, if you catch the right train, that track will also take you away to some of the biggest British towns and cities too. A daily Caledonian Sleeper service ferries people from here to Glasgow, Edinburgh, and eventually even on to the sprawling metropolis of London. I fancy, if you timed it right, you could probably go from Treig to Paris, arriving the following day.

For the folk living in those cities and coming up here, the purpose of that track is *life* itself. These mountains represent freedom from the pressure and suffocation of the cityscape. Clean air and big skies in the high north transform people within hours. You soon get an eye for it. After just a few hours, they seem to walk that bit stronger, taller, more purposefully. It is like an invisible weight has been lifted from their frame, but the train soon sucks them back down that line again. Back to work and a soul-crushing life that I could never now contemplate.

There is a small station platform called 'Corrour', located only a couple of hours' walk from Loch Treig. There's no way for the public to reach Corrour by car, and, at 1,350 feet up, it is the highest mainline station stop in the United Kingdom, and probably among its remotest too. Certainly, the bar that opens in the station house in the warmer months must serve one of the wildest pints on this island but, regardless, when that train leaves and you're left staring out into the desolate marshes and hills, the sense of isolation here can still get the pulse to tap-dance.

Aye, she's certainly got a presence, has Treig; that's undeniable. Yet what was it about this particular sheet of water that made it stand out above all my other options? That's something you have to look a little harder to find, but it's there, hiding in plain sight really, once you know what to look for.

Loch Treig tapers along its length till it forms a sharp tip at its far norward, dammed end. From above, it resembles a witch's finger, where steep slopes meet boggy banks; but there is a real gem nestled in there too.

On the far eastern shore, around the place where that witch might have worn her finest ring, lay a very dense patch of woodland. The ground there was sloping, but the trees offered a rare shelter and sanctuary against the windswept glen. There was water in abundance, food in the loch, fertile soil for planting, timber to build and burn. Crucially, it was a place where I could enjoy a real peacefulness, away from people but without being utterly cast adrift. There were no popular walking trails in that area, but it wasn't too troubling to make it out to one, and the railway line and station were handily close for supply runs too, if I needed them.

In short, those woods of Loch Treig represented the best of all worlds. A place of abundant natural resources, whilst escape from there to get food, and enjoy a civilized conversation and the occasional pint, was still possible, in one long day of tramping from the loch's banks.

That late summer, standing windward, with Loch Treig opening up in front of me, casting its wind-whipped flecks of water into my beard, it felt like the opportunity I had been waiting for was opening up in front of me too.

PAINFUL PATIENCE

15 September 1985
Well, if I'm staying in this larch wood for some time then I'd better construct a good windbreak as it's one hell of a wind hole.

Working until 2 p.m., such a good two-wall construction of ten-foot-long timber had been erected that it's begun to look like a cabin. In fact, it was beginning to urge me to build a cabin for this coming winter away from the drug addicts of Staoineag.

Boy, how I'd love it if I could become granted as such, but who does permission be obtained from?

Have you ever had it? That feeling you get when you just know you've found a place where you are meant to be? An ancient sense of peace and security, and of a future comfort. Even if your door opens to reveal the rotten shell of a house, or, in my case, the shell of a cabin, the sense of well-being and potential is undeniable.

Undoubtedly, the feeling was intensified by the wood itself. These moors and hills might have been barren, bleak and hostile at times; but step into this wood of larch and pine and I felt like I was home.

Mankind has sought shelter in the trees since the very dawn of time. The feeling of sanctuary offered by being among trees is instant. After only one night, I wrote in my diary that this place was the best wild campsite I had experienced thus far on my travels. A week later I had constructed my temporary shelter, and thereafter I decided that, assuming I could tolerate the cold, I would try and stay here for as long as possible.

21 September 1985
Wandering round camp for a moment of relaxation – mind you, I
receive that all the time – an encounter of so many sawn tree stumps
set me counting: 9-10-20-23-40-55 and finally 63 rings of circles within
the stump, making it 63 years since the larch and spruce were
planted, the year of 1922, the year both Mam and Dad were born.

When it gets dark, you actually feel as though you have a wall
around you, a reflection of white larch trunks from your roaring
fire to a black background of strength and immortality.

I might've known that the woods of Treig was *the place*, but I
still needed permission to live and build there. I couldn't stay in
Staoineag bothy for the rest of time, nor could I just cut down
some trees and throw up a cabin without asking first. First though,
I needed to find out who to ask.

As luck would have it, not more than a couple of weeks passed
that September before I spied a young gamekeeper out rowing on
the loch. He soon joined me on the banks as I cooked a sausage
on a small fire of larch, and, after comparing notes about recent
comings and goings in the valley, I asked him about the land I was
on. He revealed the name of the laird was a Mr Donald Maxwell
MacDonald, and went on to explain that Loch Treig was only a
small parcel of a wider 57,000-acre estate on the edge of Rannoch
Moor.

Known as the Corrour Estate, the land was acquired back in
1891 by Mr MacDonald's grandfather, Sir John Stirling Maxwell, a
philanthropist and celebrated botanist, who, quite remarkably, had
only been twenty-five years old at the time of purchase. It had
then been passed to Mr MacDonald, who had managed its upkeep
and activities since. The public could access it for their own
pleasure, but a mainstay of estate income revolved around the
deer hunting season, when guests and clients shot stags, hinds,
and grouse.

They seemed like quite a family, the MacDonalds, but would
they grant a request from a lowly homeless man such as myself?

There really was only one way to find out, and for that, I needed his address.

The gamekeeper explained that Mr MacDonald spent most of the year at his house in London and, to get his contact details, I would have to walk to the Corrour Estate Shooting Lodge, located eleven miles away at the far eastern edge of Loch Ossian. 'Call any time in the evening after six p.m.,' the young lad advised as he left, 'we're all out shooting until then.'

I bade him goodbye but worried about how I'd fare on an eleven-mile return journey after six p.m. now the nights were drawing in fast but, unbeknown to me at the time, Lady Luck had decided to smile down on the hopeful tramp of Treig.

At the time, Corrour train station had a signalman's house where post could be delivered. It sat five miles walk from Staoineag and was a place I'd been using as an address of sorts; keeping in touch with my family through letters and, increasingly, the government too. I'd been signed on for dole payments, an unemployment benefit, since my savings had finally bottomed out; so, regardless of whether I was likely to get permission to build the cabin or not, increasingly it felt like I might be tramping about on borrowed time. On the other hand, I felt something would probably have to swing my way soon.

I'd become friendly with the stationmaster, Jimmy Morgan, and his wife Chris and, while on my way through to the shooting lodge, I'd popped in to check if I had any post waiting. I had a letter from my brother and a card from a lady I'd help walk out to Glen Coe. She informed me she was still on her magic mushrooms, and my brother assured me that my family were all well so, with letters read, myself and Jimmy got down to a good old natter.

They say that if you want something you've been dreaming about to actually happen, it helps to start telling people about it, and Jimmy was going to be my second confessional.

'Jimmy,' I ventured, 'I'm thinking about building a place to live down by Loch Treig, but I need to ask permission first.' I explained

I was heading to the shooting lodge that afternoon for the address, but Jimmy stopped me in my tracks and shouted out to the back of the building.

Chris slopped in through the mud. 'Bloody weather,' she declared to no one in particular, 'it's too sludgy to go in the garden and my wellies have been almost buried to their tops. Anyway, here's the address . . .' She handed me a scrap of paper. 'I can't remember the house number, but I think it's number six. Write that anyway, and that should find Mr MacDonald.'

She was so casual but I could scarcely believe it. All I needed to do now was buy a stamp, pen him a letter, get it posted, and cross my fingers.

I got to it on my very next trip to the shops.

———

A month passed and I'd heard nothing.

It was 18 October 1985, shortly before my thirty-eighth birthday, when I arrived back at the station. 'Any mail, Jimmy?' I called up to the signal box, slightly less hopefully than I had been on previous visits. 'Yeah,' he called back, and took me into the ticket office.

I was actually planning on catching a train on a supply run to the nearby village of Spean Bridge, but I'd arrived early to get my post, and then Jimmy informed me that the Spean Bridge train was now half an hour late due to derailment.

I had no letter from Mr MacDonald, but the derailment was an act of bad luck that led to the biggest slice of luck to come my way that autumn. There we were, Jimmy and I, wittering away like a pair of old women, when suddenly the door opened behind us both.

I turned and there he was. Mr Donald MacDonald himself. Immaculately turned out in traditional tweed and carrying a calm, measured and outwardly friendly demeanour. Aside from my shock at our chance meeting, what really struck me was his terrific height. I came to realize that all the MacDonalds were tall, but, as I was being introduced, I can very well remember craning my neck right up to meet his gaze.

His status and stature didn't make me feel small as a person, though. I instantly felt very much at ease in his company; so much so, I opened my mouth with a potentially very cheeky: 'Ah. Just the man I wanted to see. MacDonald, is it not?'

He took it in his stride. I think – well, I hoped – he thought me charming enough, albeit a little eccentric. It transpired he was at the station to meet his wife off the London train, to celebrate the end of the stag shooting season; something that only happened once a year. Not wanting to squander this sensational piece of luck, on top of what had really been a string of very lucky events in the build-up to this moment, I brought up the subject of my letter.

It turned out that he hadn't ever received it. Could it be that the house number was actually quite important in that part of London after all? Or maybe his secretary just hadn't bothered to hand it over in the first place? Either way, I blurted out my plans and eventually put the big question to him: 'With your kind permission, Mr MacDonald, could I possibly build a cabin at Treig?'

The answer he gave in return, I am afraid to say, was not entirely straightforward. He paused momentarily, weighing it all up. 'I'll let you know,' he eventually answered, before taking my name once more and promising me a reply within the next seven days.

'I'll let you know.'

I mulled the words over. It wasn't a 'no', but it most definitely wasn't a 'yes' either. I accepted it. What reasonable alternative did I have? Seven days was nothing to me, but his reply meant everything, and it was hardly surprising that he needed some time to think. We had only just met, and what I was asking was hardly a small favour.

We shook hands and my life continued on.

I camped in the woods at Treig till the weather became so bad my flysheet was torn apart and carried off in the winter winds. That was it then. Back to Staoineag bothy for the winter.

The week passed and I heard nothing. I felt no ill-will. I instinctively felt like Mr MacDonald was a man of his word and an answer would be forthcoming when he was ready. Thinking positively, 'no' was likely to be the quicker of the two outcomes anyway; perhaps, with more time, he was increasingly likely to say 'yes'? Either way, I resolved to be patient and eke out my dwindling financial resources, dole payments and tolerance of my bothy bedfellows.

Sometimes in life you have to show a bit of fortitude to get what you really want, but that next period in the bothy would've tested the mettle of even the hardiest humans on earth.

———

There would be worse dumps of snow and storms to be endured in my log cabin at Treig, but that place was my home, created the way I saw fit. The winters in North America were unquestionably more dramatic than the ones in Scotland, too: deeper snowdrifts and severer temperatures; but you always knew what you were up against in Alaska and the Yukon – the country's citizens and structures were built to take the worst.

My time in the bothy was now pure purgatory. I didn't know when, or if, I would get a response from Mr MacDonald, and I couldn't plan anything till I did. Added to which, the bothy was not mine and I was almost flat broke and increasingly very hungry.

I was at the mercy of the decisions made by the strangers I lived with, and, with the river freezing over, I was completely reliant on the outside world and the total insanity of man for all my food. I also developed the worst toothache of my life – a rotten tooth sat on top of three pulsating abscesses – and had a pain of unknown origin in my arm that made it very hard to do any physical work at all, especially lifting; which, let's face it, was the one exercise my whole world revolved around.

It would have been tolerable, even with the heavy rain and snow, but that winter brought storms like no other too. There were some absolutely hellish walks to civilization for treatment and supplies – with a frost so bad it would turn my beard into a frigid frozen cloud of ice, and winds that felt like you were being whipped across the face by a cat o' nine tails with every single step you took.

It could scarcely get worse, but then 1986 arrived and it was as if the weather gods had leant over from their pulpit and boomed: 'Ken Smith! You think this is bad!? You insignificant little urchin! Well, have some of this!'

The new year brought the very worst period of snowfall, hurricane-force winds and plummeting temperatures. With the depth of the drifts piling hard outside the bothy door, and food supplies dwindling down to scraps, I was forced to make a decision: stay in the bothy and pray for a miracle break in the weather within days, or risk a walk to the shops before the snow got so deep I was trapped inside to my fate.

I attempted a crap outside, bearing my backside to the torrid conditions as the frost nipped at all my exposed white-arse flesh. As I went to wipe, my last toilet roll was torn clean from my hands and carried off, never to be seen again. Yep, I'd finally hit rock bottom.

On Friday 24 January 1986, I decided to go for it. It would be an eighteen-mile return journey from Staoineag to Kinlochleven, but I would be in charge of my own destiny and, if this was what finally saw me off the earth, at least it would be on my terms.

I woke long before dawn and strode out into the snow with my wellies tucked in behind waterproof leggings. The first mile passed without event. My torch beam guided me up the river and onto a set of rapids. I climbed through great overhanging curtains of ice with deep snowdrifts below; gripping my torch between my teeth, I punched my fists and feet up and up, creating a staircase in the white and making decent progress out onto the glen top.

Dawn broke grey and brought solid showers of fresh snow with it. The path was buried deep, but I knew the way well enough as I hit the banks of Loch Eilde Mor. This, though, was the point

where any semblance of 'easy going' was over. The drifts intensified and my pace slowed down. I was soon well behind time, but
focused my mind on just moving forward as I hit the halfway mark
– an old, abandoned shack that was absolutely crammed with
sheltering sheep. They startled at the sight of me, poor buggers,
and ran away in the rough direction of the path. Sad for them,
but a stroke of luck for me as they crushed the fresh snow into a
far securer track than the one I'd been ploughing on my own.

It didn't last, and I was soon back into the waist-deep drifts and
cutting a route past knolls of snow that had been whipped up into
great twisting, towering mounds. They hung over me like a white-
cloaked Grim Reaper as I stumbled forward, squinting through
the snowstorm as my beard froze solid to my face. It was with
some surprise that I gradually realized the snow had abruptly lost
its density and was slushing around my knees. I had made it to
Kinlochleven, and the few pedestrians that were out to shop gave
me a very wide berth. I heard their whispers as they passed; anxious,
hushed tones that they would likely use if a full-grown Yeti had
wandered in off the glen and down into their town. Which, I
suppose, it sort of had.

'Jesus,' I thought to myself. 'That's just taken me over four
hours. So, how bleedin' long will it take me to walk back with a
heavy pack?' As hard as it had been, staying in Kinlochleven was
absolutely out of the question. I didn't have the money or the
friends to call upon for a few nights' shelter and, given I was well
behind time already, I headed straight to the supermarket and
bought as much food as I dared.

I couldn't fill the bag up to the brim – it would have been like
loading extra bricks in my pockets right before walking the plank
into the sea – but it was clear now that this winter's weather was
here to stay, so I needed something, at least.

I needed something else too. The return walk was beyond
contemplation without a little bit of drink inside me, so it was off
to the Antler Bar for a pint and a half of Tartan special.

I sat on that stool as time ticked relentlessly forward. It was the fastest half-hour of my life, but this whole predicament wasn't going away on its own. Reluctantly, I peeled myself from the bar and shouldered my pack. I even turned down a dram from a well-wisher. I needed to be the right side of sober for what I had coming.

My god. Had I known what was coming, I ruddy well would've taken that dram and a damn sight more booze too. Forget Dutch courage: that walk back was to take me to a place that was well beyond prayer. If it wasn't for the fact that the wind had dropped slightly, the wind-chill factor alone would've killed me. It was the smallest of mercies; no, it was the *only* mercy.

It soon transpired that I could scarcely have chosen a worse day for the supply run. The freshly fallen snow had already topped up the drifts and covered my tracks. Now, even in the smallest drifts I went in over my waist, and, for the first time in Scotland, down over my chest in places. My feet wheeled helplessly below me as I grasped out desperately with my arms and hands. Some of the drifts actually felt bottomless; and with my pack pinning me down, pressing me into the suffocating cold, I took to rolling forward till I found some sort of traction to pull myself out onto slightly higher ground and into marginally shallower drifts. In short, I was drowning in snow.

The effort of inching forward greedily ate away at my reserves of energy, and slid my waterproof leggings up to my knee with every stride. My boots, I knew, were filling up with snow, but there was nothing I could do about it. Even if I pulled the leggings back down, every stride forward would pull them right back up in the gripping drifts.

Two and a half hours it took to walk just two miles, but at least the moon emerged to light my way forward. There was only one thing worse than the severe pain in both my legs, though, and that was when the pain ceased completely in my right foot. Frostbite had it gripped in its fangs, but there could be no release with so much more walking still left to do. Stopping now would've been a death sentence.

Even in the depths of anguish, you can always find visions of beauty to motivate you onwards. In that white world of hell, I watched a herd of deer stags cross the Rath River. Their antlers stood proud in absolute defiance as they carefully negotiated the great bergs of ice that sloped around their bodies as they passed across. They weren't bothered by my presence, and why would they be? They knew we were all in a dogfight for our lives; nothing still alive out here had energy for anything other than grim progress. I drank the scene in and pressed forwards. This was not my time to die.

Staoineag eventually came into view one mile away. Twinkling in the moon amongst the deep, motionless drifts, as over I went, down into another infinite pit of snow. Countless times I fell forward or back, flopping about like a gasping fish tossed out on the riverbank and floundering for its life. Ironically, this pack of food was trying to kill me but, without it, death from starvation was highly likely too. It was a beautiful piece of entrapment, I grant it that.

One final burn stood between me and the bothy, but I was well beyond negotiating it with care. My body shook with exhaustion as I simply plunged into its depths. There was no pain to feel any more, as ice-cold water swam around my waist, soaking me thoroughly, flooding my boots and submerging my right – surely now dead – foot.

Up and out the other side of the burn I went where, to my absolute shock, I saw a group of people. They were walking the bank in the direction of the bothy and seemed to be going well, with power and purpose. I moved into their slipstream and staggered forward drunkenly. I followed them wherever they went, winding through the snow, my saviours at last. I couldn't believe my luck. We broke through the ice and travelled back across the river, with me finally feeling happiness and the sense of sanctuary that had eluded me for so long on this interminable trudge. It was all over.

And it bloody well would have been, had I not then realized

that I was actually following a herd of stags and not people at all. I cried out an expletive, and gave myself the most almighty telling-off. Foolish Ken! My mind was giving over to hypothermia. I was hallucinating so badly, and now I was back on the wrong side of the river to the bleedin' bothy!

You read it often. Woeful tales of hikers dying from the cold just a few strides from safety. Often the people who discover their bodies are confused as to how, or why, they hadn't quite made it, when escape was seemingly right there in front of them. Once you've experienced hypothermia and exhaustion yourself, you very much understand how it happens. Cold and fatigue kills all reasonable and rational thought, and, once your mind has gone, your shelter may as well be on the moon. Luckily for me that night, I snapped out of it and somehow made it back.

Bursting through the door of the bothy, I let out a cry. Lumps of snow tumbled from my body and simply lay there on the floor inside the room, unable to melt. My work wasn't yet done. This was a sign it was below freezing inside the bothy itself. Hastily I removed my boots and socks and summoned my last threads of energy to build a fire.

Finally, I could relax and take stock of the damage done to my body. It took two and a half hours of massage, warmth and sweet words, just to get one of my feet pulsing with blood and life again. Six hours of torment and torture, on top of the four I had endured on the way out to the village, but I had seemingly made it back in one piece.

My right foot took three more days to recover, but I was very lucky not to lose it entirely. It swelled with blood and doubled in size, before all the skin shed in great grey flakes, but beneath it all was lively pink flesh. It didn't succumb to the plague black of frostbite then, but it had been far too close for comfort. Losing my foot would've felt like a disaster, but had that walk been any longer, it would've been my life that was gone anyway, so I knew I had to be grateful.

Count yer blessings, Ken. Then count yer bleedin' toes.

24 January 1986

When it's all over you tend to forget the passing burden, but I can't, I don't think I ever will, and sitting in front of such a red-hot fire, content and semi-lit by candle power, it was to remind me of Christmas at number nine, where you took everything for granted and never was to realize how something so small – like heat – could ever be appreciated.

I think to myself, if my destination was Corrour, a walk I do regular, that extra six mile would surely have destroyed my foot, so I can thank the existence of Staoineag, and thank also for such a small thing and much wanted in its need, and that's the glowing heat and leaping flame of fire . . .

Christmas at number nine. That was a long time ago, way back in my parents' home at Crich. Interesting that I grasped for that childish memory of a familial comfort – surrounded by warmth, dry clothes and food – right off the back of that abysmal trek.

The message I was trying to convey in my diary then was crystal clear. When I lived in Crich, I had absolutely no idea how lucky I was to have the family and all those comforts right there, whenever I needed them.

It is true that you don't appreciate what you have till it's gone, and that awful experience in the snow had stripped me right back to a respect for the most basic of our needs. As I sat there, watching the flames lick into the wood, providing me with their life-saving warmth, it was impossible not to feel a degree of life-affirmation too. It was a significant lesson. No matter how bleak things got in my life, I would always now try to find a way to appreciate the smallest of the gifts I'd been given.

Of course, there are always going to be those times when you have to look really hard to find something to be grateful for. Sometimes it can be just the lump of rock over your head giving you some form of shelter from the rain. Other times it can be a break in the storm that lends you a glimpse of something beautiful, something worth living for, like those stags among the icebergs; but sometimes there is nothing obvious at all, and that's when you have to dig deep. If you still come up short, I tell myself this: no matter how bad it seems now, it won't last forever. You *will* light that fire again, you *will* feel warmth, things will *always* get better if you can just keep going forward.

—

Spring didn't seem to want to come in 1986. Just more snow, more frozen conditions and more hardship. That storm brought slaughter and, come February, I started to find dead sheep and deer, frozen rigid to the spot and unable to rot; elsewhere in Scotland, many poor people died of hypothermia too. That February in the Highlands ended as the coldest month anywhere in the United Kingdom for a quarter of a century; a record for February that stood for thirty-five years straight.

On 1 March 1986, while clothes-washing in the only ice-free section of the river, I reached up to grab an iron post to haul myself out, only to cause a pair of freshly laundered blue underpants to freeze solid to the ironwork. It took so long to remove them from that darn post that, by the time I'd made it back to the bothy, my underpants were solid enough to knock in nails. It was a truly gruelling and miserable period, but sometimes you have to laugh too.

Unbeknown to me, just two days later, a warmth so brilliant was to break out in my entire being. While out on one long trudge for supplies, on our forty-ninth straight day of snow, Jimmy was ready to greet me at Corrour Station with an enormous smile across his face.

Monday 3 March 1986
I don't know how things have suddenly turned for good in my direction, but Jim the stationmaster at Corrour was to pass on a message to me about my cabin building upon the shores of Loch Treig. Now granted officially for whenever I wanted to build it.

Wow! That's really something, but to add more to my good luck, the rich laird – Mr MacDonald – wants me also to work for him as a ghillie during the stag shoot which begins sometime this summer.

Imagine me, Smith, the scruffy old beard of a tramp alongside the rich lairds of Ossian, living in a lodge, eating at a rich man's table and receiving a working man's wage for the summer and then, come the end of the stag shoot during August, a vast nosh-up of food, beer and wine, where all the ghillies, rich men, poor men, and all who have helped him during the season, mingle together for a big celebration within his lodge, and who else will be there but me, a lonesome vagabond in his last day of ghillie work before departing to build his cabin!

All this sounds like an untrue dream, but it's put before me and I accept it all . . .

But the day didn't end there. Upon my return to Staoineag via Loch Treig, I tried for a trout in the ice-free bay . . .

Now it was calm, but snow was falling as my lure hit the water. Wham! Just one bite and one fish, just enough for an evening snack of a three-quarter pounder.

If this world could bring forth such beauty and pleasure as it has done today, then life would really be worth living!

What a turnaround!

What a victory snatched from the jaws of defeat!

I sailed through the snow to Staoineag, so delighted that not even an ice storm sent from the frozen arsehole of planet Pluto could've remotely chilled my spirits!

A few days later and the details had all been firmed up with Mr MacDonald. I was to start the estate work as soon as the snow had melted, and I had his permission to start the build whenever I was ready. In all honesty, if my old flysheet hadn't been ripped away in the storm, I would probably have left the bothy right there and then, and immediately started building. Instead it took another six weeks, much hitchhiking, and ultimately a trip all the way to Inverness to get my hands on a new flysheet.

It was for the best. I would've frozen to death, drunk on my reverie, had I left the bothy for Loch Treig any sooner. I was, however, amazed to discover that flysheets were no longer sold separately to tents, and, as much as I bargained, I had to pay the full price for a tent, before leaving behind the groundsheet, tent and poles, in the Inverness outdoors store. Such is the rip-off of the commercial world of the outdoors, but it was better to ditch the extras than carry all that load on my back. The time and effort it had taken to acquire a new flysheet had brought me right into mid-April, and the eventual loosening of this very harshest of winters.

Given how high up Scotland I'd travelled on my flysheet hunt, I thought it only fitting that I should push on a little further and tick off John O'Groats. It had been fully seventeen months since I'd returned from North America and started my life all over again down at Land's End – some 900 miles by road to the south-west of the island and the most southerly point on the British mainland. What better way then, to mark the end of all my nomadism, by standing triumphantly on the northernmost tip?

Just a few days after leaving Inverness, I was to be found huddled under a flysheet behind Britain's most northerly pub. It didn't really matter that John O'Groats was a bit underwhelming in itself: a flat, windswept mix of peat hag and moorland; or that I'd had to pitch my new flysheet behind the shelter of a rubbish dump – my days of homeless tramping had finally drawn to a close.

I went back to Staoineag just once more. It was to permanently borrow a toothbrush that I knew had been left behind by a hiker. They were long gone now, so I was sure they wouldn't mind the donation to my cause and, as unpleasant as it was to use a stranger's toothbrush, it was in a lot better shape than the one I'd been using for the past twenty years straight.

A new toothbrush, a job, a home, and a whole new life. I pulled the bothy door closed behind me, and made a quiet prayer that I wasn't going to have to babysit any more fools in the hills for some time to come. Finally, I had found a place to put my roots in the ground and, goodness me, what a tree it would turn out to be.

———

When I reflect on it all now, the fact that I was granted permission to build my hut is quite remarkable. Just think how much easier it would have been for Mr MacDonald to say 'no' to me. I appreciated it then, but I probably appreciate it even more now, especially when I reflect on everything I've experienced since living out here on the shores of Loch Treig.

I suppose it takes a bit of guts to ask the question in the first place, especially of someone who, on paper, seems to be in such a lofty position compared to myself. Him, the owner of a great Scottish estate, and me, a homeless nobody, living in a bothy (or under a battered old flysheet); but sometimes in life, you just have to put all your insecurities about being turned down to really give yourself a shot at capturing your dream.

After all, if he had said 'no', I would have lost absolutely nothing; but just imagine the life I would have lost had I not dared to ask at all?

PART FOUR

Hermit Days and Ways

GOING OFF-GRID

I watched an eagle turn slowly and fall away, quick-sliding across the dark stands of spruce that marched in uneven ranks up the slopes. His piercing cry came back on the wind. I thought of the man at his desk staring down from a city window at the ant colony streets below, the man toiling beside the thudding and rumbling of machinery, the man commuting to his job the same way at the same time each morning, staring at, but not seeing, the poles and the wires and the dirty buildings flashing past.

Perhaps each man had his moment during the day when his vision came, a vision not unlike the one before me. A strange possessiveness seemed to surge through me. I had no right to call this big country mine, yet I felt it was.

Sam Keith, from the journals of Richard Proenneke,
One Man's Wilderness (Alaska Northwest Books: 1973)

When it came to my inspiration for the cabin build, and indeed, much of how I've chosen to live, the story of one man's life stood head and shoulders above the rest. The remarkable narrative of Richard 'Dick' Proenneke's life was immortalized in the 1973 book, *One Man's Wilderness*. It tells of how Dick first took to the remote 'Twin Lakes' region of Alaska, breaking ground and constructing his own cabin back in 1968. I'd first discovered it when I had been roaming the North American wilderness myself; an impressionable time for me anyway, but this book really set an example, and contained plenty of sound practical advice too.

Dick found the motivation for his own life-change in much the same way I had mine. In fact, our experiences were remarkably similar. He too had grown weary of the long hours and intense blue-collar labour. According to the records, Dick had enlisted in the United States Navy the day after the deadly attack at Pearl Harbor. He served there as a carpenter, spending nearly two years at Pearl Harbor before rheumatic fever saw him medically discharged in 1945. After that, the pull of the American high north saw Dick first travel to the forests of Oregon, where he ranched sheep, before he travelled even further north: right up to Alaska and the island city of Kodiak. In Kodiak he held down multiple jobs for very skilled hands – repairman, technician and fisherman – and soon gained a deserved reputation as a very fine engineer who could fix virtually anything. For me, it was falling onto that bed of industrial spikes that started the firing pistol for perpetual adventure; for Dick, it was a welding accident that almost left him permanently blinded. Following that, he took early retirement and then immediately acted on his dream.

One Man's Wilderness details his first sixteen months in Twin Lakes. It describes how he was flown in by seaplane and the steps he took to build his cabin by hand. It also details his many extraordinary experiences with the local fauna, his battles with the weather, and his great meditation on life in the company of those great mountains and vast waters.

It concludes with Dick returning to civilization to over-winter with his father, whose health was ailing at the time, but he would return to Twin Lakes and he remained there for much of the three decades that followed. He was eighty-three when he eventually left his cabin for good, and eighty-six when he finally succumbed to a stroke, but his truly beautiful home was left to the National Park Service and remains there as a tourist attraction; or rather, for those who appreciate Dick's life and mindset, a place of pilgrimage, where people can pay homage to this true backcountry icon.

Like Dick, I intended to construct solo with hand tools. I would utilize materials from the land around me, but, also like Dick, I was not precious about bringing in elements from the outside world to significantly improve my construction efficiency. Living off-grid is not about pure primitivism, rolling back to a time when we all built with only what we could craft from the natural elements. I was as happy to use a modern axe to chop and drop timber as I was to use a sharp draw knife to peel off its bark. Dick's Twin Lakes cabin stands as testament to his outstanding abilities as a craftsman, who was armed with both the appropriate tools and the knowledge of how to use them; but, make no mistake, there was no instrument on earth that could significantly ease the physical hardship of building a wooden home all on your own.

I knew from the day I started, just as Dick must have also known, that getting this build completed before winter was going to take backbreaking work and very long days; but this was my own dream and I didn't ask or wish for any help.

Secretly, I welcomed the difficulty. There is, I'm afraid, a very rare brand of pleasure to be had from building something that requires a bit of pain, and I wanted to discover it. All of it.

—

Going 'off-grid' means no mains water supply, no phone line, no gas and no electricity. Some of those essentials could be loaned or harvested from the natural world, others could be replaced with something else, and others could be forsaken entirely. My time in North America and the bothy had already hardened me. Even if I could have got hooked up for mains electricity or water at Treig (which I definitely couldn't), I didn't want the burden of all the bills, or the paper trail linked to my non-official address. I had soon come to learn that some of the conventional necessities weren't really that necessary after all; but living off-grid does not mean you can always just do what you want. Not all the time, anyway. As romantic as it all undoubtedly might seem, you can't just throw up a home *even with landowner's permission*. There is still some red tape involved; at least there is, if you want to do it all legally.

Alongside the permission and the offer of work, the estate made it very clear that the responsibility to make sure everything was built above board was mine to shoulder alone. It was fair enough, I thought, and I saw it as just another important condition of the approval they'd granted me.

I sought legal advice on planning permissions in Scotland, and was given precise details as to what was and what wasn't allowed; particularly in terms of the dimensions and height of my timber structure in the location I'd chosen. After that, I just made sure I stuck to those rules and I didn't have any problems.

Things have changed since the mid-1980s and I have heard of people having real trouble going off-grid in certain parts of the United Kingdom. All I can say is, approach all authority with positivity and a good nature. Don't take your eye off your ultimate goal, but don't get hung up on making small legal concessions that smooth the path to getting the job done. More than anything, good luck – you won't ever regret it.

Like Dick, I decided to build my cabin in the traditional Canadian log cabin style. I'd found a flat area in the woods midway up the sloping valley side. That ensured good drainage, but it was a good place to build and a good place to plant too. I have mentioned before that the soil was decent in the woods, that there was a burn close by for clean water, and how all the trees provided a natural shelter from the wind and hiking humanoids; but it wasn't simply dense forest either. There was a natural break in the treeline that offered a wonderful view onto the loch itself. It is important not to get bogged down solely in the practical benefits of where you choose to build your off-grid home. A vital part of why we all choose to go off-grid is that direct access to nature's wonder. After all, you won't be watching any television, so you'd better have something nice to look at through your window, and the changing scenes in both the trees, the water and the mountainside beyond ensured there could never really be a dull moment and it wouldn't ever feel claustrophobic.

Before I started on the build itself, I made a precise scale model of the cabin using sticks. It might sound a bit daft, but building it in miniature really helped me understand the process and design before I started. I figured it was better to troubleshoot little problems on a timber cabin the size of a shoebox, than on thick, heavy logs out in the rain. Even Dick himself had made an error on one of his timbers, and I wanted to avoid that at all costs.

Satisfied, on a beautiful early summer morning in May 1986, I erected the flysheet by my building site and began to work.

Tuesday 6 May 1986

That shovel given to me by Tom has proved useful. I've removed the turf and began a level foundation of gravel from the loch side carried by nothing more than the shovel . . . huge flat hunks of granite rocks from the highwater mark proved useful for slabs, or for use of ground level upon my cabin base.

That chaffinch keeps returning to camp and doesn't stop cheeping until it's given some bread. Each time it returns to camp, I place a small crust a little nearer until now it cheeps about four feet away. In the end I hope it will feed from my hand.

The first job was digging the foundation. With the handy gift of a shovel, I dug five feet down into the earth, right down to the bedrock, and prepared to backfill the foundation hole with granite slabs and gravel gathered from the loch side. These natural materials aided drainage in the area beneath the cabin, and provided a solid, compact base to take the weight of the timber construction above. I carried the slabs up the bank when I could, but the heaviest ones had to be rolled right up the hillside. Once there, I laid them out in neat rows and filled in all the gaps with the shoreline gravel. Once I was satisfied that the whole layer was perfectly level, I repeated the process. Layer by layer I filled and hauled. Right till I'd completed the entire foundation from bottom to top.

The construction of that foundation alone put new muscles on my body and deep, satisfying aches into my bones. Real dogged work, but there was a fine beauty in there too. You can learn all the crafting skills in the world, but you can never really better what Mother Nature can create with her own hand. Not just in the obvious splendour of a butterfly's wing or the sublimity of a frozen curtain of water left hanging from a burn in winter, it is also right there in something as fundamental as those slabs scattered along the loch's shoreline. Even as I hauled and placed, I never lost sight of how every one of those wave-washed rocks were their own original art pieces. Coloured and patterned with soft ochres and creamy grey swirls, perfectly smooth, solid and strong; all basking loch-side amongst the wolf spiders, millipedes and woodlice.

One day I was hauling rock up the shore when something shot out from beneath my foot. Its dark zigzag patterning on a serpentine form identified it, unmistakably, as an adder. Adders are the only venomous species of snake in the UK, but I wasn't concerned. Although the bite from an adder is potentially serious, they are not a particularly aggressive snake and I believe there has been scarcely more than a handful of deaths from adder bites in the last century or so.

Still, it pays to be cautious, and, given the snake was sharing my workspace, I did try and move it off with a stick. My best impression of a snake handler fell woefully short, so I soon resigned myself to allowing it to make its own way, which I had no doubt it would, given its naturally unconfrontational nature. The adder is a very rare snake up here, and quite secretive as it goes. The only other time I saw one was when my brother Dave was sitting up on a rock and it slithered out next to him. It gave him quite a fright, and confirmed they were definitely another resident in these woods.

———

With the foundation completed, I needed to source the logs for the walls. I wanted twenty-four logs in total: sixteen cut to twelve feet in length and eight cut to fifteen feet, so that should give you an idea of the cabin size I had in mind. I was going to use larch. There was plenty of it in the woods, and handily it was an excellent timber for cabin building as its high resin content makes it resistant to rotting and very durable. The key was to find long and straight sections with a uniform diameter; the last thing you want is an aggressive taper that leaves you with wonky walls; but, also, I didn't want to be chopping down living larch trees for my build. Rather, I set about looking for timbers that had already been blown over in storms and had dried out a little, of which there was absolutely not a shortage.

Extracting my sections from a great jumble of fallen trees wasn't going to be straightforward – not least because I was working solo. The area where I gathered most of my timbers was on a steep sloping bank of the loch, over by a burn that flowed down into a small bay. It took a little forethought and planning, but once I'd selected the logs I definitely wanted, I laid smaller logs in horizontal positions down the slope beneath them, to act as crude rollers. Next, I pulled the larch timber till its end was pointing directly down the rollers, and then I'd just let it slide out, and hopefully down, under its own weight.

If I got it right, I would scarcely have to pull the timber at all – it would just roll its way right down to the water's edge. I'd then float it in the water, letting the loch take the load, and tie a rope at each end to pull and steer the timber on its mile-long journey back to the building site. Pulling them up the slope to the foundation took a fair bit more time and muscle, but again, I'd use the log rollers and get the whole thing done in about one hour per timber.

The next job was peeling. Bark seals a ring of moisture into the log that can leave them prone to rotting, so all that needed to come off. I started with just a hatchet, but soon found that it was taking far too long and doing a slightly rougher job than I would've liked, so it was off on the long walk to the shops for a specialist tool known as a draw knife. It has a long cutting blade, with handles at both ends, that you simply draw along the log towards yourself, taking off the bark in one efficient glide. It was a deeply satisfying process that marked a period of huge building progress without a massive investment of my time or energy. With the wood all peeled, the difference day-to-day was about to be massive.

First, I rolled the larch logs into position as per the stick model. Two lay on the ground parallel to each other – these were the first timbers making up the first lengths of the front and back wall. Then, I bridged the gap between the front and back with two more timbers for the side walls. Those side wall timbers were lifted up at the ends and balanced in position on top of the ends of the front and back wall timbers – forming four basic corners and a full floorplan footprint of the building.

As Dick Proenneke once had, I decided to use the traditional 'saddle notch' method of cabin building. This required me to cut two half-moon curved cup-shapes at either end of each log that were designed to support a timber from above. The notch needed to be wide and deep enough to fit snugly around the log that was being locked into the corner, forming an airtight and weatherproof seal that would compress tightly over time, as the weight of the log above slowly bore down into the cup-shaped saddle below. This method uses no screws or visible joints and was beautifully simple but incredibly effective.

First, I marked the exact corner position and width of the notch using the timber above as the guide. Then I'd lift the top timber off, and set to work cutting the saddle notch into the timber that was set to receive it below. First, I'd saw a cut halfway through the log, right in the centre of the two width marks. Then I'd use an axe to hack out chunks of wood in the rough cup-shape of the notch, before finishing the job accurately and smoothly with a hammer and chisel. Once I'd repeated the task for the other end corner, I could then lay the timber above into the notches at each end, and repeat the whole process again, laying layers of logs right on top, till I'd gradually built up to the height of the entire wall.

The higher the walls grew, the harder it became to make notches and hang the timbers above. By the end I was climbing and straining, with the timbers digging hard into my shoulder blades, but every effort upwards proudly pulled my dreams towards the sky. The cabin was coming together.

With the structure standing, I used a saw to cut in the windows and my front door, and cut off the rough corner ends to give the whole cabin a smooth and uniform look. Dick, I hoped, would've been proud; but for the roof I deviated from pure tradition and went for corrugated metal coated in zinc in preference to the customary wood shingles. I wanted something that I knew could take a heavy hit from a falling branch if needed, and wouldn't rot away too easily; beneath that I insulated with moss (although much later, I swapped that out for modern fibreglass. It was just so much more efficient at holding the heat and wasn't as much of a fire hazard as moss) and then finished it all off with ply-boarding for my ceiling.

If I had been able to work absolutely flat out, I think I would've finished the basic cabin in six weeks, but the start of my estate work meant it took six months to get the structure just as I wanted it, working in absolutely all of my free time. The rest of it (the interior, the garden, the sheds, pathway, fences and toilet) would take a further two years to get to the point where I really felt it was done.

I'll try now to stick to the stuff that I think you're most likely curious about. It's the stuff my guests seem to focus on the most, anyway, but I'll throw in a couple of the things of which I am probably most proud.

Let's get it out of the way then. The toilet. Outside I have a long drop toilet called the 'Bottomless Pit'. It is not bottomless, of course, but the long drop design, and mostly single-use (bar one or two contributions from friends) means that it is never really that smelly at all, and the waste can be used as a fantastic manure. It is a simple log construction over a deep hole. Perched on top is a box with a toilet seat, and that's about it.

Cleaning out the Bottomless Pit can be hard and mucky work, though; a throwback to the 'gong farmers' of Tudor times, where people were employed to head into the pits of a toilet, long after dark, to scoop out all the contents. Argh. Okay, it's not *that* bad doing my dirty work. I'm being a bit dramatic. Those gong farmers of yesteryear were likely dealing with thousands of arseholes, and not just their own, plus they poo-dived up to their waists and were even known to suffocate and die from the odour and lethal gases. Death in a pool of poo. It doesn't get much worse than that.

They were then tasked with properly disposing of the faeces too, often taking them away for use as fertilizer on ornamental gardens and fields. I'd heard the penalty for not getting the disposal right was to be buried in poo and then made to stand in public with a sign detailing your crimes.

Yup. Cleaning my Bottomless Pit was definitely not so bad.

Moving on to happier details: water. So, in terms of a fresh water supply, I am naturally blessed here with an abundance of fresh, clean water. Obviously, there is the loch very close by, but the benefit of having the cabin located by a running burn is that just a length of pipe (handily placed at the base of a small water-fall) on a downwards angle, with a tap at one end, gives me the convenience of running water all the way to my back garden, without having to haul buckets up and down the banks to drink, cook, wash my clothes and wash myself.

The gardens, path, fence and borders took some considerable time to complete. Forty-one of Treig's slabs and almost four thousand pounds of gravel went into the pathway. The path was then bordered with old, discarded fencing poles, and I then just backfilled the whole area with soil for the garden; but I'll tell you more about the garden and vegetable patch later on.

In terms of interiors, I found an old cast-iron stove and a drain-pipe for a chimney in an abandoned hut, and made all the planks for my furniture – the doors, cabinets and cupboards – myself. I'd find the stool of a dead dry pine tree and cut the planks of wood I needed on site. I would roughly mark the width of the cut I needed, and then just slide the power saw down from top-to-bottom, right through the old tree. I let gravity do its work to get a straight enough cut, but my cabinets and doors are not exactly uniform; still, they are all mine and are full of character in a way those expensive-looking sterile units in modern homes just aren't.

What I really like with my way of planking is that it reveals to me all the little hidden images from the hidden heart of the tree. Stains and marks, knots and warps in the grain, discolouration; to me they were all unique works, crafted by the tree over decades.

You would never see the same one twice, so why on earth do people make such a fuss over having boring and plain pieces of strictly uniform planking in their homes? On my back door, right here now for instance, you've got an eagle, then there's a duck. Oh, and this one is the best – the shark. With its eyes and perfect fins. Just beautiful. All borne by the tree and brought into the light by me.

So that's the outline story of how I did it all; but the sense of fulfilment at having my home goes far deeper than a few basic instructions and fancy flourishes in the stone and wood. I don't have much to my name, but this cabin is one thing that feels like it is truly mine. Of all the stuff you can acquire through your life, there are few possessions more important than your home; and, having been homeless, I knew I would always appreciate having any roof over my head. But whether it was canvas, a bothy, the cabins of others, or a clear roof of stars, the sense of satisfaction I had from finally building my own home, by myself, was beauti-fully boundless.

GOLD IN THE MOUNTAIN

Monday 23 September 1985

Leaving the café my mind once again began to ponder – 57p, that's all I have left . . .

Walking down the A82 road towards its junction as it turns right over the River Spean, something made me stop. Would you ever do what I'd done? Stop, walk back two paces and start ferreting in grass only to find a fiver!

A £5 note, a little wet, but still wet and worth its value . . . If I fell in a muck heap, I'd come out smelling of violets.

If you live the way I do, then you don't really need very much to get by. I worked hard to retirement, and saved harder, but there have been times in my life when I have been short, and yet always somehow, just when things began to feel quite desperate, I'd somehow find some money from somewhere and everything would be all right again.

Sometimes it would be in a conventional way, like being offered lodgings and food to work in Canada, or the offer of work from the estate. Other times, though, help would come to me in very unusual ways. I mentioned before how I took to dump-diving in Canada, and in doing that how I found all sorts of things, including a wodge of cash hidden in a pack of cards, but there were times I'd just find money on the ground during my walks to town, right when I scarcely had enough to buy oil for cooking. Most of the time it was just sheer blind luck and good timing. I recall once taking a chance and exchanging £500 worth of traveller's cheques in Canada. It was a massive amount of money to me (it still is), and it was a risk to have the burden of that much cash on my person, but I didn't know when I'd be able to change money again so, on balance, it felt like the right thing to do.

The very next day a huge market crash saw the value of sterling fall right off a cliff-edge. It turned out that the 1980s recession had just sunk its teeth in back home and, had I not changed my money that day, I definitely would've been ending my travels a lot sooner than I did.

It isn't just money, though. Keep your eyes on the land and you'll be amazed at what you might find. I've found sacks of coal, old stoves, building materials, tools, deer antlers, fishing tackle, everything from clothes to sleeping bags to food and even booze. One of the finest was the time a tough fortnight was punctuated by a bottle of high-quality malt whisky coming into my hands. It had been carried across the loch by the waves and wind, before gently tapping into my bank, like a gift from God.

I don't always take everything I find. You have to use your judgement. If I ever find something that can go back to its owner, or if I think the owner might yet come back for it, then I'll hand it in to the police or leave it be. I once found a whole chest filled with brand-new high-end tools while on my travels on the Alaska Highway. I reported that to the police and it transpired that they had been stolen from a man's home back in Johnson's Crossing, some two weeks previously. The thieves had hidden the cache roadside with the intention of coming back to collect it, but I'd found it first and managed to get the whole lot back to the owner.

I used to do the Football Pools, a sort of equivalent to the lottery, based on football results, where you can win up to £3 million. I kept up the payments for many years, then, one day, I had to ask myself what, quite honestly, I was doing it for? I don't want any more money in my life. I've already got everything I could ever need, and I have no idea what I would do with three million quid. They still send me all their promotional leaflets, though. You know the kind. The ones with Mrs Such-and-Such holding a giant cardboard cheque outside their house in So-and-So. Can you imagine how daft that photo would look if it was me holding a giant cheque standing outside my log cabin in the woods? The interview would be even worse. I'd have to say I'm not leaving my home and I'm not going on a fancy holiday or buying a posh car as I can't drive. I'm not even going to bother getting electricity or plumbing. Still, I could do something with that giant cheque. It'd look right good stuck on my wall amongst all the photos and news clippings!

—

Be good to the world in your manner, and a man who has nothing gets everything.

I found that penned in one of my diaries and I've tried to stick to it. It's a basic thought that keeps me going when I do fall on hard times financially. Keep the faith, strive to be a good person, and good things will eventually happen to you in turn.

The thought of getting a reward should never be the sole reason to choose kindness when you do go about your day-to-day business; but it is remarkable what can happen when you really try and hold that mantra close to your heart. I never take anything for granted, though. All acts of kindness, goodwill, or pure good luck are always received on my part with absolute and genuine appreciation.

I found this in a diary and it sums it all up really.

Tuesday 23 June 1987
Good headway was made on my journey to Corrour and I arrived long before the train was due. Calling in for my mail, two letters proved of interest. One being from Roger, a friend from Corpach near Fort William, who wrote 'What do use for kindling for lighting your fire?' . . . But more important to me was a letter from Chesterfield, tightly closed and stuck with Sellotape.

It read:

I had intended to leave you £100 when I die, but if I do that, I don't think you'd get it. We will never meet again but I shall never forget you. I go into hospital on the first of July. I hope I shall come home, but one never knows. I am not morbid, I am just facing facts . . .

Please drop me a line to say that you have got it. This is just between you and me, just a little helping hand.

Mrs Rutherford.

That letter was almost a tear-jerker. A letter I promptly replied to once in Fort William. Mrs Rutherford and her husband met me at Bridge of Gaur twenty-three years ago, who, during those days, was just a lonesome stranger walking the shores of the Gaur. Just a stranger who had since lost her husband, and now, just out of the blue, chooses me as a receiver of some of her lifelong earnings.

These days £100 is not worth a lot, but to me, from her, it's equal to all the money in this world.

———

I worked for the Corrour Estate for seventeen years. You might wonder why I would need to work, given I have none of the ordinary big bills to pay, but even living as I do, you still need money for some things. Building materials don't always come for free and neither do your tools for growing, chopping and fixing. Seeds, clothes, fishing tackle, and the food and drink you can't easily make, grow or catch yourself – all those cost too. Then there are some things I have for my cabin that just make my life that little bit more pleasant. My replacement wood-burning stove, for example; my radio and its batteries; the film I need for my camera and the money to develop images into slides or photos for the album. I really like reading too, especially magazines about science, true crime and natural history, and will usually try and buy a few titles when I venture to the shops.

Regardless of all those reasons for earning myself some money, the agreement to allow me to build the cabin on estate land had come hand-in-glove with the offer of the work. I needed the estate's goodwill as much as I needed the income, but working hard and making friends there would later help me in ways I could never have imagined at the outset.

I started work at the same time the cabin build began. The work was not full time. I'd get a message about a job that needed doing and off I'd go. There would be periods, sometimes of weeks or months at a time, where I wouldn't work at all; and then periods where I would be absolutely flat out, especially during the deer-hunting season. That suited me right down to the ground. There was, after all, always an awful lot of work to be done around the cabin.

I was given the job of ghillie. The work of the ghillie is woven as tight as tartan into the ancient traditions of Scotland. 'Ghillie' derives from an ancient Gaelic word whose rough translation rests somewhere between 'manservant' or 'attendant', specifically within the hunting, riding and fishing disciplines. In the past, the ghillie acted more like countryside helps to the upper classes in their outdoor pursuits. Back in the sixteenth century it was a lowly position, one that involved really hard graft, and not a whole lot in the way of reward. The ghillie was expected to physically carry their master across boglands, streams and rivers; to load the guns and tie the fishing rods; to do all the dirty work preparing the kill and clearing the way for their overlord and master to act the hero and claim all the glory.

The ghillie's role is still to act as an assistant and guide on hunting or fishing expeditions but, in these modern times, the ghillie is treated with a real respect that, depending on their skills, sometimes even borders on a veneration. The ghillie should be a real steward and scholar of the land. Good ghillies will have a firm instinct for the rhythms of the natural world too. Often that will have been learnt through decades of knowledge passed down through the generations of ghillies before them; but you can't replace the lessons of the country that are acquired purely through time spent out on the fell. The very best have an intimate knowledge of their patch of land, which is often pieced together over the course of a lifetime's work and study.

The most experienced can look at a wide sweep of glen and pick out the gullies, patches of wood and brush that are likely to hold animals; or the eddies, holes and features in the river bed where a guest should cast out their line for a fish. They understand weather patterns, and how that relates to the behaviour of wild animals and affects the environment they seek to traverse, and they can recognize and interpret trails left by the very subtlest of clues: the rubbings on a tree from the antlers of a deer, delicate footprints in the mud, or the circles on the water's surface where a trout has just gently sipped down a fly. They then need to package all that complex (and often quite abstract) knowledge in a way that a guest is able to understand, whilst still moulding their hopes and expectations to suit the reality of their actual abilities with horse, gun or rod.

In essence, the very best ghillie can, quite literally, see the wood for the trees to unlock the mysteries of a wilderness landscape, and considerably boost the chances of a successful outcome for any angler or shooter. Do all that well enough and your payment from the estate might be topped up with a generous tip from the guest too.

In modern times, ghillies have a huge role to play in the upkeep of the land. Hunting and fishing in the Highlands isn't about the mindless pursuit of trophy animals: a big salmon to go in a glass-fronted box, or a set of antlers for the mantelpiece; ghillie work and conservation must go hand-in-hand and, on the Corrour Estate, the ghillie plays a vital role in habitat restoration and management for the betterment of the estate's biodiversity as a whole.

Just take the deer hunt. There are none of the traditional apex predators roaming up here any more. The bears, the lynx and the wolf were all hunted to extinction in Scotland, and the upshot is that the older, weaker, sicker deer have a drawn-out death, and the unchecked deer population explodes and causes devastation to the local flora.

In areas where large numbers of deer are present, it just isn't possible for woodland to regenerate naturally; seedlings are simply gobbled up as they sprout. My patch of woodland is an exception, not the rule, but there is still lots of deer damage in here. It is nothing when compared to the country as a whole, though. The Scottish hills and fells should be covered in far more trees than they currently are – just 1 per cent of the native Caledonian Forest, which once blanketed the entire Scottish Highlands, now remains. Obviously, not all of that is down to the deer – man's economic ambitions have cleared an almighty amount of wood, too – but we can't simply stand idly by doing nothing to repair the damage we ourselves have wrought.

The estate recently extended their tree-planting programmes and deer-proof fence building. Tens of thousands of native saplings have gone into the ground here, alongside miles of fences – but deer still cause huge damage, and their numbers must be kept in check each and every year.

When it comes to the deer hunt, the numbers of deer that are culled is strictly monitored. The estate surveys the deer population before the season begins, calculates the number of animals that need to be removed to maintain a healthier natural balance, and then the hunter, via the ghillie, simply picks up where the lynx, wolves and bears have forcibly left off.

I know hunting isn't everyone's cup of tea, but that's the reality of it. The venison is gratefully received and consumed, and some carcasses are left where they fall for the wildlife to do its work. The shooting improves the habitat as a whole and, in these remote parts of Scotland, the money generated from the hunt provides a vital income for local people. It allows the estate to funnel cash back into their conservation efforts as well, and it's working: the number of tree seedlings on this estate have near trebled in the last decade. I've never seen so many healthy trees sprouting up out of the ground as there are now.

My very first job on the Corrour Estate was with the ponies. In all honesty, I was very happy just to be working with the ponies, using them to gather dead deer off the fell and looking after them in the stables, and would have been quite happy sticking with that job for my entire career. However, after three years, I moved on to deerstalking full time. The deerstalking side of the business was encountering a few issues. The head deerstalker had a giant bunion on his foot, so the long walks had become near impossible for him; and his replacement had moved on after less than a year in the role. In my third season working the estate, I was offered a job as a deerstalker, which I was considering. But before I had a chance to get back to them, they just told me: *Ken, you are doing the job.*

In spite of all my time spent in the backcountry of Scotland and northern America, there was no question in my mind that deerstalking was going to be the most challenging part of any ghillie's job, even for someone as battle hardened as I was. In the season, it is seriously tough, relentless work, with most nights spent away from the cabin and gruelling pursuits in often awful conditions. To effectively stalk, you are required to move on foot across miles of rough ground with absolute discretion. Using binoculars and natural signs to locate the target deer, very quietly and carefully, guiding the hunting clients to a point where they are close enough to make a clear and clean shot.

The deer-shooting to be had on the Corrour Estate attracted some of the most well-heeled and powerful people in the country. I don't think that it'll come as a huge surprise to learn that someone's background meant very little to me. I rarely knew who someone was, or why they were important; I can't say I hugely cared either. I have absolutely no interest in politics and always turn the radio off whenever political topics are covered. Not that a politician would ever bother canvassing my cabin, anyway. It's a long haul for one voter, and I can't actually vote anyway as, according to the housing register, I am a person of 'no fixed abode'.

People should always be taken at face value. That's how I see it. Respect is earned and not assumed because of power, titles or some inherited privilege. I treat everyone the same, no matter who they are.

I've never really had trouble with any of the apparently important guests on a deer hunt anyway. You would not believe the changes you see in people when they get up here and sniff the freedom of fresh air. That goes for all walks of life, but it used to make me laugh with the Members of Parliament that I'd occasionally get to work with. More often than not, they were absolutely nothing like you'd expect them to be. It would never be long before they'd drop all their airs, graces and posho accents, and be leaning in to you saying, 'Here, have you heard this joke about such and such?' You could bet your savings that whatever was going to come out of their mouth next was just about the filthiest joke you'd ever heard.

It was always a really good craic, and never long before you really felt that these people were not that different to us regular folk. They could be really good to you, too. I had many an MP, or member of the upper classes, go well out of their way to give me a lift after a job, or just muck in with the dirty work out on a long-distance deerstalk.

The stag-stalking season traditionally starts sometime in August and runs through till 20 October. Thereafter only the female 'hinds' are stalked, till 15 February.

Most of the time, the guests were a good shot. Which is a humbler way of saying that we did our jobs as ghillies well, and usually got them to a point where you didn't even need to be that brilliant with a gun to finish the job. Most of the thrill for the guest was in the anticipation, the preparation, the stalk itself, and the moment they pulled the trigger was just the formality at the end. However, if they truly were a lousy shot, well, that was when things could get really ugly.

I hated that, when a deer was wounded by a stray shot. I could satisfy myself with the idea that you have to do something to control deer numbers, but I didn't want them to suffer unduly in their deaths. A good clean shot and the animal should drop dead without too much drama, or real knowledge of what has just happened. A few of the guests were crazy with their shooting, though, and very occasionally we would wind up with a mortally wounded animal fleeing for miles over wide-open ground.

Then would come the very sad work of following a trail of blood and prints till we'd finally located the animal wherever it had fallen. Sometimes they would end up dying in real lonesome spots where retrieving their bodies was a near impossible task. I've had to get deer from raging rivers, or lift them from the pit of a ravine, before they can finally be hauled back to the estate's larder for hanging, cleaning and butchering.

It was no way for them to die, but the worst moments would be when a shot was so crap that the animal was just left terribly injured, and needed finishing off by the ghillie's rifle once they'd eventually caught up with it.

One really sticks in my mind. The guest had made a simply appalling shot on this deer, and off it went, sprinting away from the hunting party. I grabbed my rifle and sprinted right after it, crossing straths and great swathes of upland moor. There was snow about, but I kept that animal firmly in my sights as it started to career up a great hill.

I knew the exact spot it was heading for. It was known as the 'window'; a mark on the hillside that gradually narrows into a gulley, before a downhill dash would bring it back out onto open ground. From there, the land of the Corrour Estate soon ended, and the land of our neighbours, on the Ben Alder Estate, would begin.

I needed to get to that animal quick, for its own sake, but I had to make sure it didn't head out onto next door's land either, otherwise the pursuit would get a hell of a lot more complicated. I could still carry on the pursuit and kill the deer, but I'd then need to call Ben Alder for permission to remove it. It was a formality, but it was one that I was keen to avoid if at all possible.

Up the hill I went in pursuit. Pumping my arms and legs, lungs burning and breathing hard, as the deer went up and over the crest. I made it to the 'window' to see the deer was already back down the hill and making its way to the Ben Alder boundary, fast. This was it then. Now or never. I lay down, gripped my rifle, steadied my sight and my breathing. By this point the deer was at least a quarter of a mile from my barrel, the absolute limit of what was a credible clean shot. Indeed, had I not been shooting from such an elevated position, it would've been absolutely impossible.

I squeezed the trigger and my bullet sailed clean and true, right across the land and down into the animal, penetrating it right behind the front leg. Its lungs and heart were punctured and it died instantaneously; right on the edge of the burn that marked the absolute outer perimeter of our estate's land.

It was the greatest shot of my career and one that I never came close to replicating again; but I bowed my head in respect to the beast, and breathed a huge sigh of relief and exhaustion.

—

Fortunately, the overwhelming majority of guests on the estate were very good shots, and those sad moments were very few and far between. Over the years, though, I started to notice a change in me.

For years I had hunted deer without any issue, then one day I started to think about deer in the same way I think about people. 'Imagine,' I thought, 'if they all rose up and started hunting us?' The life of a deer was still a life. A life like mine and yours, and once that thought gets firmly in your head it doesn't matter how righteous your justification for taking a life may be. Killing deer just wasn't ever going to be the same again.

My resolution that the deer cull must happen for the overall health of the environment remains absolute; but, by the end of my time as a deerstalker, regardless of how many deer I'd shot myself, or helped others to shoot, it was all more than enough. In the end, my own health saw me into retirement from deer-stalking in my late fifties. After that, I did occasionally take estate guests out fishing on the loch, but my paid working life had come to an end.

EVERYTHING IS GONE

You would be forgiven for believing that once the cabin was built, and the garden established, that life for me might be quite relaxing. A little bit of maintenance to keep the cabin ticking over, the odd bit of tending to the crops, but still plenty of spare time to live out my imagined monkish, meditative, and *hermity* sort of existence.

I'm afraid that's far from true.

Certainly, the build is the most intense period of work, but you never really stop working. Summer is always gruelling physically, as you plant, harvest, prune, and stockpile wood ahead of winter; those cooler months might then be a bit more relaxed, but there is always something to do out here, and honestly, I think that constant engagement is one of the main attractions for people who choose to live this way. *A rolling stone gathers no moss*, as the proverb says.

No matter the time of year, things constantly need to be replaced and repaired, or modified. Just take this building, for example. The timber in my walls and roof breathes, swells and contracts as the seasons change. Following Dick Proenneke's traditional Canadian cabin-building method to the letter, the trees should be peeled and then laid to dry for a spell before they are used in the building. In Scotland, that is a pipe dream. It is *never* dry enough for logs to fully dry out before you stack them into your cabin walls. The logs only start to really dry out after they've been resting in the walls for some time, and, as they do, they shrink, leaving gaps of up to half an inch between each of the timbers.

Now, that's far from ideal when the rain, wind or snow starts to blast through the gaps from outside, but I did find a good natural solution. Sphagnum moss forms these wondrous spongy carpets throughout wet woods like mine. You'll find plenty of it growing in places where it is damp: peat bogs, marshland, heath or moorland. I just gathered up what I needed (it soon regrows again) and wadded it into the gaps between the timbers. Its soft-but-tough structure meant I could really stuff it in tight, and often it started to grow a little too, filling even more space and giving me a living wall.

I used to plug gaps in the roof with sphagnum too, but that came to an end in 1987 after a chimney fire was accelerated onto the roof by handfuls of the dry moss. I soon replaced sphagnum's role as a roof insulator and gap-filler with conventional fibreglass and tar, but that fire was only a warning shot of far worse things to come.

A life off-grid and in nature is one where the work is constant and you survive, and hopefully thrive, by keeping ahead with your tasks – fixing an eye on the forecast and preparing for the future. There are, though, moments in your life which you simply can't prepare for, and on 6 June 1991, when I was forty-four years old, I had the biggest twist in my entire cabin existence. It was one that very nearly saw my off-grid life cut short permanently.

It was a very ordinary afternoon and I was happily foraging away on the hillside. It's funny how in the moments before a seriously traumatic event, you can remember the most mundane details with absolute clarity. I had a pair of scissors in my left hand and was crouched down collecting nettles to make some wine, when suddenly I heard the almightiest BANG!

You become highly attuned to every noise out here. You learn to recognize every crackle, every call, every whisper, and associate it quickly with the correct creature, plant, or meteorological event. Some sounds you can't place, but, if they happen with enough regularity, they can be placed in the box marked 'benign' – and considered as a future riddle to be unpicked.

This explosive noise was as foreign and as exceptional as, I'm afraid, it was violent.

Startled, I looked up, and there, right above the treeline, was one of the worst sights of my life. Blackened smoke was spewing up into the sky and I just knew it was my cabin.

I sprinted as fast as my legs could carry me, through the woods and back down the slope; but there was absolutely nothing that could be done.

My life, my work, my home, were completely engulfed in flame and all I had left were a few handfuls of nettles and the scissors in my hands.

I walked back up the hill and stood square in the middle of the train line with my arms stretched out. It should go without saying, that, by the letter of the law, no one should ever trespass onto a railway line under any circumstances; but my actions were taken in pure and total desperation.

A train soon appeared on the tracks ahead, clanking down the line with an industrial rumble. The driver could see me from some distance and his horn started to blast out with some urgency. But I was not for moving.

The tracks were trembling as the train hurtled towards me with terrible intentions, but I couldn't care less. The horn blast was soon so close it shocked my ears, but still I stood, locked in a deadly game of chicken. Finally, I heard the driver slam on the brakes and the screech ripped through the air like a stuck pig. Only then, at the last possible moment, did I leap clear of the moving locomotive.

This was no suicide attempt. I urgently needed help. I ran up the line to the driver, who was leaning forward, his hands trembling with a distress that may well have given way to an absolutely furious rage, had I not been able to blurt out a credible defence for my quite extraordinary behaviour.

'My cabin is on fire! Please, you've got to help me!' The driver stared right through me, realization dawning, alongside a whole carriage-worth of his passengers who were also pressing their faces to the window and pointing out at the flames.

'Get in!' he shouted; whisking me directly down the line to Corrour Station. I then had a four-mile run to get down to the estate's shooting lodge, where I was finally able to raise the alarm and alert everyone to the fire that was now raging hard on the land.

The fire burnt itself out, but the aftermath was awful. That night I was in a truly terrible state. I sat in the shooting lodge and, as the initial shock wore off, I resigned myself completely to my fate. My life in Treig was now over and my nomadism would have to begin again. There was no way back for me or the cabin. My mind was set.

That evening, probably over a few drams, Mr MacDonald and his wife calmed me down and slowly started to talk me around. They really needed me to stay on to do my job as ghillie, but I knew I wasn't completely irreplaceable; their words were about more than that. It was probably the moment I realized I wasn't quite as alone as I'd thought. As much as my self-reliance and independence had hardened in the aftermath of the assault in 1974, the lonely path isn't always the best one to take. Sometimes, we must put aside our individualism and accept help from others when it's offered.

The estate put me up in one of their lodge buildings and gave me money for the rebuild. As it turned out, the fire had left me with a few items other than my scissors, but not many – my tools, my clothes, many of my image slides and some of my diaries, were all but ash. We salvaged everything we could: a few building materials; some of the roofing; a few personal effects. Not a huge amount, but it was a start, and I took to clearing a new spot to begin building all over again.

I had to work extremely hard to get the second cabin in place before the cold weather set in, and only just managed it before the first flakes of snow started to fall, but the stress was so bad that my hair would turn completely grey in the aftermath.

I still don't know exactly what had started that fire. I'd had that close call with the chimney fire in 1987, but that had merely licked its flames onto the roof and set fire to one of the cross-beams. I'd been able to get that easily under control with a few buckets of lake water, and I knew for a fact that it had been caused by over-loading my log burner with salvaged coal. That day in 1991 was different. That fire was, and still is, a total mystery.

I would love to say that it was the last of my major dramas, but six years later the cabin was burgled and everything I'd replaced from the fire was gone again. The robbery had been planned. It had to have been. It just isn't possible to happen across a cabin in the middle of nowhere and take everything of value without any prior organization. Camera equipment, my radio, the fishing tackle, my rifle, tent, binoculars – I could go on. Over £2,000 worth of kit, none of which I could insure due to my living circumstances and lack of an address. There I was, empty-handed yet again, relying on the goodwill of the estate yet again. It was a bloomin' good job it was only me who was going hungry as a result of all this misfortune.

That might've been the straw that broke the hermit's back, but one truism I learnt through it all is that no matter what you're facing, always try and face forward and never back. Once I had accepted it, I wasn't going to waste any more of my time dwelling on what the fire or the thieves took from me. I'd built a home from scratch once before, and I could do it again. And again, and again, if necessary. After all, I was still here. I was still alive, and believe me, when you're face down in the gutter and you've lost all you have ever possessed, that's all you want to be thinking about anyway. The gift of your life.

There are plenty of people out there who are struggling with real sickness and injury who would give everything they have just to be in your shoes (providing your shoes haven't been nicked or burnt to cinders!). Do not waste the opportunity offered by your good health; especially if the bad times have already come to pass and can't be changed now anyway. Get right on with proving to yourself that *no matter what happens* you will always find a way back from real adversity. Do that, and I'll tell you now, as I sit here as an old man, that is what you will look back on with the greatest feelings of pride. That is the way of this hermit.

PUT YOUR FAITH IN WOOD

The wood I live in has an importance that extends far beyond providing the walls for my home. It shields me from the elements and fuels the log burner that keeps me warm, dries my clothes, cooks my food and heats my water. The wood can provide food too, sometimes drink, and a home to all the wildlife that has brought me so much joy through the decades. The health of this wood is as important as my own.

The woodland around me has a mix of species. There are the larch trees, of course, which I twice used to build my walls, but there's also plenty of Scots pine, some rowan mountain ash (useful for axe handles), silver birch, holly and beech (all useful for wine!). This wood is by no means large – perhaps only around fifty acres, give or take – but I try to plant saplings to replace what I use, and lend my support to the wider conservation work of the estate.

Ultimately, many of the plants and trees that are going in now will still be in their juvenile years long after I'm dead and buried. That's precisely the way it should be. My debt to the trees in this wood is great, and it is deeply satisfying to know that I will leave it in a better state than it has been at any other point in my lifetime.

I'll go through three or four sacks of firewood on a cold winter's night, and it takes around five whole bags to completely fill the pile next to the log burner. I did make a count over one winter's period. From 18 December 1986 till 31 January 1987, I chopped and split 5,379 chunks of wood, with 300 pieces being split in a single day. That intense physical closeness to my fuel, the calluses on my hands, the felling and regrowth, all make me appreciate it so much more than if its warmth came into my home through a simple flick of a switch. I think about every piece of firewood as being its own unique part of a living, breathing tree, and give it proper thanks when I burn it for my well-being.

I like rowan and larch. They have a good density to them and a beautiful colour to their insides – deep rusty reds, tangerine oranges, or salmon pinks – and sometimes this sweet, resinous smell too. It is a smell that heightens in its intensity just after an early summer's rain.

Splitting the wood is the activity which takes the most time, and I allow my thoughts to clear as I swing that axe and bring its heavy head to bear on the circular grain. The *thwack* as I deliver the chop echoes around the woodland and bounces off the trees. I hope they don't know what it means.

The most important thing when splitting wood is getting the shape just right. So much of the commercial firewood you see sacked up on petrol station forecourts has been sliced into the most inefficient shapes possible: chunky and thick, elongated rectangles with uniform sides – good for stacking, perhaps; easy to cut with industrial saws, no doubt, but not the best for burning.

When I cut mine, I aim to make a kind of tubular triangular shape, or ideally, a semi-circle like a setting sun; just a finger-length in thickness and no more than a foot long. With a rectangular-shaped log, the flames burn the base and a bit of the sides, but you will probably have to flip it over to burn the very top; whereas when you place the semi-circular shape on the fire (rounded side up), it burns with far greater efficiency. The flames burn the flat base but can still easily lick up the sides of the rounded cut too, creating much more heat.

The shape might not sound like such a big deal. Perhaps I sound like a pedantic old bugger. I suppose if you're just burning wood for a bit of an annual campfire, you won't need to think too deeply about it, but when we are talking about thousands of fires, set through a lifetime like mine, small changes add up to a world of difference.

Another important consideration is how you stack your wood in the fire. I stack my fire with two pieces of wood side by side, with a gap in between, and another one or two stacked in a lattice formation on top of the base. I'll maintain that formation as the wood burns away below, criss-crossing the wood into the burner as I go. I find that is the most efficient way for the air, flames and heat to circulate around the wood, and ultimately my home.

Efficiency of the burn is so important. It's important to the supply of firewood I have in my home, and it's important to the wood growing in the earth outside. I waste nothing and, once the decision to light the fire is made, I'll make sure I am maximizing the heat it generates by ensuring three or four tasks are happening simultaneously: the house is warmed, my clothes are drying, the kettle is on, perhaps the cooking pan is on too. Then I'll try to keep it going by trickling in just a single piece of wood at a time.

I take from trees that have fallen in storms or have already died. That way I'm helping clear the wood's floor for new regrowth, and there is a far greater chance that the tree will have dried a little in its death, making it much easier to burn. Once I've found an appropriate tree, I'll use a chainsaw (when it's working and I have the oil; if not, a bowsaw) to cut it up into logs, and then a long-handled axe to split the logs into the parcels of fuel.

You can't burn water. It sounds so blinkin' obvious, but you only need to hold a piece of fresh-cut wood from a waterlogged tree against a piece that has been given some time to dry, just to notice a marked difference in their weight. Superficially, they might look similar, but one is full of water and impossible to burn. Honestly, it scarcely matters how hard your fire is raging, you might as well toss a wet sponge into the middle of it, if your next piece of firewood is soaked through.

Depending on how long the tree has been down, dead and drying out, you might be able to burn its wood right away; but even if it has lost much of its moisture, you should still pick up your log, feel its weight, and have a look at the cross-section too. If it has been raining hard, you might notice the bark and surface layers have soaked in some water and are noticeably darker. As with the cabin build, these can be shaved off with your axe and the wood still might burn well, but if not (or if the wood is obviously still holding a lot of moisture), then you need to slice the log as normal and stack it on a covered log pile to dry out.

This is a process called *seasoning*, and the time it takes depends on the tree's species and how wet the wood was when you stacked it in the first place. That's why log-pile management is so important. It isn't just about the wood you stack for burning, it is about what can be burnt today, and then knowing the various stages of drying for the rest of the split logs you have piled up. I have several separate wood piles on the go at any one time, some with wood I can use right away (like the one closest to the cabin) and others that will be sorted into logs drying for three months, six months, a year, or even two years.

When I'm not out working at the log pile, you can be sure I'll be spending a decent portion of the day thinking about it. Managing the wood for the fire is something that never stops. Chopping and collecting wood is as much a part of your life out here as the wind in the trees and the trout in the loch. In wintertime this is critically important work that must be completed before the bad weather arrives in earnest. Your life may very well depend on having a ready-to-use and large log pile close to hand. In really bad snow you can be trapped inside for many days up here, and not having the ability to warm the cabin when temperatures fall well below zero can be very dangerous indeed.

There is ample here for one human to live a sustainable life if they are careful and responsible, but I know too that if too many, even very careful, humans came to my wood, it would all soon disappear. Really, these thoughts should be a part of how we all look to live in all our walks of life. A *proper* consideration for what we need to take from what's around us, versus what it can afford to give up and what we can afford to give it back as a replacement. That's where the line of what constitutes a real natural balance truly lies. But that consideration, that hard reality, is pushed *far* too far away from people who (often unknowingly) grossly over-consume the natural resources carefully laid out on this earth.

Life itself relies on the careful maintenance of that balance. Go into the woods and look for it yourself. Find the great depth in the way things grow and what they need. How wildlife behaves and feeds. The impact of the changing of the seasons and the weather all around us. You'll soon reawaken that fascination with the earth we live on and maybe discover that you don't need all the other stuff that distracts you for a few hours before it disappears off into a landfill somewhere else. You'll spend less and be happier but, most importantly, our environment and everything living within it may yet survive our self-sabotaging ways.

—

The cutting and piling aside, there's also the carrying. The area I'm cutting from at the moment is about five minutes' walk from the cabin. So that's five minutes to get there, twenty minutes to split a bag's worth of logs, then five minutes to walk it back, one bag at a time.

It can be really tiring work, the chopping and walking with bags filled with wood; worse, if the weather is foul. Sometimes I'll carry a bag and rest for a few minutes before heading out for more. Or I'll make myself some dinner, a stew or something else to cook in a pot, and then leave that cooking for the half an hour it'll take me to go and fill the next bag.

I have made that return journey for wood, on the very same single footpath, over ten thousand times. Just walking up and back sees me cover a little over a thousand miles a year. Pretty mad when it's all laid out like that, isn't it?

That wood is like an old friend. I know every inch of its skin. Its moods, and especially its temper; evidenced in all the splintered trees and craters where the roots of trees have been ripped clean from the ground in all the great storms past. My foot is moulded intuitively to the footpath's lumps and rises. My muscles flex in memory as I cross the small burn, hop the log, or pass the four-foot stone, its broken seams groaning with the quartz that crosses its surface in a patterning like a brain. I forged that track with my own feet and could walk it with eyes shut tight; and yet, there is always new growth in the wood and the potential to surprise.

The change in the deepest details through the seasons is so unfathomably complex and varied that it would take many more lifetimes to witness it all. It is *like* an old friend, but one who is both immortal and infinitely multifarious; best enjoyed in the moment then, without worrying too much about what parts of the story of its life you might miss. Carrying a great big sack of logs will quickly take your mind off all that anyway. You'll soon get used to spotting the ever-changing minutiae when your shoulders are screaming and you are head down and staring at the mud that squelches around your ankles.

Today, it is mid-July, and the woodland walk is damp but dripping with life. I note the forest floor has a thickness to it; a heaviness and rawness, as if it has taken a deep and satisfying soak in a tub, before emerging without its towel. It must've rained hard in the night, but I don't remember hearing it.

There are soaking mounds of spongy moss and knee-high grasses. The tips of the grass blades are bowing deferentially, or nodding drunkenly, weighed down at their ends with heavy blobs of water. One of the moss mounds has a glistening pine marten shit right in the middle of it. I note how it is curled around in a little circle. A crude Treig wedding ring, presented on its soft green ring-bearer's pillow.

Carpets of wild flowers are abundant. Wood sorrel, foxgloves, wood anemone and meadow buttercups, all springing out at me as I shuffle along with the empty log sack. I scuff up pine cones as I go, noting how the small alpine tree species are emerging as saplings on the spots where they've self-seeded from the previous drop. They reach skywards to the summer sunlight, seemingly in a rush to achieve waist-height before the dense masses of fast-growing bracken can sweep in and suffocate their effort.

That bracken. I bend back the sections wherever it encroaches on my path. Ticks. A tiny spidery black invertebrate that crawls to the very tips of that plant will leap onto you as you brush past. Horrible little parasitic bastards that suck your blood and leave you with an unpleasant itchy bite – or the nasty Lyme disease, if you're unlucky. They are here for the deer, but they'll make a fine snack of the hermit, absolutely no problem.

I cross an ancient boundary marker, a small wall made up of water-moulded rounded stones. They were collected from the loch edge by the hands of people who lived here thousands of years before me. Theirs were very different hands, connected to very different lives to my own, and yet we both recognized the value of these natural materials in much the same way. I collected my own smooth stones for the cabin and left their wall well alone; for posterity, and out of respect. They have passed the torch on to me now, but who shall carry it forward once I've gone, I wonder?

The mud on the track thickens as I walk past a small shelter where I've piled up twigs for kindling. They are the dried, lichen-covered outer limbs of old dead trees. This doesn't get any easier on my own old limbs. My daily duty. But this is one of the easier times of the year to do it, even with a tendon injury to my ankle (picked up from the last time I entered the infinitely more dangerous walking terrain in the town of Fort William). Mind you, the sticky mud is troublesome, as are the blasted clouds of biting midges. A painful encouragement to cut the wood fast.

Freshly sliced, I'll load up my sacks with the split wood placed lengthways in the bottom. You get more in that way, and as you roll down the neck of the sack to close it and sling the whole lot across your shoulders, I find the weight sits a lot easier on my wings; useful, for when I reverse the journey with my burden.

I head back up the small rise to my garden gate. I've propped the gate open with a lump of rock so I can go straight through without stopping. Arms are beginning to burn a little now, but I'll still mind the mint that's stretching its green fingers across the garden path, oh, and that plump ground beetle that's dancing its tiny feet across the gravel.

Cheep, cheep, goes my friend the robin. He's sitting on my garden fork, expectant of some grubs. Lazy lad could easily just eat the bloomin' beetle, but he knows he doesn't have to work for his food whilst I'm around and there's gardening to be done and earth to be turned.

It is with some sense of satisfaction and relief when I can look to the full pile of logs beside my log burner. I'll relax to my chair before tending to those garden chores. Robin can wait for his worms.

It's high time for another cup of tea, I think.

IN SUNSHINE AND SHADOW

25 January 1984
*With its unexplainable beauty all gleaming upon motionless birch,
as frozen as could be, long shadows of its reflection stretched amid
banks still white with snow, while its reflection from sunbeams
penetrated every darkened hole of it. Hidden form to create a multi-
colouring of dewdrops.*

Time, or rather the passing of time, means a lot to me. You probably know well by now that I have kept meticulous records of my
comings and goings in diaries that stretch across every decade of
my life. Writing is my way of unwinding and relaxing, but those
records underpin my life too. They are both a chronicle and
evidence; evidence of my existence.

I keep comprehensive lists of all the wildlife I've seen, the logs
I've chopped, the home brews I've kept; even the illnesses and
injuries I've suffered. Statistics keep the scores and maintain my
focus on what I'm supposed to be doing out here, even on the
days when my motivation might fade momentarily under aching
bones, or a downpour, or a swarm of midges.

My words are as much a proof of my progress as the solid
building I sit within, or the log piles dotted around my home; but
they have also allowed me to see the world in a different way.
When you keep a diary, you find yourself actively looking for a
story to tell, and soon enough, your life will fill with far more
vibrant scenes than it would if you were just sitting in your chair,
passively letting the world slip by before you. You want to impress
your reader, and if that reader is only ever going to be you, what

could be more important than creating a life story that is full of colour and resonance?

I never imagined my words would make it into this book, or my photos into a film, but I hoped the record I have kept of my life would one day form more than just a personal document for me to glance over every once in a while. I hope that doesn't make me sound conceited. Truthfully and simply, there have been times I have borne witness to something so beautiful that it would feel wrong not to have shared it with others. To encourage them out into all this too, to help them towards the wonders that this incredible natural world can conjure up. The greatest magician of all.

However, the experience of the world as one individual is so fleeting it is barely even measurable; especially when held up against the great passage of time felt since Earth's conception. As humans, we arrive and pass like a mayfly spiralling on a breath of wind for its single day of life in the sun. Our lives are so short when measured against something like the formation of a granite slab, lying out on my garden path; so short, in fact, that the revelation of this brevity can make you feel like your life is even a little pointless – but the other side of this, quite extraordinary, humbling, is to see your time as the most wonderful gift of all. And if it is so (which it really is) then, like the mayfly with only twenty-four hours to live, I am going to open my senses to everything that this day has to offer.

———

I far prefer the cooler months. Not just winter, but the whole sweep of that calmer, quieter time when the hardest of the hard work has been done, and you can enjoy a period of contemplation.

My favourite time of year begins in late September, when harvest-time is eagerly awaited. When all the trees and shrubs are laden with autumn fruit – the red berries decorating the rowan and hips upon the wild rose. Worcester berries, redcurrants and white currants, hanging so heavy I can pick vast quantities for wine – so ripe that I can stew a surplus and make a salad, so ripe that my fingertips are stained by fruit juice for days. My garden should heave with vegetables too, especially the potato patch, which will hopefully be filled with hundreds of spuds for me to dig and fry.

By the time October arrives, the mating calls of stags will be puncturing the skies with their deep-throated roars. The weather turns and the first snows and storms arrive but, sequestered safely in my cabin, with the world screaming around outside, I feel nothing but the deepest sense of comfort and security, like a small forest tortoise dug deep into earth and his shell, ready for his winter's hibernation.

It is a time for reflection and writing. Indulging and enjoying the darkness. Going to bed early and waking up late. The greatest winter days come when a diamond-hard cold is broken by a still and sunny day. That's when Treig looks its very best. I'll go out for hikes and bathe in the views around me. I may even climb to the top of the largest waterfalls. Frozen solid, waves of water ossified, as glistening icicles glint like the clinking glasses of a grand chandelier. If it is strong enough, I'll even place my water-proof jacket on my backside and slide right down the waterfall's slope; whooping with the absolute joyfulness of it all, till I meet the shores of the loch at speed.

Do not forsake the beauty hiding in winter's darkest hours though. When a full moon illuminates the snow, casting light on the white like a projector on an old cinema screen, there are many wonders to behold. The night sky can be at its finest in midwinter. I have seen the Northern Lights at Treig, a dull green smear throbbing in the sky; stunning enough, but spoilt, only slightly, by the experience of having seen them at their most spectacular – dancing and swirling through the skies in northern Canada and Alaska. However, in the late December of 1993, at a little before four o'clock in the morning, I saw something altogether more extraordinary right here at Treig. A great blue orb descended through the trees and slammed into the snow before me. It looked like a meteorite, some said it might even have been part of a satellite but, given there were no experts around to identify the rock, I was left to admire it from a distance, as it hissed away on the ice.

Winter may deliver the magnificence, but it can also occasionally bring an unrelenting brutality and extreme hostility. Three consecutive winters, 1991, 1992 and 1993, acted as a sliding scale of what I could withstand out here. The winter of 1991 saw me snowbound at the shooting lodge for nine weeks and two days. New Year's Day of 1992 sounded not with fireworks, but with torrential rain and storm-force gales of such an intensity that I was forced from the cabin, fearing it might be crushed by a fallen tree. I would spend two nights in a sodden sleeping bag, dossing beneath a cobweb of fallen larch, the only safe hiding place I could find. Three weeks into 1993, and an exact repeat of the cabin abandonment happened again, only this time the winds exceeded 100 miles per hour. Back I scurried, right under the crude larch shelter.

That winter was the worst of the three. Seventy-two hours of solid snow at one point, the depth and severity of which I didn't even see in the Alaskan winter; there were blizzards, freezing conditions, waves on Loch Treig large enough to smash right over the dam wall. A snow plough was dispatched to clear the train line.

It took a month for the ground to thaw out that spring, with snow returning again in late March and then on into April. It was the longest Scottish winter in some twenty years. I can tell you now, when I heard the cuckoo's call pierce through on 4 May it cut through the air like the final bell in a heavyweight boxing contest. We all fell into the arms of the referee with bloodied noses and blackened eyes. It was an almighty battering, but it was nothing, *nothing*, compared to the meteorological holocaust that beleaguered these woods on the eve of Valentine's Day 1989.

I have written before about the sensation of deep comfort to be had by entering any forest, that they can offer a natural shelter from the wind and rain without you needing to do anything at all; but there are conditions – rare conditions of such extreme force – in which that feeling flips on its head. When that happens, being amongst the trees is to willingly place your head on the woodblock of an axe-wielding executioner.

Monday 13 February 1989

Winds are now reaching 104 m.p.h. and, as broadcast upon Radio Scotland, will reach their peak within the next four hours.

Although late evening, a dim greyness of light shows the holocaust, and an unusual one at that too. I'm observing trees falling, one just 20' short of my garden, an 80' Scots pine, but the larch are holding well. A huge 12' long branch tumbled upon my cabin roof around an hour ago, with one heck of a crash, and splitting into 3 sections upon impact. I shot outside with fright thinking the end had come, and also giving a silent prayer.

While writing prayer, one more branch hit my roofing but much smaller. I'm watching 3' branches being ripped from trees as easy as spreading butter; they're travelling horizontal and I'm in fear of a broken window.

Yet this wind two hour ago was blowing north, and within minutes, so abruptly, it changed to south. This was some great contrast as I glared through my window with bulging eyes of fear to visualize one giant wave so suddenly tower into the air – maybe 15' high, maybe more, I don't really know, and in it came to the shore followed by smaller ones about 8', and its entire background became obliterated by white spray 50' or more into the air.

Radio Scotland keeps broadcasting the news of road blockages, fallen trees, A706 closed, all ferries closed, British Rail Argyle railway line delayed due to fallen cables, two lorries blown over – so no wonder I'm so worried.

More news just through on wireless 'Storm force winds will reach their peak around now and continue for the next 4 hours.'

Four hours of fear and it's now dark outside, black as black could be, so no wonder I'm drowning my fears with a bottle of Muscadet primeur, but it's only 12% vol.

I'm going to try and write again but I'm horrified. An 80' plus

*larch tree just fell on my roofing. About 8 trees fell in one gust, with
one hazardously wedged up to support another.*

*With such a great risk of having my cabin flattened, I ventured
out in winds of well over 100 m.p.h. to be battered with either
hailstones or rain, for whatever was hitting my face was really
painful.*

*Holding a torch within my mouth, two hunks of timber became
wedged vertical beneath this tree. One more gust slithered it 3' nearer
my cabin and a 100' larch became uprooted to my left, crashing
earthwards with one hell of a thud. Three trees behind my cabin
fell into the loch.*

I can still hear the terrible sound of those trees cracking clean
off at their stumps. It was like it was nothing to that wind. Many
tons of tree, decades of growth, obliterated as easy as you'd swat
a fly. The Met Office described it blithely as a 'significant weather
event', with record gusts in Aberdeenshire and nine serious injuries
when the roof of a hospital ward was blown clean off in
Dunfermline.

I knew I had to flee the cabin, but there was going to be no
safe larch hollow to hide amongst this time.

Tuesday 14 February 1989

I didn't finish writing yesterday's events, I just fled.

*A massive stretch of trees right to the edge of the woodland
became uprooted. Debris and branches fell all around me, huge 80'
to 100' trees became snapped like matchsticks, the whole forest around
me was gradually falling apart.*

*I knew my stove must be doused with a bucket of water, in fact
two. The whole bucket-full became slung onto my blazing logs, giving
a back throw of smoke that engulfed my entire room.*

*Running to the burn, one more gust bent every tree above me.
My only way to see what way they were to fall in the blackness of
night was to glance directly into the sky to watch their silhouette,
and fear was so great I began to yell.*

I managed it back inside, engulfed my stove with one more bucket of water, bundled my sleeping bag, camera equipment and valuable data like passports, bank accounts, etc. into my rucksack. That only took me seconds and I was gone into the outside hell.

Trees were just lying everywhere. I couldn't get through them and had to make a return journey to find a further route. Within 100 yards of my cabin, in came a prolonged gust of hurricane-force wind, and you could hear trees cracking off their stumps from every direction.

Wind began to lift me, I hung onto a small 20' pine, looked upwards to distinguish falling trees and yelled into the deafening roar and blinding snow, NO! NO! NO!

I've had so many things happen in my life but fear like this, never. I began to pray, that's how frightened I was. I didn't even look back to see if my cabin still stood. All I wanted to do was get into a clearing away from falling trees.

Somehow, I managed to reach the edge of the wood. A train was stationary on the above line and I began flashing my light in hope of reaching him.

Three more gusts came. I just watched trees bend, crack and fall to the earth. A birch tree fell upon the small footbridge over the burn, preventing me reaching the train as it began slowly to move up the line and vanish behind the pine forest.

By the time I was on the line, a decision came to reach the work hut 1/4 mile down the line. It would do to protect me from driving snow, and no trees were around it to fall.

That's why the train had stopped. The cabin had disintegrated upon the line, scattering its beams and hunks of boarding to prevent passage without its removal.

Maybe I could doss under the bridge?

Reaching the bridge, I climbed beneath it, but driving snow was so wild I flew horizontal, right through the arch from one side to the other . . .

I'd try the next two huts upwards. Maybe not the first one as it was close to the woodland, but the second one, around one and a half mile away, that would be free from trees and wind, plus it was made of railway sleepers.

A huge 100' larch lay protruding 9' above the line to cause a head-on collision.

Upon reaching the wood end, winds were at their peak.

By now, few trees surrounded me, yet fear returned. With winds so fearful I flung myself flat upon the railway banks and hung on to what grass or bushes could be found. One gust caught me by surprise, lifted me, turned me round, and placed me – still standing – in the opposite direction. Another one caught me unaware and I soon found myself arched with a pack on my back, holding onto the iron railway line until it temporarily lessened.

Around 10 p.m., I arrived at the hut and bedded myself in for the night.

I slept cold and restless. Winds continued their turmoil throughout the night. Noises were deafening, branches rattled my roof, and roaring sounds grew with intensity. Work trolleys moved along the line and power saws were used for removal of felled trees; then slowly came the greyness of dawn.

By now the winds were lessening but snow still fell.

Opening the door, rowan trees lay uprooted in the snow. Packing my gear, heavy eyes made uneasy walking, but approaching the woodland hurried my step. Arriving its edges to visualise 1/3rd of it devastated to the earth, and there, sat amid its uprooted evil were sheep, chewing their cud and most unconcerned, but hundreds must have lost their lives.

One section of forest was obliterated from the railway line to Treig. Not a tree standing. The railway hut, which I had refused to doss in, had its gable end missing, and most of the railway fence was destroyed by falling trees.

I was sure my cabin was going to be intact, and it was, as clear as it came into view from the railway line.

Arriving at my cabin proved most difficult, but far easier than getting away from it, as was last night, and regarding my prayer, it became granted.

If counting a 50' radius of my cabin, 30 trees had fallen, two upon my roof. One 100' larch fell directly towards my roof but became intercepted by another larch which fell and lodged in the V of an upright 30-footer. If not for this my cabin would now be non-existent, and so would I, for I was in it at the time.

I said my prayers last night and they became granted.

After all this passing holocaust, I'd say now it's the happiest time of my life. It's so great to be alive.

I mentioned that hat-trick of consecutive winter storms in the early 1990s. In 1992, that extreme winter was followed by the wettest Scottish spring in sixty years and then a six-week drought from mid-May to the end of June. In 1993 the storm was followed, just a couple of weeks later, with the highest temperature of anywhere in the UK, only for the snow to then return once more.

That was bad, but things are even harder to predict now. I can feel how the seasonal rhythms of this land are becoming increasingly warped and distorted. Warmer, wetter winters, long periods of heat in the summer, occasional random mega-freezes, even more violent storms, drought, and flooding.

An erratic climate stifles the young: the plants can't sprout, the fruit can't grow, the insects and animals can't feed and breed. Sadly, those extreme swings in the weather have started feeling like they could come along at some point almost every year.

I can't accept that as my new norm, but as time elapses, I feel powerless to stop it.

It troubles me greatly.

29 June 1985

My leg for some reason was itching badly, and, in fact, had been itching for some time. Rolling up my trouser leg I saw it. Ugh! An 'orrible tick, Ugh! All red and bloated with blood from its original size of 1/16th of an inch to its now blobby posture of ¼ inch with its buried head in my blood vein.

Snip! Squirt! Minus its body, as blood ejected outwards after

*severing its head with my scissors. But the hardest bit was removing
its gnashers as they were buried deep.*

I did it though, but it was hard to cut ya skin away with a knife.

Summer is glorious when it's good, but bloody awful most of
the time.

I'm sorry, I know how much regular folks love it, but summer
is just not for me. I've said, several times now, that summer is the
time of the most constant and continuous graft. The long daylight
hours forcing work deep into the evenings with cabin repairs, the
log piles, the vegetable plot, and everything else I might have going
on with the estate; and the night, which may never achieve total
darkness, is far too short to truly rest the body and spirit.

Summer is at its absolute worst when it is baking hot and dry.
My meat, butter and cheese soon spoil; and sweat steals fluids and
energy from my body, spilling it out onto the floor in great streams
of salty water.

But none of that is what bothers me most about a sultry still
summer's day. By far and away the worst thing about summer is
the rise of the pests. Midge, fly, cleg, ked and slug. They read like
the poisonous brew of a witch. Quite honestly, they may as well be.

Each one brings their equivalent doses of psychological or physical discomfort and it is quite hard to say which one is worst. The
midge is certainly the most enduring, and is probably the one with
the biggest celebrity profile outside of the Highlands. Anyone
planning to visit here in the summer will invariably be met with
a wide-eyed: 'But what about the midges!?' It is fair enough. A
steady day brings them out in their millions, alongside their
dastardly partners the cleg and the ked, both of which can have a
bite like being slapped with a needle, and all of which are a massive
pain in the arse. On their day, those three are abysmal, but at least
the worst they'll do is leave you a little sore. Whereas the slug,
house or bluebottle fly can seriously damage your livelihood.

I'm going to take all these little bastards in turn, so let's start
with Public Enemy Number 1.

Saturday 22 August 2009

Midges are evil little insects, 1/60th of an inch in size, that descend around you. Invisible almost to the naked eye, they crawl on your arms, face, and hands with a prong that enters your poor pore with a jab that prolongs the day. And that's how it was. Hundreds of 'em, bringing a drone to my ears.

By heck, by the time I was home, midges had penetrated the knackered zip of my fly hole to much discomfort.

The midge is actually a tiny species of fly. Not all midge species bite, but of the ones that do, it is the female midge that seeks out your blood. Your claret gives her the nutrients she needs to grow her eggs. At just a couple of millimetres across, they might sound insignificant, but believe me, when they gather in great cloud-like swarms and land en masse on your body, their sharp bites are enough to drive you insane.

Just talking about the little buggers is making my skin crawl. I have experienced bites that cover every piece of flesh exposed to fresh air, and I don't need to elaborate on the time they flew right in through my blasted broken trouser fly.

The bites leave painful and itchy lumps on the body, which will go red raw when scratched; but they are not half as bad as what the cleg and ked can inflict when they are in the mood. The cleg, or horsefly, is pretty large as fly species go. That is its only redeeming feature, as it gives you a small chance of you feeling it land on your skin and blasting it with a swatting hand before it has a chance to bite.

If it goes unnoticed, it'll slice your flesh with its minute stabbing blades and lap up your blood with a horrid straw-like mouthpart. Horrid. Horrid. Horrid. As is the ked, the blasted deer fly. These flies look like a cross between a fly and a spider. They'll land on you, mistaking you for their usual host, the deer, drop their wings, and then crawl all around your hair. If you are very unlucky, they'll give you a bite, and that bite is possibly the worst of the lot – a big red welt that comes with an intense itch that might last a fortnight. It must be absolutely awful for their prime targets, and in the past I've seen deer that are covered in hundreds of them. Death would be a relief, quite frankly.

There are repellents available, and some people seem to get bitten by this ghastly triumvirate more frequently than others; but for me, the best thing you can do is cover up or seek out the heat and smoke of the fire. If I need a repellent, I'll look for a sprig of bog myrtle. This sweet-smelling plant loves the acidic soils of a good old Highland bog. Head into the quagmire, then just crunch up a few of their leaves and rub them onto any exposed skin – you'll soon find you're getting bitten less, and I may add that this wonderful plant makes a decent gallon of wine too. Regardless of anything, though, if there is a warm, sticky and settled summer's day, you know the midges, at least, are very likely to be out in full force, no matter what precautions you take. When it is really very bad, you just have to beat a retreat and pray it rains soon.

Mind you, really heavy summer rain can bring on a plague of slugs.

Slugs. I hate 'em. Long, black and slimy moustaches that slither all over my vegetable patch, eating their way through everything I've ever grown. One particularly bad infestation saw so many slugs enter my garden and home that I ended up having to go out with my scissors and attempt to eradicate them by hand. I stopped counting when I had sliced through 140 slugs in my morning mass cull, but it didn't seem to make an ounce of difference. They were simply everywhere: across the garden, in my house, on my clothes – one even slithered into my frying pan and ended up getting sizzled up like a little black sausage.

It may sound disgusting (it was) but it was potentially disastrous too. With no vegetable reasonably able to withstand the slug onslaught, if it had carried on, I could've easily lost an entire harvest. Luckily, the weather cooled, and the slugs slunk off to hide once more.

Monday 29 June 1987 was a date to remember. Blimey. It was the heart of a heatwave that was steadily cooking the entire country, and it brought another cursed pest to the cabin in biblical proportions.

It was so hot and clammy today that my return, with a burden upon my back, gave me itchy heat lumps and a wet shirt. Orgh!! It was terrible, and once in my cabin that became worse.

Opening my cabin door was like entering a greenhouse, but it wasn't green, it was black with houseflies enjoying their sawner bath – 'sawner', can't find it in the dictionary, how do you spell it? – anyway, as I was saying, my cabin was full of bluebottles and housefly, crawling my window as though covered in ink spots, crawling on my clothes, wardrobe and door. They soon began to crawl on me. Brrrrrh! It makes me shiver. So, quickly unpacking my rucksack, I found what I was after: fly killer, a government-approved device similar to a cup that lets out vapour that kills flies.

So far, after five and a half hours upon my shelf it hasn't worked. Therefore, many tiresome hours of towel-swatting polished off about 500 of 'em, and if you think I'm joking then come and see the change of colour to my gravel floor that once was white, AND STILL THEY CAME IN. It just wasn't on.

Just when I was on the verge of lunacy, I said a silent prayer, and peering from my cabin the sky grew fearfully black with rising winds whipping sparks from my everlasting outdoor fire of bark chippings.

The heat of the heatwave began to vanish. Rain pounded from above, and all outside insects scurried away to hide in whatever shelter they could, and no longer did they enter my cabin.

However, I'd say maybe a hundred or so still crawl my walls, but I reckon there'll be nil upon my departure to the land of nod.

I got that wrong.

That infestation kept going. It endured through rain, prayer, chemical warfare, and the efforts of my heavily bloodied swatting towel. Still they came. Later, I learnt the flies had actually infested the entire Highland district that summer. A pestilence of Old

Testament proportions, which didn't end till the mercy of the cooler weather finally arrived in earnest.

I have saved my most hated miniature miscreant of summer, possibly the leading arch-villain of the entire gang, right to the very end. Ladies and Gentlemen, I give you the tick.

In Scotland, anywhere where there is thick bracken or brush and animals present, you can bet this horrible little parasitic arachnid will be hanging around somewhere; poised to pounce on any warm-blooded creature that slides past.

The initial bite is usually painless, and, early in its feast, the tick will resemble nothing more than a fleck of dirt on your skin. Rest assured, though, you're unlikely to miss it once it starts guzzling your blood. Out they swell to the size of a brown pea and, if undetected, they can gorge on you for a couple of days before dropping off. A tick bite wouldn't be the end of the world, just unsightly and a bit creepy, but then there's the Lyme disease they carry.

I've been bitten by hundreds of ticks through my lifetime, and, as far as I know, I haven't ever contracted Lyme disease. It is pretty rare. But nonetheless, the symptoms of this bacterial infection can be life-changing, and include recurrent bouts of swollen joints, fatigue, headaches and even paralysis of your facial muscles. The good news is that an infection with Lyme disease can be spotted early. One of the most obvious indications is a large red rash that looks like a bullseye on a dartboard, spreading out from the site of the bite. See that, get treated with antibiotics early, and you will significantly lessen the chances of having any of those awful long-term problems.

The obvious way to avoid a tick bite is to steer clear of dense areas of vegetation, but given where and how I live, that's impossible. I wear long trousers to lessen the chance of getting bitten, and you should too, but aside from that (and the use of insect repellent, if you have it), you just need to be vigilant and try and quickly remove the little bastards, if they've latched on.

I do have tick tweezers, but usually I'll just rip them off. That's not the recommended method. They say you should gently grip the tick with a fine-toothed tweezer, as close to your skin as possible, and then pull steadily without squeezing the creature, less it ejects its innards into your body. The traditional methods of using a cigarette lighter, a lit match, or a dollop of Vaseline are all out of favour these days too – probably for the best with the lighter, you wouldn't want to add a bad burn to a bite; plus, I've known 'em scurry right into people's arse cracks before now.

Midge, fly, cleg, ked and slug. Nah. Give me winter any day of the week. With a full log pile and larder, and those devilish beasties firmly in the ground, there is nowt more for the hermit to do but luxuriate in the seclusion of the Scottish Highlands.

MY WILD NEIGHBOURS AND ME

There are many creatures that I truly love seeing around my home. The birds, in particular, are constant sources of entertainment and wonder. I have a bird table set up outside my cabin window and, in 1994, I decided to begin listing every single species I saw. Come 2016, I had extended it to ninety-nine separate species. The list included birds of all designs – big and small, scarce and common, timid and tame. Tree creeper, great tit, cuckoo, chaffinch, siskin, robin, mistle thrush, great spotted woodpecker, collared doves. In winter I recorded wood pigeons roosting, and the lonesome call of the tawny owls on a near nightly basis. I soon branched out from the bird table and started including all the birds I encountered on my travels.

By Treig's shoreline I ticked off the geese, the gulls, the sand-pipers and the herons; and out on the uplands the meadow pipit was very simple to find. They are probably the most common songbird outside of these woods. They burst up from the brush with their skittish flight pattern, opening their white-edged tail fan as they zigzag about the sky. Industrious birds that are always on the go with something: gathering flies, spiders, beetles and grubs, or plucking out nest-building materials. Real stalwarts of the glen.

I spotted some rarities too. The lesser redpoll and its young visited the woods one day. It is a tiny finch species with a distinct-ive red patch on its forehead. They hang upside down when they eat, but they are now on the Red List – the International Union for Conservation of Nature Red List of Threatened Species. In 2002 I saw another rare finch, the strikingly orange parrot crossbill, and then there were all the birds of prey: golden eagles, hen harriers, buzzards, white-tailed sea eagles, goshawks, kestrels, sparrowhawks, merlins and ospreys. Some you'd expect, some you might see regularly in other parts of Scotland, but all still had the ability to thrill me whenever I received a privileged glimpse into their predatory world. Especially so, if I could get close.

The golden eagles have a special corner of my heart. For years I would climb the crags to observe their nesting site, high up on a precipitous cliff ledge above the loch. From there I watched them tenderly raise their young, a pair of fluffy white chicks, and would be sad when they all left. In 1997, a fire raged through much of the uplands and I was sure they were gone for good, but back they came in 1999, to mate and breed once more on their coveted spot of granite overlooking Treig. A golden phoenix from the flames.

Unquestionably the strangest bird was the puffin I found dead against the dam wall in 1997. I can't imagine what tragic circumstance brought that puffin, a seabird, inland some seventy miles east of its closest colony on the Treshnish Isles, south-west of Mull. Perhaps it had simply been badly disorientated in a storm and blown into the depths of the Highlands? Regardless, there was something undeniably sad at seeing this extraordinary seabird, with its iconic technicolour bill and clown-like eyes, downed amongst the gorse at Treig's end.

I have seen all the famous Scottish Highland mammal species: hare, rabbit, red squirrel, otters (in 1985, one even stole a fish right off my fishing line), the invasive mink, the threatened vole, many of the bat species, the fox, badger, ferret, stoat and weasel. Of course, the cabin is frequently visited by rodents, shrews and mice, and the garden is home to many moles too.

I have seen tens of thousands of deer in my life, both our native species here – the red and the roe – and the non-native fallow and sika. For a four-year period from 1993, I would regularly see a pure white roe deer in the hills above Tulloch too. Any albino creature is an extraordinary sight, but white deer have an exceptional place in folklore. In ancient Celt culture, the presence of a white deer was considered a sign that a taboo had been broken. Many of the Native American tribes still hold them as a sacred symbol of their spirituality; others believe a white deer will lead you to enlightenment, bring messages from another realm, or carry some supernatural powers. All agree it is extremely bad luck to kill one.

I enjoyed watching that deer on the few occasions I saw it. There was something quite other-worldly about it; certainly, if you didn't get a clear view of exactly what this large white shape was, you could very well imagine it would be ripe for a yarn.

There have been many occasions where snatched glimpses, odd sounds, or strange markings in the grounds have left me scratching my head as to exactly what creature from the animal kingdom had just sloped past the cabin. Indeed, I had a peculiar one when writer Will and I were working on this book together.

We had left the cabin together to collect logs late one morning. It was a wet start to the day, with that misty sort of rain that clings to your clothes and soaks you right through in seconds. There were globs of cuckoo spit on almost every clump of grass, and a wind pushing some white waves right along the surface of the loch. It wasn't the sort of day where you delay yourself whilst out on a task, but there – pressed directly into the mud outside my front gate – was one of the most unusual animal prints I've ever encountered.

It was very large, seemingly five-fingered, with long claws and a narrow pad. The closest animal in terms of size would be the badger, but it was far too narrow in its shape, and lacking those heavy pads set into the palm of the foot. Superficially, it was similar to a grey squirrel, but at five inches from claw-tip to heel it was clearly from a *far* larger animal. Later, we found a flattened area of grass that was as long as my garden fork. A real mystery, but with no further pugmarks in the mud, and just that single patch of crushed grass, it wasn't something we were likely to be able to solve.

Wild calls and flashes of animals that you can't quite place. Living here, you soon get used to the mystery of the wild and must accept that, to a large degree, you are not going to know it all. Mind you, just because something sits in the box marked 'unsolved', it doesn't mean you start blathering on about your brush with Big Foot. Especially when a perfectly ordinary explanation is still most likely. You don't immediately and completely discredit the extraordinary, either – if a puffin can come to the dam and an albino deer can wander about the local hills, what else might be possible?

There's only one hairy sasquatch-like humanoid living in my small patch of wood – and his name's Ken Smith – but some very strange things have happened in the wider Scottish Highlands, some of which did prove to be wilder than fiction. The most famous case came after a few years of consistent reports of a big cat roaming the Cannich countryside, some forty miles due north of here.

It all began in 1976, when an elderly resident claimed to have seen a big black cat, and followed that up with several more sightings around the forest near her cottage. Other reports trickled in, but no credible evidence was found until 29 October 1980 – the day after my birthday, in fact – when local farmer Donald 'Ted' Noble baited a trap with sheep's offal and, quite sensationally, captured a huge puma.

The cat became an overnight celebrity; but this was no savage beast. Experts agreed that the female puma, soon to be named 'Felicity', had been in the wild for possibly less than forty-eight hours. She was well fed (to the point of actually being quite overweight) and was found to be rather tame. Apparently, she was quite partial to having her ears tickled.

Clearly, then, this cat was once a pet who was well used to people and being hand-fed. Felicity found a new home at the Highland Wildlife Park, but her story confirmed long-held suspicions that the 1976 tightening in UK law, over the keeping of dangerous wild animals as pets, had seen the liberation of several big cats directly into the remotest parts of the Scottish, Welsh and English countryside.

Over the decades, big cat sightings continued to trickle in, with lynx, puma, black panther and mountain lions all being put in the frame at some point – but nothing as undeniable as the capture of Felicity has ever been achieved again. However, as the campaign for re-wilding the Highlands continues to gain momentum, it hasn't taken too long for the subject of the reintroduction of apex predators to be raised too.

Scotland was home to bears, wolves, and the lynx, all of which once played an important role in controlling the numbers of herbivorous animals such as deer and rabbits. Natural control could benefit the environment in theory, but any suggestion of small-scale pilot projects in the Highlands have been met with ferocious opposition from Scottish farmers. It doesn't feel like something that will catch on here anytime soon. Still, it isn't impossible to imagine at least a few lynx being released on the sly at the hands of overenthusiastic animal activists, just as has happened with the beavers that popped up recently in the River Tay.

Felicity passed away in captivity in 1985. Her body was stuffed and remains on display in the Inverness Museum; but there is one true Scottish predatory cat species that is so rare it really does border on the mythological. Armed with lightning-fast reflexes and sharpened retractable claws; muscular, with thick fur and distinctive black and brown stripes extending down its body, the Scottish wildcat is the true Highland tiger.

This feline is no lynx or puma. At a glance, our wildcat could even be confused with a domestic tabby. The pure wildcat, though, has a larger, flatter head with ears that stick out to the side (instead of pointing upwards on the tabby). It possesses no white markings on its underbelly or feet (like the tabby) and is up to double the size of your average pet cat. But the biggest difference comes in its absolutely savage ferocity. This animal, the only native species of cat still in the wild anywhere in Britain, will comfortably kill and eat rabbits, hares, reptiles and birds. It will even eat roadkill.

Their aggression is the stuff of legend – one eyewitness reported how a wildcat all but removed the face of a German shepherd dog when cornered; others even claim the very largest of specimens have taken down deer.

One thing is certain; the Scottish wildcat is critically endangered. Its life is compromised to such an extent that the only credibly identified populations cling on in the quietest woodland edges of the Highlands. I have been extremely lucky to see them in my life, but all my sightings were when I was fifteen years old and out working in Rannoch. That was a very long time ago, and today the specialists say they are no longer considered viable in the wild, as fragmentation of their habitat, feline disease, collisions with cars, and especially, hybridization with domestic and feral cat species, marches them to the point of no return.

Their solitary lives and elusive behaviour make them extremely hard to spot in the wild anyway. Despite having spent more of my life in these woods than anywhere else on Earth, I can't honestly say for sure that I have ever laid eyes on a Scottish wildcat at Treig. That's probably as damning an indictment of their survival chances as anything; these isolated woods would provide perfect cover for an animal or two, but there have only been a couple of 'maybe' moments during all my decades in these trees.

The Scottish wildcat spends most of its life alone and in silence; but, during the winter breeding season, a female wildcat may wail to attract a male, and in 1993 I did hear a feline call that was quite unlike anything else I have ever heard here before. That call re-occurred periodically through the years, and I never was able to pair it conclusively with any of the mammalian woodland species that I know so well. My most likely sighting came before that, though – back on 5 May 1987. I was walking the shoreline of Treig in spectacular weather conditions – clear, still and bright – when I sighted a movement along the earth in a patch of pine.

It took a moment to really get a good look at it (and even then, it was very fleeting), but I did see a large rounded and cat-like head, with thick fur and a thick tail. It could've been a wildcat, but some years later, my bird table was frequented by a cat that was definitely more tabby-feral than wildcat. It must've wandered some distance from its home at some stage in its life, and there it would remain, killing birds and taking scraps. It wouldn't take much to put a cat like that in the frame for what I'd seen in these woods that day but, even if there was a pure wildcat at Treig, the presence of just that one feral cat alone would raise the threat of a cross-breed exponentially.

Unless something dramatic happens, we are likely to see the end of the line for the true Scottish wildcat soon, but something magical endures in the wilds up here; and when you've gone weeks without seeing a soul, and had nothing but the trees, mountains and this expansive loch for company, you can still believe it might yet have the power to conjure up something special. I can but hope.

———

My relationship with wildlife is not completely harmonious. I have told you about the worst of the biting and slithering mini-beasts, but there are plenty of other creatures that are capable of raising my blood pressure on their day. But no matter how reckless and murderous they may be, and how angry I might feel when they undo all my hard work, eat my crops, or ransack my home, I still find myself hoping they are doing okay. I just can't help myself.

The chaffinch and bullfinch are plenty capable of stripping the garden of its berries, and the rodents will clean me out of food (if I let them), but when it comes to thievery, the pine marten is the undisputed king of the lot. They may have a cute and cheeky appearance, with their soft brown fur and teddy-bear eyes, but they are sleek and athletic killers too, armed with sharp paws and dagger-like teeth. Determined, intelligent, and powerful, I've actually been forced to store any meat and cheese within a second-hand gun locker. They might not be able to get in, but they have a habit of pissing on it, soaking urine through the joints, and rusting them right up. I am absolutely convinced it is a deliberate act; but, yet again, I frequently find myself worrying about them when the winters are at their very worst – and, in 1993, I would say I even went as far as making friends with one.

Well, if not quite friends, we definitely declared a truce.

Through the spring and summer of that year, a young pine marten came as close to being completely tame as I would say it is possible for a creature of that disposition to become. It killed the cabin's rodent pests, and would happily feed on leftovers, without taking the leap to either pillaging my larder or killing birds fresh off the bird table – as so many of his ancestors happily had.

We had a truly appalling winter that year. One evening, I returned from ghillie duties at the estate to find him sheltering in deep snow beneath my bird table. He was truly dishevelled, and far more nervous than he had been throughout the summer, but he came around again and, all too soon, proved he was an absolute warrior of an animal.

The new year of 1994 brought in a storm with 100 m.p.h. winds. The violence sent huge waves down the loch and brought its levels up by thirty feet – but, even in the teeth of that tempest, the marten remained. Stoically, under the bird table, gritting it out. It survived that, but then came a full month of snow and intense blizzards. It disappeared then, and I was sure it would be dead, but a rapid thaw in March saw it back yet again. As cheeky as ever, it stood up on its back legs right under the bird table, as if nothing had ever happened. It had my respect, for sure; but I am afraid to say our relationship was swiftly tested when he proceeded to dig up my entire seed bed.

From that point forward, the pine marten rediscovered the true ways of the pine marten. Falling into ordinary rank and file, it proceeded to steal from the cabin, raid my meat stores, and would spend its nights running back and forth across the roof till it had cracked the zinc sheeting.

Three years later, I was stunned to discover that 'he' was in fact a 'she' – and in the spring of 1997, she squeezed into the gap between my roofing and ceiling and made a nest in the insulation. Her litter of kits brought absolute chaos to my life. As soon as they could, they had gnawed a hole in my roof, and I found them running all around my shed wreaking total havoc. I rushed around, trying to drive them all back out before they completely destroyed the place, with their mother, my former friend, sitting watching (and doing nothing) from just a couple of feet away.

There they would remain till July, when they all eventually left the nest. I wish I could say they were good house guests but, pine martens being pine martens, I was left with the gift of a highly warped plyboard ceiling (due to all their urine), an extremely messy shed, and the chewed-up corpses of thrush, chaffinch, various mutilated baby birds, and one very sorry-looking frog.

For years, they would continue to visit the cabin as a family, causing bedlam on the bird table, slaughtering birds, running across my roof night and day, and peering in at me through my windows.

It is never a good thing to have wild animals quite *so* fearless and tame, but I have to admit, much against my better judgement, I was always secretly quite pleased to see them back again, just as long as they didn't come back into my cabin or my shed. Which thankfully, they never did.

———

Of all the animals I've looked out for over the decades, one stands head and feathers above the rest. Simon, the hooded crow.

I need to take you back to the aftermath of that great storm I described earlier. It was in February 1989, when I fled from my cabin and it felt like the entire forest was crumbling to the earth around me. I survived unscathed, and so did my home (just), but among the wreckage I found an animal that hadn't been quite so lucky.

Thursday 16 February 1989

Thousands upon thousands of trees lay flat from the railway line to Treig, all tightly twined together to prevent an easy passage. Even roe deer had trouble of movement jumping over the slippy white tree trunks.

Looking for dead stags and sheep none were found, but they'll be there, but not so noticeable due to snow.

What I did find, though, was a hooded crow, hopping around with a broken wing, where after chancing it (and receiving a peck on my left hand), I took it back to my cabin.

You don't get hooded crows in England, just carrion, and all are supposed to be vermin. Actually, I can't ever recall a crow doing damage, but more so good, while devouring rotting carcass from moorland and scattering bones within the earth to rot.

So here I am, with a hooded crow beneath a supermarket basket in my living room, which up to now is OK – crapping all over my slab floor and eating bread.

If it survives its overnight shock of meeting me, I'll use the outside cage nailed to a tree – if you remember it? The cage once used for keeping meat in, away from predators like pine martens.

I'll remove the cage from the tree, line its bottom with wood, put a perch in it and keep it within my living room until the crow's wing heals.

I surely hope that, if it does heal, it will be able to fly again – for I don't want to end up with a tame hoodie that can't fly.

———

Friday 17 February 1989

With heavy snow until early afternoon, little outside work could be done. When changing to showers, out I went to collect a good supply of logs to keep me and my pal warm. It's called Pal because a hoodie is hard to distinguish in its sex. How do you tell a male from a female?

Seeing Pal still alive, but rather dismal beneath his shopping basket, I began construction of his new cage and perch.

It didn't actually take long, and Pal stuck lump hammer noise rather well as it became hammered to my wall, with a follow-up of rattling falling objects by his side – his or her side I should have wrote – but anyway, even when picking Pal up, all that really happens was a bent head of hissings. Nothing quite so serious this time, like a nasty peck.

It's a better view through my living-room window, perched and glancing to outside snowfalls instead of standing on cold slabs. A nice full stomach of bread, sausage, and dog biscuits I once bought for Morgan's dog, B.R., but if not for me walking through woodland yesterday I'm sure Pal would be a frozen block of ice by now.

———

Saturday 18 February 1989

Railway workers have been using power saws on the above line for most of today, only to be accompanied by repetition of a O24 AV chainsaw, as Ken Smith cut two fallen trees into a good supply of future logs, and – as regarding Pal – Pal didn't mind one little bit, for Pal was busy stomach filling with dog biscuits and the remains of a hock end.

What a dismal face greeted me this morning, though, with a body covered in dry urine after the perch had broken overnight. A depressing night indeed, sleeping as done the previous night without a roost, poor soul, so another became added but made secure for a change, along with sawdust to mop up whatever droppings may occur.

What a change came over Pal, and I'm sure as I left the room a faint croak was heard.

Having survived his trauma, and two weeks of excellent recovery in my cabin, I rewarded Pal with a proper name. Henceforth and forever more, he was to be known as Simon.

Quite why I chose Simon, I can't say I can recall, but by this point I was quite taken by my companion, although it had become clear by now that his wing was truly broken beyond repair.

My diary continued:

> I didn't know until told by Chris and Theresia that no one had encountered me since the passing storm seventeen days ago, and because of this I was thought to be a victim of the storm and already rotting to the earth. Therefore, if nothing was heard of me soon then members of the Mountain Rescue would be paying my cabin a visit.
>
> It's nice to think everyone was concerned, but I think in seventeen days I'd have long since been dead if a tree had pinned me to the ground.
>
> Well, now I'm back at my cabin after walking five miles of snow-infested land and my pal, Simon the crow, has eaten well.

Our time together, as a pleasant duo, would continue on for some time. I can't tell you exactly how long, as the diary ends a few weeks later, and I fear the next instalment of our adventures may have been lost to the cabin fire that came a couple of years later.

What I can recall vividly though, is what a wonderful companion Simon became. He was completely tame after just a few weeks, and was back to full physical strength by the summer. His wing, though, was irreparably damaged. Sadly, this is a trait that is very common in injured birds. Their lightweight bone structures, evolved for flying, are very brittle; once damaged, that is ordinarily a death sentence – whether in the wild or the veterinary surgery.

I couldn't keep Simon. As much as I would've liked to, and as much as his injury necessitated care, I could tell within his little heart that he longed for the freedom of the wild. It is all too easy to project our own will onto nature, to imagine animals as we imagine ourselves. Often, we do this to fill a void in our own lives and, in doing so, we unwittingly deprive nature of the right to behave in its most natural way.

The odds are stacked unfathomably high against a bird that cannot fly, even one as tenacious and intelligent as a hooded crow, but I knew I was doing the right thing as I released Simon from his cage early one summer's morning. He'd rather die on his terms than die in a cage. Me, of all people, had to understand that.

I didn't think I would ever see Simon again, and assumed it wouldn't take too long before a fox picked up what would be a very easy meal. Given a fair fight, hooded crows can actually live for sixteen years, but I didn't hold out much hope for Simon. Then, to my utter shock, three years later, we were reunited.

I was on my travels and had just come across the carcass of some animal that was being picked apart and consumed by a whole murder of hooded crows. As I approached, they all flew, bar one – a bird with a broken wing and no fear of me whatsoever. I walked right up to the crow and we looked each other in the eye. 'Hello Simon,' I said, and sat with him talking for a while as he ate.

That would've been one of my most wonderful moments with a wild animal in all my time up here, were it not surpassed by yet another chance meeting with my friend. By this point, I was almost a decade clear of that storm and out walking in an entirely different part of the glen, behind the Corrour shooting lodge on the banks of Loch Ossian, miles from Treig, my cabin, and where I had first met Simon all those years before.

I was working, taking guests out, and we had ascended onto the open moor to look for stags. We were all sitting in position, watching the land and waiting, when out of a nearby bush hopped a hooded crow. It saw us immediately, but instead of fleeing (which it couldn't do anyway, owing to its broken wing), it hopped straight down the path towards me.

It was Simon. I knew it was him before he'd even had a chance to come close enough for me to know for sure. He came right up to me, to within an inch, and we greeted each other as the old friends we undoubtedly now were.

He stayed with me a while before about-tailing and heading off up the bank of a steep-sided stream. We followed him up, but as we reached the summit he was already gone; and that, truly, was the last I ever saw of him.

His survival against the odds was a miracle.

In spite of his injuries, he had found a way to adapt to a life on the ground. He had evaded death by starvation and predator, and he had actually managed to do rather well for himself. I felt very emotional. Perhaps, after all, I could see a bit of myself in this wild animal? Perhaps, too, you'll forgive the further indulgence, when I add that I felt that day, out on the glen, Simon had hopped over to me, simply to say: *Thanks*.

BROWN GOLD AND WILD BREWS

My cabin would be nothing without a solid foundation and I approached my garden in much the same way. The garden surrounds the entirety of my home – with the largest patch of earth sat squarely outside my front door. It is quite small; probably little more than an eighth of an acre; but it is prolific, and that is all down to the soil. There's lots said and written about all the things you can grow in a garden, but not enough said about the essential element that sustains all that life. The brown gold. The muck itself.

Your soil needs just as much care and attention as what you grow in it, if not more so. I'd learnt enough in my years working for the Forestry Commission, the nursery, and on my allotment, to know what constituted good soil. It was finding it that was going to prove the issue. The original soil around my cabin just didn't have the depth to grow all that I needed. The good news, though, was that you didn't have to travel far in this wood to find some lovely thick patches of earth, filled with nutrients from decaying organic matter and, crucially, worms. I would find an area and scoop some into my bag before transplanting it into my own garden, and then I'd be on the hunt for natural fertilizers.

Before the sheep were moved from the mountain, my major source was sheep dung – a lovely, slow-release fertiliser, high in potassium and phosphorus; but I've always used my own fertilizer too, harvested from the depths of the Bottomless Pit, or from my dedicated food-waste compost heap.

It has all worked wonderfully well over the decades, and today I've got all sorts out there in my garden. Some of my plants I've grown from seeds I've collected and set, some are from shoots and saplings I've bought (or been given), and others are from cuttings I've borrowed and grown on. There's that much out there, and that much been and gone, it's very hard to keep a track of it all.

I used to be able to remember it all quite easily, but some names do slip the mind. I did diligently write tags for all the plants as they went into the ground, but bad weather, wind and small creatures have all played their part in mixing those tags up.

In spite of the shelter offered to my plants by the wood, it is naturally a lot colder here, so things tend to burst into life just that little bit later. Really, it's only just warming up in the day now, in early summer, and it is still quite cold at night; but there's still a whole lot of greenery erupting outside in my small woodland garden.

I planted this season's seed potatoes in late May. Each seed potato should produce roughly 3 lbs of potatoes, so I need a fair few to build up for a decent harvest – but as with all of my fruits and vegetables, they are a supplement to the food I buy in the shops, and not intended to provide me with all the nourishment I need year-round. It is much cooler up here than the lower-lying parts of the country, so food will last longer, but without any refrigeration that only goes so far. I have to plan my planting year carefully and eat what's available when it is in season. Once winter is passed, I'll be looking to the vegetable patch to cover a lot of my needs. Carrots, turnips, onions, parsnips, rhubarb, beetroot, radish, kohlrabi – all hardy root vegetables capable of surviving the occasional savage twist in temperatures. Root vegetables have a natural density to them and they are very filling – a very good thing when you are out here and food supplies are dwindling – but their weight makes them a good practical choice to grow as well, as when I go shopping I can focus on buying lighter vegetables, like salads, which are much easier to carry home.

On the fence line beside the potato patch, there's a whole mix of herbs springing up. The names of most of them escape me now, but I know the largest one in the bunch is comfrey, and there are thirty-five species of that alone. I've made wine with comfrey in the past, and if you rot down its leaves in a bucket of water, it can make an excellent natural fertilizer. It isn't a herb that foragers generally recommend you eat, though; apparently there is an enzyme in the plant that can harm the liver if it's eaten in large amounts. I've got plenty of other herbs, too; ones I've planted myself in makeshift planters from crates, old tubs and recycled pots.

I have lots of fruit for my wine-making. Redcurrants, white currants, blackcurrants, damson and elderberries; all in varying states of growth; and I've even got Worcester berries, a cross between a gooseberry and a blackcurrant. The damsons are struggling though. We had a late frost this spring, so only one small shoot has made a bid from the earth to the sunshine, but the blackcurrant berries are already starting to show on one of my garden's most exuberant residents: a giant fifteen-foot blackcurrant bush, sprouting from behind the vegetable patch.

The elderberry trees are slowly beginning to flower come early summer. The elderberry will produce its fruit after the blackcurrants in July, but I'll still have plenty of mixed fruits to harvest throughout the midsummer and into early autumn for making wine. Really, the elderberry is more of a bush or a shrub than a tree. It has green leaves with these serrated saw-like edges, and it grows these great clusters of tiny black berries. You must take care, though: every part of that plant has the potential to be toxic to humans – the berries, the stem, the root and the leaves; so, when making your wine, jam, pies or syrups, just make sure your berries are cooked and prepared correctly.

In terms of the trees, I have to be a little careful – I don't want them throwing shade over this hard-won patch of earth; so I grow miniature species, things I can keep small, or things I can plant in the wider wood once established and strong.

I have a few hollies scattered around, a rowan sapling by the back fence, and a plum tree by the cabin corner. That plum was flowering in April and I had been keeping a very close eye on it to see which flowers might have been fertilized. Out there now, there are signs of success, with some immature fruits showing. Minuscule they are. Just an eighth of an inch in size; half of a little fingernail, or smaller; but rounded and green. And hopeful. I get an awful lot of pleasure from growing maple trees, too, and have several varieties potted or planted around the garden, in various stages of growth. It is a nostalgic indulgence, I suppose, taking me back to those Canadian days, but the maples are truly beautiful trees, with their iconic lobed leaves, as depicted on the Canadian flag.

I've also got a lovely young willow tree growing from a cutting I'd been quietly loaned from a tree in a town square close to Fort William, where I do my shopping. That's now planted next to a truly beautiful rose, whose flowers are a golden honey yellow. I've got a few other roses, but at the moment I'm trying to focus on growing a pair of roses to form a lovely archway of blooms. Sadly, they've stalled in their growth. Barely a flower, let alone an arch. I think the birds might be eating the petals, but it is all a bit of a mystery. There's still time, though.

A lot of the things I've planted are practical: things to eat; things to drink. Other plants are grown purely for their beauty, providing forms of nourishment other than just the stuff you shovel into your belly or pour down your throat.

I have other flowers, pretty plants and shrubs, aside from those beautiful roses. All sorts: wallflowers, wild tansy, balloon vine, foxgloves, scarlet pimpernel, nasturtiums, cotoneaster; rhododendron bushes, too, which will be bursting out their magnificent purple flowers any day now.

Do you talk to your flowers? I believe in talking to them, especially the roses. I'll give them a little stroke, and tell them all about whatever's on my mind. They seem to respond to that bit of extra-special attention; take on a little bit more colour, grow a little bolder, and look generally happier.

I don't know. Maybe in seeking out a flower for a chat you

A stunning windless day turns the loch into a millpond-calm mirror.
I fell in love with this part of the world from the very first time I came here,
aged just fifteen, when I discovered a very special sense of freedom.

The view up the slope behind the cabin, illuminated by a band of sunlight.
The train track runs in the shadow beside the treeline and snow fills the gullies
and creases on the mountain tops.

Home sweet home. I live a simple life but it is not without its comforts.
This is my room, with my armchair facing the fire and a piece of carpet covering the
gravel floor. There's a barrel of booze on the go in the corner, my calendar to keep
the score, tins on the shelf. Perfect for a long winter's hibernation!

Fish and chips made the Ken Smith way: a pair of fresh trout fillets and
a pan of boiling spuds over an open fire. Perfect!

Right: One of my store cupboards: tins at the bottom, magazines and reading materials at the top, and a whole lot of home-brewed wine in between! There are very few edible berries or plants that I haven't tried to make into wine at some point.

Below: Chopping timber for logs with axe or chainsaw is a never-ending but very necessary part of my life out here. A well-maintained log pile is vital for heating my cabin through long winters, and for cooking my food all year round.

A bucket of freshly harvested home-grown spuds. If planted well, and correctly cared for, a single seed potato can yield me up to three pounds of potato to boil or fry. Delicious!

A crop of juicy raspberries successfully grown. Wonderful to eat raw, make into a jam, or use as a base flavour for an excellent home-brew wine – I just need to make sure I get out there and pick 'em before the birds get to work!

Above: The scarlet berries of the rowan tree burst through and mark autumn. The wood around my home has a mix of species, but mostly the larch and Scots pine dominate, alongside silver birch, and beech. I've planted a few species of tree myself – hollies, plum, willow, and especially maples.

Right: A lovely smear of fat, likely from a recent bacon sandwich, thickens up in my frying pan. I try not to waste anything. Fat can be warmed again and used as a cooking oil – especially useful for adding a meaty flavour to bannocks, a simple hand-made flat bread.

Here is a pine marten enjoying scraps off the bird table. He's welcome to them of course, but when it crosses the line and goes for the bounty in my meat locker, or worse, takes up residence in the cabin roof and soaks my ceiling with pee, then we have a problem!

There have been many times when the local birds have become so confident around me, that they have actually come to my hand for food. This is a male chaffinch, just one of almost a hundred species of bird that I've recorded over the years here at Treig.

A red deer calf gets hand-fed some milk. Although the populations of deer on these fells must be managed for the health of the herd and the wider environment, that doesn't mean we don't care about them deeply.

The culmination of a lifetime of careful study as an angler – at 12 lbs exactly, this giant ferox trout remains the Loch Treig record. I never came close to meeting a ferox of this size again.

A blizzard begins. There won't be any birds visiting the bird table on days like this.
All animals, including hermits, must seek shelter and wait for it to pass through.

Sometimes the rain falls so heavily that it looks like the surface of the loch is actually
smoking. The sheer amount of water in the Scottish Highlands is what brings the land so
much of its beauty – but there are times when it feels like it won't ever stop pouring!

subconsciously wind up giving it a bit more practical care: the removal of a stray weed that might hamper their progress here, or a useful prune to support their growth there, and that's what really makes them grow better. But I personally believe that it is the affection in your words and feelings towards them that stimulates them to grow too. You shouldn't feel self-conscious about saying a few kind words to the things that grow in your garden. You shouldn't feel self-conscious about saying kind words to anything.

Friday 12 March 1993

One demijohn was overflowing with birch sap. The other half full. Bunged up holes in birch trees with spearmint.

Some to drink. Some as a gift.

Siphon off birch sap wine, the last of my siphoning which I'll exchange for a watch with Sandy, the estate butcher.

Two gallon of wine for a watch was our deal.

—

Sunday 12 April 2009

Such a fine dry day of sunshine and I wondered if birch sap was running from the trees. Yup! It was, two holes drilled into nearby trees, fix tubes and into demijohns. They should be full by midweek, I hope, then the beginning of wine-making will begin.

While at it, I washed out a drum, brewed hops, added yeast extract and made five gallon of beer. The way I'm going there will be enough for an army. Just counted 'em – sixty-three gallon of wine and three barrels of home-brew beer.

I've already told you how I cultivate a few berry and fruit species in my garden specifically for my wine-making, but I've also foraged from a fair few species in the wild for the same boozy purpose. The blossoms from rowan trees, roots of nettles, jack-by-the-hedge (also known as garlic mustard), the pretty pink flowers of the rosebay willowherb, horsetail weed, even the yellow flowers of wild gorse and the purple heather flowers – all have been collected by my hand and brewed at some point in the past.

One of the finest wild foraged ingredients for the wine, in my humble opinion, is the sap of the birch tree – and to get that, like a miner prospecting for oil, you're going to have to get to drilling.

Now, there can be no hanging about when it comes to tapping a silver birch for its sap. It's not like wild berries, roots or flowers, where you might have weeks on end to complete your work. With birch sap you might only get a fortnight, or three weeks at a stretch, to complete your tap and start pulling that nectar from the silverine trunk of the birch tree. Usually it is somewhere around early spring, depending on how warm it is out; but this isn't like seeing a flower, tree, or bush in fruit or bloom, and thinking: 'Oh, now's the time to go for it'. No, knowing when and where to tap is not as easy as that, I'm afraid.

Birch sap is a solution of water and sugar that is held within the tree's trunk. Trees pull in the water through their thirsty roots. Most of that will later evaporate through its leaves, but for the birch, a little bit of it gets made into sugars and stored for the winter. Now, as soon as the tree senses spring is coming, up the tree trunk all that water and that store of sugar flows, giving the energy that the silver birch needs to start shooting out its fresh leaves for the warmer months. That's the moment you start your tap.

With the early spring birds chirping in the background, and us all thanking god we made it through another winter, I'll be shuffling through the woods with a glass demijohn, tube and hand drill. I'll be looking for a silver birch with a foot-wide trunk, or preferably wider. Next, I'll clear the drilling area at about waist height, ease off any moss from the creamy-white papery bark of the birch, and then start to drill a hole, on an upward slant, a couple of inches deep into the trunk.

Usually, you'll see the signs you're onto a winner fairly quickly. The sap will start to bubble up around your drill bit as you ease it on its way through the bark, and then it'll dribble out in steady drops. If nothing comes out at all, plug the hole and look again in another week.

If I've hit sap, I'll push one end of my tubing into the hole and then put the other end into my demijohn to collect the fluid. If you're in luck, you might get a good few litres of sap from a single birch; if you're exceptionally fortunate you might even fill your demijohn; but, once I feel the birch has donated enough, usually after a day of dripping, I'll cap off the demijohn with something porous like a wad of muslin or a bandage – something that helps all those sweet fluids breathe. It is then really important that you carefully seal up the hole in the tree you've drilled. You don't want to leave the tree bleeding out all that sap it has made for its good health, once you've collected enough to toast your own. I'll usually bung mine up with a good wodge of spearmint.

Brewing the birch sap is pretty straightforward. First, I'll pour it into a deep pan and bring it to the boil. This kills any nasties that might be hiding away in it. Your belly will be bad enough if you overdo it on the booze; last thing you need is the squitters from some little bugger of a bacterium too. Once that's done, take it off the boil and let it cool. Next, I dissolve about two pounds of sugar per half demijohn into the mix; sometimes I'll squeeze in the juice of a lemon or two (if I'm lucky enough to have them). Finally, I'll add my yeast. It is *vital* that the sap has cooled down by this point, otherwise the heat can kill the yeast. I'll use a packet of high-alcohol wine yeast. I used to buy them from Boots the chemist, but I get my friends to send away for them now, using the 'Internet'. With the yeast sprinkled on, I'll return the mix to a demijohn and fix a bubble-trap valve and leave it for about a year before cracking it open and having a party.

You will probably have gathered that there are very few things, whether flower, fruit, root, or shoot, from which I haven't tried to make wine at some point. My more unusual brews have come from coffee, tomatoes, the daisy-like feverfew flower, pansies, potato, cress, lovage, comfrey, ginger root and horseradish. I have a list pinned to the door of my cupboard-cum-cellar detailing everything I've tried through the years.

All that booze carefully recorded in biro. One page alone details a period of some sixteen months where I produced some seventy brews or so; plenty enough to see a small garrison have a fair few heavy nights and days, at any rate, and an honest testament to just how much I really do enjoy trying to find a new alcoholic wonder.

There have been many brews that would fall well short of prize-winning standards. Writing this, I passed through a fair few diaries from the cabin days of the 1980s and 1990s and noted many guests were laid *very low* following a long night on my home-made wine. This diary note from the 1990s seems fairly typical, if not a little unfair. I believe it was during a visit from my brothers and their friends:

Night on raspberry wine until 4 a.m. Everyone reckons my wine smelt like Bostik glue, the raspberry wine that is. They reckon my other wine, heather, was an 'unusual acquired taste.'

Perhaps I'll concede and admit that it's true to say a few of my brews were definitely an 'acquired taste'. That was never going to stop me experimenting, though. You never know what you might end up liking if you don't give some experimentation a go. I'm sure some of the finest culinary discoveries on earth had their origins when someone just looked at something growing in the earth, on a bush, or up in a tree, and thought to themselves: 'I wonder what that might taste like if I did this . . .?'

In the end all that really matters is that *I like my wine* and I will certainly continue to enjoy the brewing, gathering, tapping and drinking. I hope, for many, many, years to come.

CATCH IT. COOK IT.

If you want to truly live in the wilderness, you must first learn how to hunt, fish or gather. In North America, I sustained myself off foraged plants and fungi, and used traps and a slingshot to harvest the occasional duck or rabbit. In Scotland, the deer aside, I needed to be much more opportunistic. I have eaten fresh road- and train-kill when I've found it, and continue to forage seasonally, but my most regular source of wild food has always been the loch.

There is something vital about choosing to take the life of an animal. Something that is lost on the vast majority of meat-eaters on this planet, whose only real engagement comes when they choose their cut from the butcher's or supermarket aisle. You can't really blame people for being out of touch with what they put in their bellies. The gulf between the consumer, the producer, and the consumed could hardly be greater. The hard work is outsourced elsewhere and the animal is absolutely unrecognizable by the time it reaches the bottom of their baskets. All neatly presented; free of blood, guts and gore; lying on a plastic carpet with a price tag stuck blithely on the front of some shiny pack-aging. Everything that animal is, or was, has been stripped away, as is everything it has taken the farmer, fisherman or packer to get it to that point.

Eating meat is a privilege, and that animal's life should *always* be remembered, whenever, and however, you choose to take it. I would encourage anyone to learn a bit more about the meat they buy to eat, not just where it's from, and how it was looked after or caught, but something of its life too. What it meant to be that fish, cow, pig or chicken. You might just find you have a bit more respect for the animal *and* its home; and that can only be better all round.

—

The depths of the loch hide beautiful brown trout, monstrously dark pike, thick, snake-like eels, pretty three-spined stickleback, and three separate species of Arctic charr – a hangover from the Ice Age. One species of those charr was believed to be extinct here, until a netting survey hauled them right up from the frigid lake bed. Such are the mysteries of Treig; but I always knew those charr were there, as – come the cold weather – they move up from the deeps onto shallow sandbars to breed. A well-placed worm brought them to my net (and the lens of my camera) long before their official rediscovery.

There are many ways to catch a fish, and I've tried a great deal of them through the course of my fishing life. Over the years, though, my fishing techniques have narrowed to either lure fishing or fishing with bait. Fishing with bait is nearly always a static method. You cast out your baited rig into a favourable area, and leave it there till you have a bite from your target fish species. In the Canadian winter I would use cuts of dead fish to tempt the serpentine burbot out from their icy lairs. They were ugly-looking buggers, but my goodness they tasted nice, with their big meaty chunks of cod-like white flesh, which I ate fried or boiled up in a stew. In Scotland, I've employed worms for trout and perch, or small fish to snare a pike – but usually, if I'm going to fish, I don't muck around looking for worms, or waste fish I could eat trying to catch fish that are invariably too big to knock on the head anyway; instead, I use lures.

Inside a series of small plastic tackle boxes and old tins, I keep all my lures. I must've gone through thousands in my life, but there are plenty in there that are decades old and still more than capable of catching fish – just like me.

Lures are designed to mimic the actions of small prey fish, something that a larger predatory fish would like to eat. The way the various different lures achieve this are many and varied. One of the most popular here are metal lures, which are shaped to spin, flutter and flash as you reel them back through the water. Usually, they are 'spinners' or 'spoons' that resemble a small silver fish fleeing in open water. Another type are 'plugs' or 'crankbaits', built to look almost exactly like a fish, with a swimming action that wobbles through the water as if it were injured or weakened. Colours and patterns can be added to these lures, too, as well as feathers, and the hooks can even be baited with worms; anything to give your lure that added bit of attraction: a splash of blood-red, or a trailing wormy scent that a predatory fish will likely follow.

The very best lures cover several bases: they move in an attractive 'eat me' way *and* are coloured to provoke a predatory response. However, it is always worth remembering that a lot of fishing tackle is designed to catch the angler and not the fish. I have modern lures in my boxes that look very pretty, and are made with very fine materials indeed, but are only really good for stripping down and building back into an old lure that I know will work on this very specific water.

I generally like lures that are made of metal and on the smaller side. That way, if a fish decides it does want to eat it, I know it'll be well hooked. A lot of big fish anglers use very large lures. That's all well and good, but patterns that are particularly long are always giving the fish that chance of taking it right across the middle, avoiding the hooks placed on the ends of your lure. You lose fish (or have to put more hooks on the lure) when you could just fish with a far smaller lure and hook that fish first time anyway. Remember: big fish will eat small fish too – you just need to find the right lure.

I will spend money on fishing tackle – it is an investment, as it goes towards providing a source of my food – but I'll do everything I can to make sure I don't end up losing it all to the many snags hidden beneath Treig's surface. That means fishing with strong line to lessen the chances of it snapping, but, if the worst still happens and I lose my lure to a big rock or a submerged tree, I'll mentally mark the spot where it is and, as soon as the water level drops low enough, I'll go in and retrieve it.

I hand-make many of my lures and am always on the lookout for everyday materials that might be attractive to fish: coins, spoons, old name tags, key rings; anything with a good shape and a bit of a shine. Then I'll add the holes for the hooks and swivels, and usually put on an extra bit of attractant in the form of coloured beads, paint, or fur; anything that will give me that extra edge.

On Loch Treig there are fish to catch everywhere, and a few hotspots that they seem to frequent with real regularity, especially the mouths of the burns and all the big bays. Of far greater importance, though, is the weather. The very obvious difference between a pure pleasure angler, and someone like myself, is that I catch to eat, whereas they just fish for fun. For a lot of those sort of anglers, just being waterside satisfies a lot of what they are looking for: a day away from stress and time spent in nature; the fish are just a bonus. That means they'll usually choose the nicest days on which to head out with a rod in hand, favouring warm and dry weather, and the comfiest spot they can find on that stretch of bank.

For me, I won't even head out if I know I'm not likely to catch. Sunny weather is actually the absolute worst possible for catching predatory fish. I have nothing whatsoever against fair-weather anglers, but when I've got so much to do day to day, and I'm reliant on catching to feed myself, I just can't afford to waste my time trying and failing.

You *must* think like the fish you are hoping to catch. A big fish-eating trout isn't going to bother hunting on a day when its own prey is hard to sneak up on. In bright, settled conditions, a small fish can see a big fish coming, and they will flee from the area; but when it is murky, overcast, with a good ripple on the lake, predatory fish will find ambush a hell of a lot easier. I would actually go so far as to say: the more violent the conditions, the more violent the take from the fish. As long as you're not daft enough to head out in truly severe weather conditions (that could see an errant lightning bolt mould your rod permanently to your palm), never overlook the fish-catching power of bloody awful weather.

With the right time and place ticked off, next think about what lure you are using and how it will work in the water. Too many anglers get *time* and *place* right, and then just cast out and reel their lure straight back in. You need to *work* that lure through the water. Think about the water in three dimensions, not just the blank surface stretched out in front of you. Fish the lure at different depths, counting down the seconds as it falls, and then wind it back towards you at varying speeds. Properly cover the area, fanning your casts out like you are fishing the face of a clock. That way you know you've put the lure through everything out there and, if anything *really* wanted it, they would have had it.

Finally, basic watercraft. Use stealth, wear dull clothing, and be quiet. Even if you can't see the fish, they can see you. Here in Treig, they will often chase your lure right to your toes, so if you are being noisy and wearing garish colours, you'll certainly blow it.

—

My greatest fishing haul came off the back of one of the worst winters in living memory. The year 1994 opened with a month of solid squalls and snow storms; frozen ground then gave way to endless rains. It was that rain – the dark skies, and even darker waters – that brought the biggest of Treig's trout into the loch edges to hunt and feed.

And I was right there, waiting for them with my rod in hand.

Monday 7 March 1994

A fantastic day today. Out with my rod and home-made lure to fish nearby bay. Large trout attacks but misses lure. Keep casting, and on fifth cast hook, play, and beach it. Back at cabin it is weighed in at 6 ¾ lb, my largest trout so far from Treig.

Rain still pounding down, must try again tomorrow.

—

Tuesday 8 March 1994

Down fishing the bay again in pounding rain and a torrent of flowing water. Hook trout on very large spinner. Play it out, beach it, and was to weigh in at 7 ½ lb. Again, I break my trout record for Treig.

—

Wednesday 9 March 1994

Hailstones, snow and sleet, we had the lot today, and I walked 17 mile in the bloody stuff by 8.20 a.m just to see what letters had arrived for me at Spean.

I also carried the two fish with me for Alistair in the Spean Hotel. I was given free alcohol during my stay in the pub.

—

Friday 18 March 1994

Any form of outside work is now beyond all hope until the thaw. As temperatures never rose above freezing and heavy snow continued its fall to a depth of 10'.

Because of no hope of work, I picked up my rod and walked to the boathouse. I fished right the way to Rath River and back again without a bite, that is until back at the boathouse.

Six casts, one hell of a bite, one hell of a fight and a long time to land it. Where back at my cabin was to weigh in at an 8 lb trout, my largest in Treig so far.

By this point, in just a week and a half of fishing, I had broken my personal best Treig trout three times. To give some context to this, quite remarkable window of good fortune, your average-sized wild brown trout in Scotland is likely to weigh less than a pound. A real specimen would be around three or four pounds, and catching a fish double that, truly, would be the fish of a life-time. So far, I had caught three 'fish of a lifetime' on three back-to-back trips. That haul in itself stretched credulity, but what came next was nothing short of a miracle.

On Saturday 2 April the snow was so awful that all work was out of the question again, so I picked up my rod and went back to the boathouse. There were some campers from Holland already on the spot, proudly displaying a nice two-pound trout they had just caught on a lure. I asked if they wouldn't mind me fishing there, and they were only too happy to make way. I could tell from their faces that they thought I was unlikely to catch anything, but I had been watching them fish and could see that they were retrieving their lure far too quickly. In essence, they might have covered the bank, but they had only really fished the upper few feet of water that dropped to several metres deep. There, down in the dark, I felt instinctively that something mighty could yet be stirred.

Within just a few casts, my rod hooped over and my reel screamed urgently into life. From the off, I was left in absolutely no doubt that, whatever this was, it was likely to be very large indeed. It fought, as many of the very biggest fish do: dogged resistance at depth, like a super-heavyweight boxer leaning back on the ringside ropes and throwing thunderous blows every time his opponent tried to apply any pressure; but there was something about this fish that was different too. It held its ground and would not yield. It was almost like being attached to the whole lake bed of the loch itself; but then it would move, chugging up and down like a heavy goods train, seemingly unconcerned about anything I attempted to do to bring it up through the water column.

I had to keep going through the stalemate, bending the rod as much as I dared, as Treig's wind whistled ominously through my line with a whine. The spot where I had hooked this fish was littered with snags – enormous boulders and doubtless a few trees too – and if this giant fish made it into any of those, my line would snap like cotton, but there was only so much pressure I could apply without the hook pulling clean from the mouth, or the line breaking purely under the strain of this fight. When playing a big fish, this is a balance of power that you must learn; a great game of cat and mouse with repeated advances and calculated retreats.

Twenty minutes passed and, very gradually, I started to gain line, but I still had very little idea of quite what I was attached to. Not once did the fish leap or swirl on the surface, it just thundered back and forward, giving me incremental gains till finally, mercifully, I pulled it clean onto the bank by my feet.

I have never, and will never, see anything like that fish. My jaw dropped, and the Dutch campers gasped in amazement. It was the trout of many lifetimes.

In bodies of water where the water is murky, stirred up with silt or sediment, the fish that hunt there will often appear quite dull in colour. They need not take on camouflage in their skin, as the suspension in the water column has effectively done it all for them. The gin-clear clarity of this loch, though, often means that the predatory fish have taken on colour of their own. Hold a brown trout from a turbid water next to one from Treig, and you could be forgiven for thinking the two fish were different species. The one from murkier water may be a light brown with creamy yellow flanks and the classic red and black spots, but the other could be coal black and dark – so dark, in fact, that its spots would blend seamlessly into its dark sides, were it not for the fairer rings around their perimeter giving it away as a trout; like sandy beaches ringing a series of volcanic islands in a sea of ink.

This fish was a ferox trout. A brown trout that has evolved over time to develop much larger jaws and amass a far greater size than a conventional brown trout. Ferox are found in deep glacial lakes and lochs, and have a diet made up almost exclusively of fish, especially the Arctic charr. The one that I cradled in my arms that day was extraordinary. It felt like a relic. A dinosaur. A true loch monster. It was covered in jet black spots and had a real slab of a head. Its jaws were plenty capable of swallowing trout that would ordinarily make your day and, quite clearly, it had been feeding very well indeed. Its body was dense and muscular, thick as a breeze block, right down to its tail root.

I clonked it on the head and took it back to my cabin to weigh it on the scales. It was 12 lbs exactly. Larger than any trout I had ever caught before, larger – even – than any trout ever caught in Treig. I lay it down amongst the snow and pine needles, admiring it, right till a cheeky pine marten scurried out and attempted to steal it whole.

It was far too big for me to eat (and far too big for that marten), so the next day I walked it out to my friend Alex, who lived at the nearby village of Fersit. I knew Alex would be grateful and put the whole fish to good use. I never ask anyone for money for anything. I still believe very much in giving, loaning and lending whatever you have to people, so they can use it at the time. Perhaps there is an unspoken agreement that, if and when the situation might arise, they could gift back to you in kind. Reciprocal agreements were once the foundations of what made human society tick through the ages; it was something I had experienced all the time during my travels in North America; the overt gift of something practical, with the inexplicit tightening of the bonds of a true friendship. It is a shame we have since moved so far away from it.

Not all of Treig's trout are as powerful as that giant, but even the smallest will bristle with a ferocious brand of wild muscle. The line sings off the reel and the fish will likely either be going aerial, or charging directly towards line-severing snags, from the very moment they are hooked. Hanging on to land a very big Treig trout takes strong tackle, experience and skill, but often you need a good bit of luck too. I certainly had it that day, and was very surprised to learn, as I read back through my diary, that the line I had used had a breaking strain of half that fish's total weight – it was, it seemed, simply my time.

My ferox still stands as the loch record, and is, unfortunately, very unlikely to be bettered. The truly giant trout of Treig are a distant memory these days. That is because nearly all the trout have, I am told, been infected by some god-awful parasite. This bug leaves them with fleshy lumps inside their bodies that resemble pink scrambled egg. As a result, they just don't seem to be living long enough to grow to such a massive size any more. You'll catch a one-pounder and it'll be clean, a two-pounder might have a few signs of the bug, a three-pounder is markedly worse, and then a four-pounder is riddled with it. These days, the trout very rarely seem to get any larger than five pounds without succumbing. As a result, I haven't fished the loch for almost two years. It is such a pity.

———

Despite that single monstrous trout, the biggest fish in this loch by far are the pike; and, of all the native freshwater fish that swim through British waters, the pike sits as the top dog. The true predatory king.

In Latin, the northern pike's name, *Esox lucius*, translates literally as 'water wolf'. It is a well-chosen label for this fish, given their entire being is tailored towards remorseless killing and eating. They are elegantly camouflaged, with mossy green flanks mixed with creamy yellow spots and stripes, and have a rear-loaded tail-set, perfect for explosive forward momentum and ambush. Most ominous are their fang-filled jaws, which sit inside an arrow-shaped head placed at the front of a long, streamlined body. Those teeth are razor-sharp, but they are backed up inside the mouth with bony pads that contain rows of yet more teeth. That cavernous mouth is the last thing many a hapless fish will see, right before they are clasped, instantly split across, then turned and swallowed whole.

They will happily kill the living as they will devour the dead and decaying; and, as such, have a lot of responsibility for maintaining the health of any ecosystem where they are present. I have eaten Treig's pike in the past, but mostly it is a fish I avoid. That is partly because killing off such an important cog in the wheel would be a mistake, but also because even an average-sized pike would represent more meat than one man could eat in a single sitting, and there are few sins worse than throwing out wild meat that you haven't been able to finish.

Amazingly, a pike of the same weight as my record trout is only really a modestly large specimen. Pike have been caught in Treig to almost 30 lbs, and the world record is double that again. These are truly giant fish, with heads like a prize bullock and bodies thick enough to place a small saddle across and ride. If ever I am tempted to fish for them, it will purely be to catch, admire, and slip them back to fight another day. Pike fishing is as close as I'll get to pleasure fishing. Make no mistake, though – even when fishing for fun, there can be moments of absolute heartbreak, especially if big fish are involved.

I have been blessed with a lot of great fish throughout my life but, as the famous biblical saying goes: 'the Lord giveth and the Lord taketh away'; and for every leviathan landed, there is always an equivalent yarn of a leviathan lost. After fishing for so many decades, really, a lost fish shouldn't be something to worry about; but some fish burn as harsh in the memory as they did from the moment you first parted company – and the biggest fish I ever lost from Highland waters was one that will haunt me to the grave.

It was back when I was living in Rannoch, working in forestry, and a young man at the absolute peak of a pike-fishing obsession. I was fishing an island on the wide and slow-flowing reaches of the River Gaur, and I was utterly fed up. I'd been fishing the place for weeks and couldn't seem to catch a pike over 8 lbs, no matter what I'd tried.

When out piking, you might catch lots of juveniles, known as 'jacks', of a few pounds or more; but you only really start to get excited when they are topping 15 lbs, with a real specimen generally considered to be any fish of over 20 lbs. I'm not a greedy man, I wasn't looking to set new records, I just wanted a fish that was undeniably in the class marked 'big'.

When it came to my date with disaster, the conditions looked spot on, and I set out more determined than ever. 'Ken,' I remember saying to myself, 'today is *big pike or bust.*'

My method was crude but effective. I fished my way around an island with my lures, till eventually I'd caught a trout that was far too big for any small pike to fit in its jaws. I placed sharpened treble hooks under its skin and slung it out towards the island, full of hope.

There was, however, a considerable flaw in my plan. The trout bait was so heavy on the line that the float I was hoping to suspend it beneath was dragged right under. Your float sits on the surface and acts as your bite indicator. It should only slide under the water if a fish has grabbed the bait below, so with mine disappearing alongside my super-sized trout, I was effectively fishing the river blind.

With no float, I decided to feel for a bite instead. This is achieved by putting a little tension in your line between your rod and your bait, and then placing a finger on the line next to your reel. It is a really sensitive way of fishing, as you *feel* every tremble and knock on the bait right through your fingertip.

I worked my way down the island, moving twelve feet after every cast, and carefully covering all the water and likely pike-holding areas. Eventually, I ran out of river to fish and was standing on the bank right at the point the Gaur met the mighty Loch Rannoch. This was my last cast, and probably my last attempt to catch a big pike in these waters, but I focused, and made sure I fished it all properly.

Out went the trout, under went the float, and on went my finger. I felt the trout move across the depths, being gently pushed along by the water flow as it exited the Gaur's mouth and entered the loch proper. Initially, the fish swung smoothly across the water, just as it had all day, but then I felt a sudden tightening on the line. I released my finger and watched, in some astonishment, as the line purposefully yet persistently peeled off my reel.

Something down there had picked up the big trout, and was now heading right out into the loch with it.

'Oh!' I exclaimed aloud. 'There's one on!'

I felt my heart leap as the line continued to trickle away before me, knowing that the only fish capable of inhaling a trout of that size was likely to be a *very* big fish indeed. My hands started to shake, but this was no time for panic.

When a pike takes a fish to eat, it first grabs it lengthwise across its toothy jaws and then moves away with it. Only then will it start to turn the fish in its mouth before it swallows it, usually head first. What that means as an angler is that you don't strike straight away, as the hooks won't properly be inside the pike's mouth. You give it some line and you wait till it has turned the bait and is about to swallow, and then you strike. Strike before, and you are very likely to lose the pike; strike too late, though, and you are risking the pike swallowing the bait, and your hooks, deep down its gullet. You don't want that either. The hooks will be very hard to remove and you could easily end up killing the fish by doing fatal damage to its throat.

Practice and experience teach the optimum time to set your hooks. The line spilled from my reel beautifully and, before I knew it, I looked up and realized it had gone a full thirty yards up the loch in no time at all. 'Now's the time to strike!' I shouted, reeling up the slack and heaving my rod skywards with all my might.

Nothing.

I felt absolutely *nothing*, just more slack line. 'What the bleedin' heck has happened here?' I cursed, staring at my tackle, but before I could cry about the missed fish and lost opportunity, I realized the giant had actually made a smart U-turn right in the middle of my strike. Now, it was running straight back towards me.

Frantically I reeled, taking in all the slack as fast as I possibly could, and, just as I felt I was catching up, the float, the only indication of where the big fish was swimming, suddenly started to kite hard to my right.

I cried jubilantly. *The fish was still on!* Reeling down on the very last of the slack, I struck hard once more—

Spladoosh! Shocking cold. I was thrown into the water.

As I'd struck, the force of resistance had been so great it had literally launched me off my feet. Striking that fish was like I'd been momentarily attached to a wild horse as it leapt cleanly off a cliff and now, I was in the loch.

Taking a moment to gather what was left of my senses, I realized the line was hanging limp all around me and what was left of the trout had already floated to the surface. The pike was gone, and the bait it had discarded looked as if it had been thumped with a cleaver and run through a clothes mangle. A pathetic-looking trout mashed into oblivion by a Goliath of the deep.

Some fish, I learnt, are just not meant to be caught.

I squelched out of the loch and reeled up. It was the last time I fished with such an over-sized trout, and I never did hook a pike of that size again.

———

There are more effective ways for man to catch fish than rod or line. I could employ nets, but it would strip away something that sits at the very essence of what it is to go fishing. It is, as they say, *fishing and not catching.* When extracting from the wild, a degree of failure should be as acceptable and natural as it is to any predator whose hunts can result in disappointment. It is only our warped sense of superiority to the animal kingdom that makes us believe otherwise; a sense that has since seen us empty our oceans of so much of their fish-life.

Even with the benefit of skill, casting a single line into a great deep dark loch still feels like an impossible act of faith. The catch is even more miraculous when you stop to consider that you're fooling a fish into choosing your lure or your bait over all the natural food items that they have at their disposal. There are times, even, when catching any fish at all feels like a divine intervention – but when skill and luck eventually meet, an angler on Treig can reap some fine rewards for both the stomach, and the soul.

BY FOOT AND BY THUMB

21 January 1985

Come dusk, I actually held back my head to yell to all this wilder-
ness of nothing in a more emotional voice of anger than ever done
before, a voice of anger not a soul could hear in those howling winds
of torrential rain.

'Ya bast—!' Not God, but to the winds . . . and they returned
in power.

That last two mile was hell, or very near it, for not one inch of
moorland or peatbog was free from water, whether running or
still . . . But ya know, once you've changed clothing, peeled off your
wet socks and put on dry ones, with a roaring red fire before you,
then it's all forgotten.

It's the memory of an achievement, and what more does a man
want than heat from a roaring fire and internal warmth from a
bottle of Hannesen dry wine?

Where I live, it just isn't possible to sustain yourself entirely from
the land. I'd either need access to a lot more land to work, hunt
and grow on, or it would need to be a different sort of land entirely
– one filled with natural bounty of the sort that sustained the
hunter-gatherers of yesteryear. The reality, in modern Britain, is
that environment has not existed for several hundred years. Our
island is increasingly crowded and our wild places are struggling
more than ever. I've been extremely lucky with quite how much
I have been able to take and grow wild from this land, but I still
rely on access to the world outside the shores of Loch Treig for
many products and foodstuffs.

Every few weeks, I'll venture out to town for my shopping and post. In spite of my lifestyle, I don't hugely mind going to the shops and seeing people. I hear that everyone is doing much of their shopping on the internet with computers. I have never been on the internet, or on a computer, in my life; and it all sounds very strange to me. So there are all those people living near to shops, but instead choose to do it all without leaving home? Is that really how we are supposed to live these days? Without seeing a soul, having a conversation, or experiencing life outside? I'll go down the shops, hitch a ride, have a chat, get a backslap off old mates, sample a pint, maybe; and yet I'm the one who's supposed to be the antisocial old hermit. Odd, in't it?

That trip to the world outside is always a big adventure. On a shopping day I'll rise before dawn, usually at three or four o'clock in the morning. I'm a lucky person in that I don't need an alarm clock. Before bed, I'll just say to my body, 'Right, we are up at three a.m. tomorrow,' and at three a.m., I'll wake.

I'll almost always walk the first eight miles, northwards through the glen before climbing up and out onto the A86. I could just pick up the train a couple of hours' walk away at Corrour, but then I'm spending money and bound by train times and the all-too-infrequent service. Walking out is better as I am in total control of my time. I've also seen many amazing things as the world wakes up around me. Perhaps a herd of red deer will trot dozily past to the orchestral tunes of the dawn chorus. I might see an otter or lake trout feeding in the upper layers of the loch. Frequently, I've seen the most beautiful sunrises. Gentle hues or deep reds, embracing the land in a glowing performance for one very lucky set of human eyes.

Sometimes, though, those walks can become very long. Occasionally, excruciatingly so. The plan, usually, is to get those eight miles done and then thumb a lift to Spean Bridge Post Office for my letters; a pretty village with a pub and small shop; then thumb on to the busy town of Fort William for my food from the supermarket. If that doesn't come off, though, it's nine miles walk to the Post Office and another nine miles on top of that to get to the supermarket at 'Fort Bill'. If I can't then get a return train to Corrour, or thumb a lift back to the spot that meets my trail on the A86, then I am looking at a round-trip, on foot, in just one day, of more than fifty miles.

There have been several occasions where I've had to walk the twenty-five miles one-way without a lift, and two where I've done the full fifty-odd miles on foot. I shan't forget those two days in a hurry. There are few natural vistas that'll put a smile on your face when you're returning on foot with a huge load of food and letters, I can tell you; and there are many days the rain is adding to your pack weight too: coming down in sheets, soaking your bag and your good self.

Those are the moments when you've got to haul up the last desperate, hard-won drops from the very depths of your well of determination, as – once I've started back out onto the glen, all alone, tired, and in foul weather – I know I must never stop moving, *no matter what*.

It does not matter how slow you go – if you've got somewhere you must be before nightfall, and you are all alone in the wilderness, *especially* if the weather is bad: DO NOT STOP.

Whenever we are pushed to pain, our mind will inevitably start to nag: 'Just take a break. Sit down. Rest a while.' The more you indulge that voice, the more loudly it cries, until eventually you convince yourself that a break won't hurt; but if you're not very careful, then it can indeed wind up doing you an awful lot of harm.

The bridge between taking a rest and giving up entirely is a cruelly short one, especially when the weather is awful and you're knackered, cold, and feeling very sorry for yourself. Once you've stopped, though, one of your biggest tools for warming up, which is natural body heat generated through movement, shuts down immediately. Your body temperature quickly drops and your mind can start to play cruel tricks on you. You can lose track of how long you've been on your break, and, as you remain in that stationary position, your body loses more heat than it can generate. Without immediate action, you'll start to shake, your breathing will quicken, and a sense of confusion and disorientation can soon set in.

If that is allowed to deepen further then you're really in trouble. You will enter a serious hypothermic state where the shaking stops. You might believe you are getting warmer, whilst actually being colder than ever; some poor souls have even been found dead and undressed in the snow, having torn clothes from their body in the belief they were burning up, even while the deepest of colds was sinking catastrophically into their core. After that, your blood pressure plummets to an unsustainable degree. Your body becomes overwhelmed. You suffer cardiac arrest and then you die.

Honestly, for the overwhelming majority of people reading this book, a bit of careful planning, appropriate clothing and weather forecasting should avoid you ever having to worry about being in such an awful state. I chose a unique way of life which has meant there have been times where I've simply had to go out in bad conditions, but that will most likely never be you. But if it is, try to keep that most basic of my survival rules in your head.

Silence that little voice asking for rest. *Just keep moving.* Keep those arms and legs pumping. Flex your fingers and toes. Keep that blood flowing and retain all the body heat you have, and all that you can generate. Even if you are going as slowly as a snail, every step forward is one step closer to your safety.

You've got to arm yourself with some tools to shut out and silence those negative thoughts, though. Devastating death aside, every time you give in and stop, you are psychologically conditioning yourself to stop every single time it gets hard on the trail. I'm sure you've been there before, on a run or a long walk, and you just feel dog-tired and not up for it; and then you get distracted by something as you move along your way. You see an interesting plant, a nice view, or an animal; maybe you have a daydream, hum a little tune, or give yourself a talking-to; and hey presto, before you know it, you've just knocked off a mile or two without even really thinking about it.

Give in to the nagging voice and you'll struggle with your walking forever. It'll always feel like a trial and you won't find what you need to push through when times get truly tough; but, more than anything, you'll never achieve your full potential in the outdoors.

I say silence the negative thoughts, but if you feel the need to shout out and curse, then do it! I don't think it is good to keep any extreme emotion bottled up in the body anyway, so if you have the opportunity to release a forceful 'F' into the wind then take it. Don't ever be afraid to let all those emotions out. Sometimes, you might find yourself laughing at the daftness of it all too. Or, if you are religious, and the depth of your desperation is making you want to speak to your god, then go ahead and pray.

Use all that raw emotion and instinct as energy to fuel yourself forward. Right into the source of your suffering and right out the other side to your safe place. Do whatever it takes. Just don't stop.

———

I don't mind walking. I've done it my whole life, after all, and I'd generally rather be out here, experiencing nature and the wild environment, than hemmed in within some vehicle; but a hitched lift in a car, or a well-timed train ride are an absolute blessing on a shopping day.

Hitchhiking is something that is in real decline. In the 1980s and 1990s it was very common to see other people hitching lifts on the roads, but not so any more. I don't think it is necessarily that the world is a more dangerous place, but people have certainly become more mistrustful and reluctant to pick up strangers.

I have met some incredibly kind people while hitchhiking. People who didn't even know I existed before their day began. People who have driven many miles out of their way to help me out. People who have given me food and sheltered me from the roadside rain. Strangers who became friends, sharing a moment of their life with me, pouring out their hearts and problems in our car-shaped confessional before we parted company again.

I do accept that there is a risk attached to hitchhiking, and that it is easier for me, as a lone male, to stay safe. That's not to say that there were never times when things took a deeply uncomfortable turn while I was in the car with a stranger, though. There was the time with that horrible lorry driver and Mam, back when I was five, plus, when Roy and I were travelling in Canada, we were involved in a traffic accident when our drunk (and probably stoned) driver fell asleep at the wheel and careered off down an embankment. There were two other occasions here in the UK that stick in my memory too.

The first was shortly after I'd returned from Canada and I was free-wheeling across the country, trying to thumb a lift not too far from the Forth Road Bridge that skips over the mouth of the River Forth just west of Edinburgh. This old fella with a flat cap pulls over in his car and offers me a ride. 'Brilliant,' I thought, keen to get away from that comparatively built-up area of Scotland and back out into the countryside.

At first, all seemed well. He was seemingly just a friendly fella who was happy for the company and, in all honesty, a very normal bloke. We had hardly gone far though, when he leant in and asked me, as casually as you might ask someone what they'd had for breakfast: 'Do you ever have a wank?'

Beyond jumping in the car with a murderer, this is just about the worst-case scenario for someone hitchhiking. *Bloody heck, who've we got in with here, then Ken?* I thought to myself, already considering how I could escape his – now moving – vehicle. Luckily for me, I didn't have to think too hard. Just before the bridge crossing, the man pulled over, and again, as breezily as you like, he said: 'I'll just pop in here for a wank. I'll be back in a minute.'

I can't tell you where he was popping in for his sexual gratification, as I wasn't exactly keen to find out, but as soon as he was gone, I grabbed my rucksack and ran off over the bridge.

The other rough-time roadside was when I was living up here. I was in a layby near Fort William, thumbing for a lift, when this car suddenly screeched to a halt right in front of me. These lads all started piling out, and it was quite obvious they weren't about to offer me a lift. Their body language was menacing and they started walking towards me as a gang – a throwback to the beginnings of that life-changing street beating I took when I was twenty-six. Just at that moment, another car swings in behind me and I thought: 'Oh no, that's me trapped then,' but, as I turned to face the new vehicle, this man opens the passenger door and urges me to 'Hop in, mate.'

I didn't need asking twice. I was certain I was about to get mugged at the very least, but it was the fundamental kindness and quick thinking of a total stranger that rescued me there.

On a more positive note, the truth is that I've had thousands of lifts through half a century of thumbing, and can barely recall more than a handful of tricky moments. Lord knows it only takes one disaster to completely ruin your life, but I've since come to understand that there are *many* more good people out there than bad, and you shouldn't let your concerns about what a tiny minority could do, stand in the way of you experiencing all the love, kindness and opportunity that are offered up by everyone else.

Terrible people can do terrible things (and I'm truly very sorry if they ever have to you), but never allow yourself to think that their faults and flaws as humans are yours to bear any responsibility for. Certainly, don't let the thoughts of what they might do dictate your life. You rule your own life. Not them.

LOST SOULS

Thursday 17 June 1999
There's pain and there's pain, but toothache has a pain of its own.
A warmer night and a drier night, sitting by my outside stove trying to rid my body of an aching tooth when 6' away sits a chaffinch asking for a peanut and saying 'ignore the pain man'.
It's alright for them buggers, they don't have any teeth.

—

Tuesday 28 September 2004
That troubled filling fell out early this evening while eating a bacon sandwich. Some size it was, and worst of all I swallowed it. I suppose it'll come out the other end sometime or other.

It's the little things out here that can wind up being big problems: the colds, the flus, the shits, the splinters, the burns, the occasional trapped nerve. If it gets really bad, I'll take the long walk to town to get it sorted. That is not easy when you're really sick, but bear in mind too, with no phone, I am often looking at making the walk just to make an appointment, to then come back again some days later to actually get fixed up. That return journey, when whatever I'm suffering with has had a few more days to sink deeper into my body, is the absolute pits.

Colds and flus are infrequent as I have such limited contact with the masses, but when I do get them it is much more of an issue for me. Aside from Covid last year, January 2009 brought me the worst bout of flu I have ever had. I caught it from a shop attendant who sneezed into her hands and then handled my tin cans of food. My coughing was so bad I stained the snow around the cabin with my blood. I don't know if I suffer more due to my lack of exposure to your everyday bugs, like a wee mountain gorilla hidden away in the remote recesses of some African jungle, or whether it is that it just *feels* worse as I can't dose up on pills and put my feet up when I have so much physical work to do every day. Either way, it's really bad.

Food poisoning from a bit of meat that had gone off made me extremely ill on one occasion; then, on another, I thought I might have inhaled a puff of weedkiller from the sprayers up on the train line. Both brought such awful diarrhoea I dared not cough. I scarcely left the Bottomless Pit for twenty-four hours and I lost so much weight. It took the almightiest effort to haul myself to the doctor for those courses of antibiotics; but mostly I'll just grit my teeth and hope it goes away on its own, or I'll try and fix it myself.

Quite recently, actually, I became aware of a scratching sensation on the inside of my eyelid. I had a look in the mirror and, would you believe, I could see a tiny stump of metal sticking out of my eyeball. I got a pair of tweezers and teased out a small splinter. I'm sure it had come off my axe when I was out splitting wood many moons ago. I taped it into my diary to keep and my eyeball healed up just fine. Some people have tattoos as permanent reminders of moments in their life, but I have a body filled with lumps, bumps and scars. A tapestry of time spent out here, carved into my own skin.

It can all get quite ugly at times, but it is part of the trade-off to live in all this beauty, and it teaches you some very serious lessons in self-care and self-reliance. Above all, your level of risk needs to be managed as much as possible, and that starts with shutting up the voice that says, 'It won't happen to me.' It bloody well will. So, take responsibility for yerself and do everything you can to avoid that trip to the doctor's in the first place.

We departed at Corrour pub and in I went for a pint as a hiker came in, somewhat worried after losing his companions on Beinn Na Lap, and so followed two hours looking through binoculars.

Beth ran him down the new road to Loch Treig searching, me as well, for it's my direction of home and we found 'em, two bedraggled hikers on their way to Corrour. We parted company and I was home by 8.30 as rain tippled from above. My specs are now squint since I trod on them.

So many people arrive in these mountains, ill-prepared and with an overly romantic notion of what this place is really like. People like to imagine that the land watches over us all with some sort of benevolence or a sense of compassion, when in reality it disregards us entirely. As I am sure you know by now, when the weather turns out here, it truly turns, and it is all too easy to find yourself badly caught out.

I can scarcely begin to list the number of times people have been rescued up here, or the amount of close calls I've witnessed. The Highlands don't discriminate by age, gender, or fitness, either; even the military have had problems – in the winter of 1997 two members of the Army were helicoptered off this area with severe hypothermia.

Most search-and-rescues end with a happy outcome; thanks largely to the dedication of a hardy band of volunteers from Mountain Rescue, and whoever else is experienced enough to lend a hand.

Many years ago, before the cabin, and before I'd even been to North America, I was out climbing a mountain over in Glen Lyon, sandwiched between Loch Tay and Rannoch.

I'd not long summited when I saw a bloke lying in the deep snow with his eyes shut. My immediate thought was that he must be dead, but, as I knelt down next to him to check his pulse, his bloomin' eyes burst wide open and he almost gave me a heart attack.

I heaved him up from the spot and carried him all the way back down the hill to safety. His name was John and we would become good friends. Later, he explained that absolutely nothing bad had happened to him. He was just feeling tired and had simply sat down for a break and fallen asleep in the snow.

I've lost his last letter to me now; but I remember he was moved to say that if it wasn't for me finding him that day, then he wouldn't be here now. That really meant a lot. Tragically though, there are far too many cases of people who aren't as lucky as John was.

Ten years ago, a young man died just weeks into what he hoped would be a year-long survival challenge in the Scottish wilderness. He was up the track from my cabin when he apparently froze to death in a railway hut, just a half-hour's walk from Rannoch Station. I remember another too, a really fit man trying to do as many Munros as he could. He was running up here in the snow and I was out on the estate with some guests. It was the start of the weekend, so I was off back to the cabin after the hunting had finished, but I wasn't back long before I was told the alarm had been raised and that the man hadn't made it to his final destination over at Ben Nevis. We went out on the search, and there he was, dead on our land.

It is quite terrifying how easy it is to make a mistake that winds up costing your life. I wrote before about how I too was once caught out on that awful frost-bitten walk from Kinlochleven; where I thought I was following people, that turned out to be deer; and how easy it can be to give in to the voice that tells you to sit down and rest.

So to reiterate: it isn't always an avalanche, a fall, or some catastrophic event that'll kill you out here; more often than not, it is that toxic mix of tiredness and extreme cold that just causes you to lie down and give in. It can happen in the most trivial-seeming circumstances too. I recall the story of a local man leaving a pub in Roybridge, just off the River Spean. The weather was bad, but all he had to do was cut across a field and he was home safe. When he didn't make it, the alarm was raised and the search party headed out.

He was found dead, sitting on a rock. He'd probably just dozed off and the frost had got him. Heartbreaking, but it happens more often than you'd probably imagine.

———

Thursday 6 November 1997
Emmanuel, the man who shot himself on Ben Alder with a black powder pistol has finally been identified . . .

On extremely rare occasions, the lack of preparation is quite deliberate. It seems to border on the suicidal because that is actually what it is. I have heard it said that when people decide they've had enough of this life, they will often take to the mountains to end it all. A place where they feel happy; at peace, alone, with little chance of being disturbed or discovered.

I dearly wish that they hadn't got to that desperately sad point in their minds and lives, but I completely understand why they would come here. Of course, I do.

There have been a few poor souls who have killed themselves in these hills, but none created quite as big a stir as the story of the young Frenchman, Emmanuel Caillet.

I saw him that day. There was nothing untoward about him whatsoever. Just a normal man walking out for Ben Alder Mountain from Rannoch Station. I remember he was roughly shaved (I think he was wearing a hat) but that's about it.

It was June 1996 when his body was found up near the summit of that desolate hill. The authorities reckoned he'd been lying there for months; but no one had the first clue who he was. All the labels had been pulled off his clothes, and I'd heard his bank and identity cards had all been destroyed too. According to the reports, he was wearing slip-on shoes that were completely inappropriate for a day in those mountains, carrying a sleeping bag but no tent, and three big bottles of water in an area where there is water everywhere. None of it made any sense, but then suicide rarely does to those left to pick up the pieces.

The most surprising bit of all was his gun. The investigators said he'd shot himself through the chest with an antique black-powder pistol. You can imagine what the headline writers made of all this. They had a field day.

It took seventeen months before Emmanuel was formally identified. It wasn't easy because he had left so few clues as to who he was, least of all the fact he was from a suburb in Paris and had only told his parents that he was going to Britain on holiday. Not that he was coming up here, or what his true intentions were.

The exact circumstances of his death are still shrouded in mystery. Apparently, his parents believe Emmanuel was murdered, or at the very least aided in some sort of ritualized suicide. I heard all those rumours. Some people round here had said that another person was involved; someone mysterious who was then never seen again. Emmanuel's mother and father came here several times to conduct their own investigations, and his father claims my friend Jimmy at Corrour Station had said his son had been seen with another man while he was in the area. Jimmy would later say to a journalist that he couldn't be sure if Emmanuel and this man were travelling together, or if they'd only met that day. According to Jimmy, this mystery partner had said he was going to Fort William anyway, and that Emmanuel was headed to Ben Alder alone. Apparently, Jimmy had then asked Emmanuel whether he was afraid of ghosts. That figures, given he knew full well what had happened to me at bloody Ben Alder Cottage.

I don't know. Sometimes we look for the fantastical when, really, the most likely answer is the one that's right in front of your nose. Whatever really happened has long disappeared, alongside that poor lost soul who took himself to that lonely mountain.

I felt so sorry for his family whenever they came up here looking for answers. You could see how much the terrible grief had affected them. They were among the only people I've ever seen that could never find any solace in this place.

There can be no question that life out here can be hard. Given the right set of circumstances, it can be almost unbearably so. But life away from this place is undeniably tough for many people too. It makes me so sad to think of them, and how they might gravitate towards these wilds for respite, and then wind up never returning home alive. Our life can be a fragile flame that sometimes requires cupping in the hands of others when the winds are at their most powerful; but knowing when people need your help isn't always as easy as finding someone asleep in the mountain snow. The most important thing is that we are always ready to be there whenever and wherever we are needed; whether that's lending a supporting shoulder out of a storm, or even just a nice mug of tea.

ROYAL TEA

21 February 1987

Rest day for me spent only chopping 167 logs, supping coffee, finishing
a proper gutting of the roadkill hare, and cooking.

First it was sausage for breakfast, six of 'em, all sizzling away
nice and brown, following up with my dinner, and finally stewed
hare with carrots, turnip, onions and parsnip.

I live like a Scottish laird!

In spite of the occasional hardships of a life lived by this loch, you might be surprised to learn that there is room for a little indulgence.

Some of the food and drink I cook up here is far nicer than any grub that gets served up in a restaurant for the top brass. Try a vegetable fresh out of the ground, grow some salad or herbs, and if you're ever up in my part of the world, sample some fresh water straight from a burn. I guarantee you'll taste the difference, and it'll cost you pennies, not tens of pounds.

Food aside, I like songs, rhymes, poetry, and music – and used to be able to play the harmonica with some skill. My radio is my window into the world and frequently my only company on the long winter nights. It is always tuned into BBC Radio 4 on 198 long wave. I'll enjoy listening to the documentaries and the plays, and will very rarely miss the news (as long as it isn't all about the politics). The only problem is when the Test match cricket is on and I have to suffer through weeks of drone every summer. I'm sorry, but I can't tell you how boring I think cricket commentary is. Pigeons and buses, and whoever bowling to whatever on some sticky wicket. What a load of bloody rubbish.

My great love is the weather forecast, in particular the shipping forecast. I'll sit back with a mug of something and recite its precise list of the thirty-one maritime areas of Britain. *Humber, Thames. Southeast veering southwest 4 or 5, occasionally 6 later. Thundery showers. Moderate or good, occasionally poor* . . . and so on. Surely, I can't be the only mainlander who takes comfort from hearing the meteorological comings and goings out there on the high seas? There's something hypnotic about that rhythmic, even tone. Even when it is describing some god-awful tempest tearing through the Faeroes or Fair Isle, it's still like a lullaby, and, if I am up late enough to catch the 00:48, it'll be the last voice I hear before I welcome sleep's embrace and the last log peters out on my fire.

Out here, the forecast is your friend. Warning you of dangers yet to come and telling me, as the captain of my own good ship, exactly when it is best to batten down the hatches and ride out the great waves of the occasionally awful Scottish weather.

I have the further luxury of an extra log burner too. A second stove set up outside in the garden. It is my old one, replaced with the one I'm using now, and it means I can sit out late into the summer night after a long day tending my crops or fishing. Just enjoying the very late light and keeping away all those dastardly midges with the smoke. I can cook on it too, if I fancy a meal in open air.

I wash my clothes in an outdoor bath and hang them out to air-dry up the side of the cabin, right next to the antlers of a large red deer. I built a log burner around the base of that tub so I can warm the water and have a good hot soak myself. What I didn't realize, though, was that your standard bath plug is not fire-retardant at all; so, after I'd picked out a well-melted molten rubber plug from the hole, and replaced it with something a bit hardier, I had my very own open-air hot tub. All it then takes is for me to place my thumb over the outdoor tap piped back to the burn, just to increase the pressure and hone the direction, and I can get a good arc of water up and over the bath's edge to fill it right up.

That bath, placed with its elevated view of Loch Treig, would probably fetch a pretty price on all those cabin and hot tub holiday rentals you hear about these days; but I'm very happy keeping it all to myself.

I don't think you could ever accuse me of being a snob. I've got a straightforward and functional palate. My culinary luxuries, for what it's worth, are probably stews, pork hock, bacon and beef – eaten before they spoil, obviously – and the occasional tin of beer and a few 'Lucozade Originals', whenever I can get hold of them. I don't like spicy food and I have a bit of a sweet tooth, but the one thing I will *not* compromise on is how I make my tea.

How you make your brew is something you are absolutely in control of. You don't need to be living in a palace or off-grid in some Highlands log cabin to make a *really* nice cup of tea. Yet the vast majority of tea drinkers ruin their drink from the second they enter the tea aisle in the shop.

I was always told that the tea leaves reserved for the tea bags were the waste tea that had tumbled from the sacks as the tea was being offloaded from the docks. Muck is money, as they say, so, having been shipped here from the plantations of Asia or Africa, it seemed too wasteful to keep sweeping the leftover tea into the sea, so some bright spark suggested scooping it all up and putting it into tea bags.

Whatever the truth, tea in a bag is *never* as fresh as loose tea, and the bag restricts the brewing process and alters the true taste of the tea. If you are making tea, *always use loose tea leaves.*

So that's my first tip. The second is: use boiling water. I know this sounds obvious, but when I say boiling water, I mean *boiling water*, and not the water from the kettle that boiled however many minutes earlier. The moment that the water is bubbling vigorously, get it straight on the tea leaves in your cup. Some say you should wait, as boiling water scalds the tea, but they are wrong. Personally, I don't fanny around with strainers either. I just put two teaspoons of tea straight into the mug and pour the water right over them.

Next is your milk. Use whatever you like, but I use the creamy long-life stuff that comes from a tin. By the way, if you're punching a hole in a tin to pour out a liquid, make sure you punch one in the rim of the lid for pouring, and then another smaller hole on the opposite side of the lid; otherwise you'll struggle to get anything out. Add your sugar and give it a stir, but make sure you dry your spoon after. In my situation, a sugary spoon left out on the side is an open invitation to pests, but, far worse than that, you might make another cup of tea and end up sticking a damp, sugary spoon into the dry tea leaves. Do that, and you've possibly spoilt the whole bag. I suppose if you can just go to a shop and get more tea in minutes, it shouldn't really matter too much (or maybe it really should?). Anyway, just dry the spoon.

Tea aside, another great drinking pleasure, clearly, is my home-brewing. I should say, though, like all the new trees going into the ground around the cabin, many of the brews I am making these days won't all be for me to enjoy. I am saving some for the guests at my funeral. But I don't want you to be sad about the thought of that.

PART FIVE

Go Now

STAGGER ON

I was sixty-three years old and it was Christmas.

My weight had plummeted and an urgent crap in the snow soaked the soft white a crimson red.

I stared down at all my blood as it spread out in a circle. I don't know much about medicine, but I knew it signalled very deep trouble indeed.

Saturday 1 January 2011

Fit as a fiddle I feel, slim as a pole and bleeding at the arse.

—

Friday 8 January 2011

It's -4 °C and outside deep in snow, twinkling from above stars. It was 4. a.m. I lit my stove, put on the kettle and waited its boil. Town today. Departing an hour later through crunching snow, I observed the above heavens displaying their beauty of shooting stars.

Shopping done and stacking my rucksack out she came, the post office attendant, one letter and yup! Cancer.

They want me inside for operation soon, just phone or visit, but how can I with such a huge rucksack of food? So, heading back home, I intend to return to Belford Hospital come Monday.

Cold wind and snow bit into my eyes, but I couldn't work it out, was it the cold or a tear?

I reckon the robins will miss me.

—

Friday 14 January 2011

I was told four ways my cancer could be removed. One, to be safe, would leave me with the colostomy bag for life. Another was radiation, but because of past brain operations with metal in my head . . . something I knew not of . . . this would not be possible.

Back in hospital come evening.

—

Thursday 17 February 2011

I feel the pain, it's nagging me, it's a pain in the arse and a flow of blood is unique, it's like diarrhoea flowing freely. Some days I'm fit, others I'm in the armchair, you get throbs that don't go away, while other days I can outwalk a long-distance runner.

The Aurora Borealis is expected tonight, sigh! . . . No hope, the sky is hid by cloud. Even the moon doesn't show itself.

I believe though that, despite the Aurora hope, my body has more troubles of body lumps that worry me.

Worry and hope fit together.

—

Saturday 5 March 2011

It's thirteen days now since departing my cabin and only now does my body feel more stability . . . I went to hell and back, living in a world of no colour, a world of black, white, and morphine, where noises creep from every corner of the room.

—

Tuesday 5 April 2011

Capecitabine chemo 500 mg is beginning to tire me out. I feel like a flabby cabbage with a hangover trying to be sick.

—

Tuesday 16 August 2011

A good bath and hair wash this evening as it's hospital tomorrow, an appointment with the colorectal nurse so I won't be taking my rucksack, she'd give me hell if I walked in with a rucksack of supplies on my back.

———

Wednesday 17 August 2011

Wow! What a greeting I got, jumped the queue and in for colorectal. I was told by the nurse that due to where I live, everything could be done in one go, but with other nurses on holiday X-rays were impossible. Therefore, I'd have to come back in a fortnight. However, she did other unpleasing jobs, mostly up my backside.

———

Friday 26 August 2011

Starting up my power saw and distant cracks of thunder were heard and a downwind black sky brought in the rain but I worked through it.

A ¾ of an hour job with this 60' dead tree across the nearby gorge and once done, switching off my saw, I heard Roger pass below in the boat. Still raining I picked up my binoculars for a spy and damn, my colostomy bag burst and spent the next 30 min sorting out the problem.

Off with my clothes and hose-piped 'em in the bath, new bag fixed and new clothes that I dressed myself in, so obviously it's wash day tomorrow.

———

Wednesday 31 August 2011

Up at 4. am and lit my stove for an early morning brew. Departing up through woodlands, I shone my torch but a dimness of dawn was beginning. Three hours later, and a ten-mile walk, I received a lift. A slow walk into town. I had no energy left.

X-ray department 1 hour prior where nurses gave me liquid, a litre to drink within an hour, whereas I was led away for a CT scan. This will be ready in 10 days and will be given the next move if cancer has diminished or not.

I've never had so many injections and blood samples taken, so it was late afternoon as I departed hospital and nurses were dubious as my temperature was two degrees above normal. No train so I booked a taxi to Spean, thumbed it to Tulloch and walked . . . so exhausted upon arrival back home I didn't light the stove, I just hit the sack.

———

Friday 2 September 2011

I was up twice in the darkness of night, sweating profusely, it was sticking my shirt to my back and made my way to the outside loo to empty my bag.

By dawn recovery must have overcome fever for I rose a stronger person, peeled off my wet shirt and wiped away the sweat. I must have been recovering for come the end of today, I'd carted 4 bags from my log pile and split more from cut logs done the other day and besides, I totally feel better.

———

Friday 9 September 2011

I don't think a colostomy bag would suit me for the rest of my life.

———

Friday 16 September 2011

When I rose from dreamland at 3.50 a.m. this morning to light my stove, I switched on my radio and a good forecast of the Northern

Lights enticed me outside, but all I could see was a partial moon hiding behind thin cloud. Departing at 5.15 a.m., and within the hour a splendid sunrise moved above the hemisphere. Red sky in the morning, shepherd's warning.

Hospital by 11. a.m. and in there for three hours undergoing checks of my back passage and scans, for those deep X-rays a fortnight ago have uncovered another cancer – cancer of my liver. Once all done, Doctor had me in his room for more surgical uncomfort and says the cancer is small. 'We'll leave it for now but keep a regular eye on it with a six-month scan.' He says it does not interfere with the bowel cancer, which is now gone, and has arranged for me to be in Belford Hospital on 27 Sept and operation the next day re-joining my bowels.

I was overjoyed.

Lift by old friend, then walk home with energy – energy soon is sapped, for lock was up the creek and took an hour to file off. Then down came the rain.

———

Monday 19 September 2011

A dry day, no sunshine, just clouds rolling above hills with mist down to 2,000 foot and spent a whole day log-cutting with my power saw and swinging the axe.

I've cut enough to last my freedom before carted away to the rectum patch in eight days' time. It'll be great though, no more hypotension or neutropenic infection, I'll be free of carrying such things, my body will be renovated.

All cut logs were rolled down the embankment to the burn below and I reckon there's more than enough to last my freedom before hospital.

———

Tuesday 27 September 2011

Admitted to hospital on the 27th, operated on the following day, one day of recovery before body went downhill, temperature slowly rises, deep body scan or X-ray was required.

Body changed colour to a purply blue and felt pissed as a newt.

X-ray shows my inside as a black hole filling with pus. The consultant rushes me away in wheelchair, I continue to vomit, tube fed into arm, one down my throat and put on drip. A pint of black fluid was drawn from my stomach and was continued to drawing it for many days. Also, a tube was put into my bladder and a notice above my bed saying, 'No food or water.'

The surgeon stayed until 10 p.m. in case he had to operate, but my body stabilized and he went home.

I was released from hospital ten days later.

———

Tuesday 18 October 2011

Living in civilization is hard for me, a world of electronics, red and blue lights and a super lock on the front door I can't fathom.

Thunderstorms and lightning overnight with snow down to the sea, storms of 60 m.p.h.

———

Tuesday 1 November 2011

No intruders during my five-week absence from home but the needles have fallen to cover the earth. I fed the finches with nuts, I stacked damp logs by my stove to dry and I'm home, a hot, warm blazing stove of enjoyment.

———

Thursday 10 November 2011

Sunshine and no wind, much difference to yesterday's wind and rain. By 1 p.m. I'd removed half the larch needles from my cabin roofing, 4 cwt bags full but still a lot to go and don't know if I'll remove the rest tomorrow as larch are still casting their needles.

Hard to believe that this morning I had a strange overwhelming feeling in my body. Something not felt for a long, long while . . . I felt normal.

Suddenly, a stoat runs past carrying a mouse.

—

Monday 20 February 2012

A year ago today I left my cabin behind and lodged outside Belford Hospital, heading the following day for Raigmor Hospital ready to be operated on for cancer. Just five days ago they informed me the cancer has gone and I was overjoyed, I'm still floating on clouds.

Heavy rain and 50 m.p.h. winds plastered my body with wet, wet, wet as I worked outside in the rain . . .

—

That was the story of my bowel cancer a decade ago. In spite of my undoubted joy at the outcome in the end, I am afraid to tell you the cancer was simply the core of a very bad apple that had first begun to rot back in 2005, as I approached my late fifties. Whether I liked it or not, my health was in decline.

It started with a double hernia operation and my first hospital stay since 1976. Even in the aftermath of that, try as I might, the writing was firmly on the wall for my job at the estate. I just couldn't keep up and carry on like I had in the past, so, after seventeen years of service, I very sadly handed in my resignation letter.

Six years later, they discovered my bowel cancer. The surgeons defeated that one too, but I was just getting started. As I entered my seventies, I suffered a head injury, then the first stroke, then the second, then my log pile fell on me, and then, in 2022, I suffered a serious urinary tract infection and had yet another operation on my bowels.

I was hospitalized for three consecutive February the seconds. On the fourth, I thought they would probably put me in the *Guinness Book of Records*. I'll admit I was nervous that day. So nervous, in fact, that I opted to only chop wood by hand and left my chainsaw in the corner. 'Anything could happen', I noted in my diary; and then stayed up till midnight to make sure I'd seen off the curse of 2 February.

I sat down and wrote up all my scrapes and hospitalizations on a piece of paper. It added up to one hell of a rap sheet, filled with what you'd call 'near death' experiences, and over seven months of my life spent in hospital. Still, I don't look at any of it and feel unlucky. In fact, I've been incredibly lucky. I'm still here, still living, when so many others haven't made it through a fraction of those maladies.

Those strokes though. They did change me, and I had to accept that.

———

I've just noticed the 'r' has fallen off the sign on my front gate.

It should read 'The Stagger Inn', but now it just says 'The Stagge Inn'.

I think 'Stagge' is Old English for stag, so it's not too bad considering, just not very funny. Perhaps the sign itself has taken the tongue-in-cheek name of my residence a little bit too much to heart? Could it be a bit drunk? Ah no. Let's just face facts, Ken. That sign is no more than a metaphor for the gently sliding state of things. My joints are aching a lot more these days and my eyesight has gone a bit funny. I get these weird colourful zigzags periodically, spreading right across my eyeballs. They look very pretty, but it isn't a good thing. I'm much more forgetful too; my movements are slower, a lot more laboured. Sometimes, it feels like my whole mind and body is swimming in the same sweetened condensed milk that I pour into my tea.

I still take the trip to town to buy my food, though. I try and catch the train when the times are favourable, and will still do the long walk to the road and thumb a lift, if I'm feeling fit enough. The world has changed a lot since I started getting sick, but people still have that kindness when they see someone in need of a bit of help.

Just a few weeks ago, just before my last stay in hospital, actually, I'd walked the seven miles out to the road near Tulloch and was trying to thumb for a lift to Fort William. Time elapsed and I was thinking that if I didn't get picked up in an hour, I'd have to walk back to the train station and get a ride in on the train.

A few cars went by and then this Land Rover comes along in the opposite direction to where I wanted to go. I didn't think much of it, and was just waiting for the next vehicle, when suddenly that Land Rover reappears right in front of me. It had turned around further up the road and come all the way back to where I was standing.

'I've seen you on the television,' says the driver, beaming, 'I'll give you a lift to Fort William.' I got in, and the driver admitted that they were supposed to be heading out into the Highlands to bag a few of the Munros, but had added an extra hour to their journey just to help me out.

Lizzie MacKenzie, a brilliant film-maker, spent many years piecing together a film about my life. I am sure it brought a few of you to spend some of your hard-won money on my book. It has not long won an award at the Glasgow Film Festival, and I've been told it has even been on BBC Two a few times – I bet that's how the Land Rover man saw me anyway. The film did more for me than a hitched lift to Fort William, though. It chronicled a tough personal period either side of my first stroke and I've since had hundreds of letters from well-wishers.

I do wonder whether the troubling question of whether or not the lead character was going to wind up dead before the end might've kept a lot of people glued to the screen. It took some time to battle back from that stroke, I can tell you. I really was not well at all. But I hugely appreciate all those people who took the time to write, even if I can't afford the cost of the stamps to reply to you all!

No matter how bad things have ever got, it has always been very clear in my mind that I don't want to wind up in some old people's home in town. Civilization was comfortable, and I liked watching the television during my stays in hospital, but bloomin' heck it's boring too. It would be the end for me really, the boredom. No medicine gets me better quicker than the motivation I have to get back to nature, and this cabin, as soon as I possibly can.

Given my unique way of living, it always takes a bit longer than with normal people before the doctors are comfortable with me being released back into the wild. The occupational therapists need to see that I can walk properly, carry a load, even cast a line; but I get there in the end. Nonetheless, things have changed with age and ailment, and I know that taking the help that's offered is the best way to keep my way of life going.

The estate and their employees, both in the field and at the Corrour Station House, have been fantastic with lifts, not just to town for food, but also for my medical appointments. They visit me in hospital and bring me things too. I've had a big slab of tins for winter and they also help cut trees for firewood; as does another good man, Davy, who also lives wild in the area and has helped me out a lot in the past. The estate is no longer under the ownership of Mr MacDonald. It changed hands in 1995, but the new family have continued to be very kind to me. They have even made copies of many of my diaries too. I am so grateful to them all, really.

There is a very kind ultra-running vet who makes the thirty-four-mile round trip just to bring me my post from the Spean Bridge Post Office too, so that's one less job now; and real modern technology came into my life for the first time a few years ago. I have a GPS tracker and locator beacon that has a button on it that I can press to alert emergency medical staff when I'm severely ill. It probably saved my life when I had the stroke.

My family continue to visit, my brother and nephews all came this year, and the estate are going to help me with a gas cylinder and gas stove, so I can stop cooking off the top of my log burning stove. Gas cooking will make an enormous difference. It took me an hour to boil my kettle on the log burner today, so it will save wood fuel as well as all my time and energy chopping and carrying timber.

I've had trouble accepting help with the cabin in the past. It used to be easier to be completely self-reliant and in the debt of no one; but that matters far less as time draws inevitably on. Life out here isn't about living in the most uncomfortable way possible, it's about leading the best life you can by striking the balance between what you really need and what you can afford. With my life savings restored, and a state pension, I can afford a little more now. I'm a hermit, not a masochist.

I know I'm getting older, though. I know my problems with my memory and mobility have grown more profound, and I know that for all of my adjustments, none of us can trick death. It's coming, and I want to be ready for it – but when my death comes, like my life, I want to meet it on my terms.

LIVE TO 102

'It's not the cough that carries you off, it's the coffin they carry you off in.'

I don't know who said that originally, but they've got a very good point. Apart from being a good rhyme, I think what they are getting at is that it's not about what killed you, it's about how you choose to depart the earth. How you wish to be celebrated, and how and where you want to be laid to rest.

I am now seventy-five and, quite frankly, a lot better than I was this time last year. I am now hoping I live to 102. I think, or at least I hope, that the longing for more from my life will keep me going for many more years. It makes a real difference, you know. Wanting to stay alive and digging in. Finding reasons and inspiration to carry on. I've seen it so many times, that people get to an age and keel over through willing the end on themselves because they don't feel they have anything left to live for. My life is too much of a gift for me to think like that. There are always more things to see and do, more stories to make and tell; but I know none of us live forever and if the end of my grand adventure is coming soon, then that's okay.

I do believe in a heaven and god, and I am a Christian, but I don't believe that to be a Christian you must go to church and subscribe strictly to an organized system of belief. No. I have my own Christian beliefs and that's that. I've tried my best to be a good person and to be kind, but none of that has been with any thoughts of getting some sort of everlasting reward in heaven. I've said it before in these pages, but you should do good because that's the right thing to do. No organization, religion, person or group has the monopoly over goodness; and no one should be made to feel like they haven't got it quite right in their life, just because they haven't followed precisely whatever those sorts of people have said you're supposed to do. Just strive to be kind and don't worry about anything else.

I don't know where I'll go when I die.

It might be heaven, it might be hell, or maybe it will be somewhere in between. I thought I saw the light once. As I slipped into an unconscious state on one of my many trips to hospital, I could feel my vision narrowing into a tunnel with a bright light at the end. I thought that could be me climbing the staircase to the grand adventure beyond, but the hospital later explained that it was a common symptom when your brain shuts down. Your eyes are forced into focusing through a tube with the loss of all that brain function. It isn't you ascending to the pearly gates at all. Either way, I think it is better that you focus on creating the best life you can for yourself right here on earth today. Don't waste time thinking about all that other guff and what it all means.

I'm not afraid of death. After that brain haemorrhage in 1974, I was told I was unlikely to make it to sixty, so this year, as I prepare to celebrate my seventy-fifth, I know I've been very fortunate to last as long as I have. I have led the life I wanted to live and, no matter what happens now, I can depart this earth a deeply satisfied man. Not many people can say that.

I've already started to prepare, just in case it happens before my plans to make it to 102. There are plenty of demijohns of wine ready for my funeral guests to enjoy. I want my friends and family to be happy when I shuffle off this mortal coil. Laughing, dancing, someone on the ukulele or, better still, the banjo. I hope that a bit of my wine will put a big smile on their faces too.

Lizzie the film-maker helped me out by finding a reverend to come and consecrate the ground where I wish to be laid to rest. It is a lovely spot, about 600 yards from the cabin, up on the hillside with beautiful views right out across all the land I consider to be home.

It is a clear spot. I didn't want to be buried amongst the trees, I wanted all that open space and freedom; a metaphor, if you'll grant me it, for the way I've always lived my life. The loch is right there, of course, lying beneath me, lining the bottom of my coffin. It will be a coffin too. Let my body give a good feed to the Highland worms. A final gift back to all these soils that have gifted me so much in return.

The only issue is that the bracken up there is absolutely heaving with ticks; but you know, you can't have it all.

———

I can understand very well why people might look at the way I live and shudder a little.

There are some pretty extraordinary stories about things that have happened to me through my unconventional life, and I am sure that at a surface level you might think my life could sometimes be lonely, uncomfortable and tough; quite dangerous too.

In truth, there have been days out here when it does get tough and I have been worried, but for me it is nothing compared to the stress of being trapped in a cycle of debt, unable to heat your home, feed your kids or pay your bills. The extreme times I've experienced have been fleeting, not life-long burdens.

I haven't had the perfect life but no one has it all. I know I could never have been married, but that doesn't mean it isn't something that I've never considered either. There was one girl in my life who I really liked. It was before I left for Canada, all those years ago. My brother recently found the photo of me and her together and brought it to the cabin this summer. I think he had discovered it lying in some old boxes and there she is, all tangled up in the memories of that person I used to be, and could easily have been. Pictures of us on nights out, down Blackpool in the clubs and pubs, surrounded by gangs of friends and family. Me and her, smiling to the camera, with her sat on my knee. Cuddling each other. It is like looking at another man, living another life completely.

We were in love and she did talk about us getting married, but my mind was firmly set on travel by then. I told her that if she still felt the same way about me when I came back, then we could think about it. But I never really did come back, at least, the person I was back then never did. You can't live as I do, travel as I did, and somehow still settle down and have a family. Not without someone being really unhappy in the end. It just isn't fair.

Of course, many people do wind up making big compromises in their life, and still find a true happiness. That's because what makes you happy can evolve over time. You might be drawn to travel and the wilderness as a young person, and then find yourself longing to settle down and have a more conventional life afterwards. That's fine, we all change, and there are plenty of ways to experience a little bit of what I have without going as far as I have. However, if you are one of the few people like me, or think you might be, then convention would always mean conceding something fundamental about who you are, and are always going to be. This was always the path I was going to choose and I don't regret a thing.

A different kind of love has long since been born in me. A love of this place, the earth under my feet, a love of the wild and the wildlife (well, the wildlife that doesn't eat all my vegetables, ransack the cabin, bite, sting or maim!). Then there's the best bit of all. The peace and quiet. There are times when it is hard work out here, and it can be uncomfortable, but it is an insignificant price to pay for peace. It is nearly always peaceful. The faint sounds of a lapping loch and the burn water tumbling down the slope. The hush in the trees, broken by the occasional train rattling on the tracks, a hoot from an owl, a honk from a goose; the death crackle of the last piece of wood as it dissolves into ashes. We do have our place in the natural order of things, you know, but it isn't the one most think. Our true place is lined up against everything and everyone else as an equal. We are just one creature in the great sweep of nature on the planet – and once you realize how small you are, you realize how great you are too; to be just another animal rewarded with the privilege of walking the earth.

I wouldn't ever profess to be better than anyone else and I'd never dream of telling someone else how to live their life. I'm not stuck up my own arse, believing what's up there smells better than everyone else's. I just feel very sure of my place and what makes me happy, and I think a lot of people could be a lot happier too.

Some people spend their entire lives dreaming of finding freedom, of travelling, or of making a major life change, but for the overwhelming majority it just never happens. For so many, sadly, it isn't something they could ever really do. They become trapped deep in the cycle, sometimes from birth, with dependants and responsibilities that make a life like mine simply unobtainable; but for many others, their dreams of living differently are voluntarily resigned. Dreams become something that they imagine they'll find time to do later in their life, or once they've retired. Good luck to them, I say, and I really hope it works out, but that isn't always how life is. I did my roaming when I was in my prime, and at retirement age I immediately contracted cancer.

Life is a gift, but it is so fleeting and fragile too. If you've got a dream, something you really want to do, and you have the means to do it, then you need to get out there and do it while you still can.

Don't let your life pass you by while you wait for some imagined 'best time' in a future filled with so many unknowns.

Go and do it now.

—

People talk about 'footprints' on my radio in a way that means more than just a footprint made by your foot. What I will leave behind, the footprint of my life, only extends as far as the physical print of this cabin, and when I am gone, I imagine this place will be reclaimed by the natural world and it'll all vanish into dust.

What of the record of my life, though? Well, I hope you've had a little bit of it in this book to carry forward with you, but the best thing you could ever really do is take the spirit of a life like mine and make it part of your own.

This book won't allow you to taste a wild berry picked straight from its bush after an autumn shower, nor will it bring you the joy of something home-grown from your own garden. It won't gift you the sense of self-confidence and comfort to be had from living simply and compassionately, nor will it provide you the connection with humans of the ancient past, by staring into flames sprouting from a lump of wood that you yourself have cut from a tree. All these are treasures woven deep into the fabric of this poor man, who has lived a life of richness that a millionaire could never understand.

Don't be afraid of letting down a greedy system that rewards fewer people than there are hermits on earth, or fall into their trap of making you believe that your future happiness rests solely on you buying the next best expensive thing, or having the biggest shiniest whatever it now is, whilst your entire liberty is thieved away, alongside the rest of this planet's resources.

Those letters, piled up over there, all have a variation on how the writer wishes they could live like me, but feel they can't. That they are scared to make the leap. That there is a battle between what is expected of them by the world that lives outside of their head, and what they really think and feel instinctively inside their soul. They suffocate the little voice inside their heads. The one that speaks the truth. The one that is the most important of all.

Don't be afraid of putting that voice first, from the very moment you hear it calling out to you. The true happiness to be had from a real life lived in the real, raw world is already out there. It's just waiting for you to pick it up and pull it deep into your own life's story.

I've told you once, but I'll tell you again:

Go and do it now.

ACKNOWLEDGEMENTS

Thank you so much for reading Ken's book, we both appreciate it enormously. I have tried, without success, to get Ken to think about who he would like to thank, but as the naturally self-effacing gent he is, I think he thought the whole 'acknowledgements' thing was a bit daft. He does, it is fair to say, have more important things to be getting on with. However, there are some people I would like to thank on both my and Ken's behalf, so I hope he'll forgive me for gate-crashing these final few pages of his book.

The Corrour Estate have been wonderfully accommodating. Thank you for sending me your copies of Ken's diaries and special thanks to Allan MacLeod for keeping me across Ken's comings and goings. Shona, Harry, and the whole team at Corrour Station House always offered such a warm welcome; I hugely appreciated their company at what must be the finest coffee house/pub/ restaurant of any train station in the nation, and I know Ken values everything you all do for him too.

It was a pleasure to get to know Davy at the loch head on my final trip. Thank you for your insight and knowledge. Thanks to 'The Runner' Mark Leggett too, for taking Ken his post and sharing our messages.

This book took a huge leap of faith from Sara Cywinski, Publishing Director at Pan Macmillan. Fortunately, Sara shared the vision for what this book could be and pulled out all the stops to make this happen. I am so grateful she put her faith in us, alongside the rest of the Pan Macmillan commissioning team. We have also been blessed with the supreme editing talents and wisdom of Lydia Ramah. Thanks for all your support Lydia, and for your huge contribution to the work and words from the first day in the woods, right until the very end. Often a thankless task, but our copy editor Penelope Isaac made a very thorough sweep of the first draft, finding the holes and offering sound advice. Thanks to Emily Macinnes for the stunning cover photo of Ken, and the graphics team for their work pulling together all the art and imagery throughout the book.

Lizzie Mackenzie's truly beautiful Scottish BAFTA-winning film *The Hermit of Treig* provided the inspiration to seek out Ken to write this book, but her time, and above all, her trust, was absolutely invaluable. Thank you for everything Lizzie, I know you are going to do great things.

'He's working day and night in his attic, reading two million words in my diaries, writing away, and never seeing his wife or children,' was roughly how Ken put it in a letter to a friend. It wasn't quite that intense, but I do owe an awful lot to my wife, Emma, for her enduring patience and encouragement. I dedicate my portion of bookwork to her and our two beautiful children, Macsen and Grace. Hold on to your dreams, my loves.

I first met Ken at his log cabin home back in the late spring of 2022 – having followed some roughly drawn instructions down to the banks of Treig and on through his woods. His cabin and garden emerged on a small patch of raised ground, and there the great man was: hunched over and planting the first spuds of the season. I felt incredibly nervous. The book deal was agreed but due to the unique nature of Ken's lifestyle, we hadn't yet spoken, let alone met face-to-face. Ken though, could not have made me feel more welcome.

Ken is a man of the very deepest humility. I can hear his sarcastic stock response to my praise already: 'I'm good, aren't I?' delivered with that playful twinkle in the eye – but I really am going to have to go there, I'm afraid, my dear friend.

Ken is a legend in every sense of the word but he is also a man of true kindness and absolute integrity. I am so grateful to him for his generosity, both in opening up about his extraordinary life and for opening up his home with such warmth and kindness. Working with Ken has been the most incredible privilege. It is no overstatement to say learning about his life has already changed my own.

Go well, Ken. I hope you make it to 102.